The Institute of British Geographers
Special Publications Series

23   Rural Change in Tropical Africa

 *The Institute of British Geographers
Special Publications Series*

EDITOR: Dr N. J. Thrift
University of Bristol

For a complete list see p. 222

Rural Change in Tropical Africa
From Colonies to Nation-States

David Siddle and Kenneth Swindell

Basil Blackwell

Copyright © The Institute of British Geographers, 1990

First published 1990

Basil Blackwell Ltd
108 Cowley Road, Oxford, 0X4 1JF, UK

Basil Blackwell, Inc.
3 Cambridge Center
Cambridge, Massachusetts 02142, USA

British Library Cataloguing in Publication Data

A CIP catalogue record for this book is available from the British Library.

Library of Congress Cataloging in Publication Data

Siddle, David
    Rural change in Africa / David Siddle and Kenneth Swindell.
        p.   cm. — (Special publications series / The Institute of
    British Geographers; 23)
        Includes index.
        ISBN 0-631-15855-3
        1. Agriculture—Economic aspects—Africa. 2. Rural development—
    Africa. 3. Africa—Economic policy. 4. Land use, Rural—Africa.
    I. Swindell, Kenneth. II. Title. III. Series: Special publications
    series (Institute of British Geographers); 23.
    HD2117.S53 1989
    330.96'009173'4—dc20   89–15171
                                                                                  CIP

Typeset in 11 on 13 pt Plantin by Vera-Reyes, Inc.
Printed in Great Britain by Dotesios Printers Ltd, Trowbridge, Wiltshire

Contents

Introduction

Considering its political balkanization, ecological diversity and the heterogeneity of production and exchange relations, writing about Africa is fraught with difficulties. While it is true that all African countries have come under the sway of the international capitalist economy, and most have experienced colonial rule, nonetheless the larger structural changes have been refracted through prisms of African experience and history. Therefore it is necessary to accommodate both structure and situation and to understand how external and internal political and economic forces have shaped African environments and rural communities. The difficulty of coming to grips with African rural society is one of reconciling individual actions and perceptions with the larger structural forces of society and the state and how they have developed historically. In contemporary Africa the pace and direction of change would appear to be variable and patchy, something which invites caution when discussing the destination of specific polities, economies and societies.

Because of the history of African studies, together with the availability of data and their form, one frequently encounters either macrolevel analyses (usually of the nation state) or microlevel studies of specific communities or villages. Indeed one of the problems in writing about Africa in general lies in the construction of relevant paradigms or levels of description and analysis which reveal the configurations of social and environmental processes in such a way that they can be used at a comparative level and yet avoid the over-generalized or the too specific. Macrolevel analysis ignores both local and regional histories, environments and interests, while household, village and even regional studies are exposed to the dangers of extrapolating trends and generalizations over wide areas from case study evidence. Too much emphasis can be placed on cases as examples of stages in the development of a universal convergence where the characteristic of every individual case becomes either an example of the general, or an idiosyncracy of the particular (Guyer, 1987). The most revealing insights into the workings of African rural society have come from analyses of rural communities, households and farming systems, but the strength and usefulness of such analyses occur only when they are contexualized within larger frames of reference.

Other difficulties can be encountered in the use of categories such as 'peasant', 'proletarian', 'middleman', or positing dichotomies like private versus state enterprise or urban against rural. While these are sometimes useful heuristic devices, they may obscure important processes which are part of classes, societies and environments in the making. So although this book is about rural Africa, it will be obvious that in many instances it is neither easy nor useful to separate rural from urban as categories. Towns are *loci* of political power, merchant capital and markets, and their bureaucracy can exert profound influences on rural societies which lie within their orbit, while in turn many rural households are either dependent on incomes from urban employment, or use them as part of a process of accumulation. It is the heterogeneity of rural communities which is often so striking: households produce both for subsistence, and buy and sell labour, while there are the land poor and landless, the latter category often obscured by their relationships with those who still have land (Mintz, 1979).

In this respect much of what we write in this book is expressed in terms of the resolution between internal and external forces of change. Indeed the lives of most rural people in Africa represent a dialogue between these forces. Certainly some societies in West Africa have been involved in trying to balance these two pressures for well over a century. Household food production has been expanded to meet the demands of local and regional markets, while export crops have also been grown primarily by domestic producers. On the other hand, in East and Central Africa some households have been involved in the market economy for only decades. Their involvement has been less as household commodity producers, than as agricultural labourers on large-scale European (and now African) commercial farms and as migrant workers in mines and factories. Some local systems of production have been by-passed rather than incorporated, and it is quite clear that in these circumstances external pressures have been too strong for adaptation. The social life of Africans might seem to present us with an array of systems of farming and household production and reproduction which range from those primarily, but no longer exclusively, geared to subsistence and local exchange to those large-scale farms operated by capitalist farmers or the state using wage labour. But between these polar opposites lie myriad rural communities where peasants and small commodity producers are either operating simultaneously (or at different points in time) several farming systems and who are involved in different production and exchange relationships in order to reproduce their social lives. In some places households may be preserving a 'balance' between the household demands of food production and the 'external' demands of exchange crops to meet their commitments for taxes, consumer goods and social services. In other places the cultivation of exchange crops for local and international markets, and an involvement in off-farm work have superseded their ability to produce the bulk of their subsistence or deal with economic and environmental deterioration. Thus rural societies have been modified, transformed and some have virtually disintegrated.

With all these ideas in mind, we have chosen to pivot our approach on a discussion firstly of the major basic dimensions of rural production and exchange – labour, land, non-farm jobs, animal herding, markets – while drawing attention to some of the spatial environmental and historical variations within tropical Africa. In specific terms, the structure of the book as a whole moves from the particular to the general, from the endogenous to the exogenous. In this way a point is made, as far as it is possible, of trying to write from the perspective of rural Africans themselves. For this reason theories of change and development, with their Euro-American bias, are relegated to a post-dictive final chapter.

We begin by presenting an overview of agricultural practices and systems of cultivation; how people collect food and grow crops and what skills and techniques they use (chapter 1). Both in discussion and in diagrammatic form we identify a matrix of crops, techniques, scales of operation and production relations which run from the polar opposites of simple household production, reproduction and local exchange through to the commercial large-scale farming which has been promoted over the heads of African household producers. Between these extremes we point to peasant and small commodity producers operating to grow varying amounts of household food, but also to create surpluses or specific crops for regional and external markets which link them to a wider economy, with all its implications. This approach incorporates several possible scenarios of change, as well as establishing the parameters and themes of the book.

In the first place, however, we confront the issue of the potential of African farming to sustain change. There now exist within African studies divergent views on the resilience and potential of African farming and production systems and these alternative views have been evident in the literature over the past decade (see Richards, 1983, 1985; Watts, 1983; Watts and Shenton, 1984; Williams, 1982). It has also been fashionable to view the change from hunting and gathering through shifting agriculture and bush-fallowing to permanent cultivation as a function of population pressure. Many classificatory schemes are based on the apparently reasonable premise that the higher the density of population, the more intensive the system of landuse. Boserup (1965) is the best known proponent of the anti-Malthusian argument that increasing population brought about not famine, but the technological and social innovations to promote changes in the economy. Thus population is an independent variable and its growth becomes exogenous in models of cultural change. The notion that population growth is a necessary and sufficient condition for agricultural growth appears to us to be an overly myopic view of a complex process which involves a wider range of variables and leads to quite different responses in different physical environments expressed in the style of settlement, kinship and social structure. Population growth has no doubt assisted changes in human society and there is empirical evidence in Africa of an *association* between population density and cultivation systems. But population dynamics change in each epoch and need to be understood in the context of particular sets of social relations of production. In both colonial and pre-colonial societies intensification has occurred to provide surpluses for tribute and taxation and the supply of urban food markets. We also need some knowledge of the potentialities of the social and political systems that facilitated, enabled, or required the growth of population (Faris, 1975).

The 'population growth approach' also implies that the intensification of production is a laudable response in itself. One premise of our first chapter is that there is no real justification for this assumption: that intensive doublecropping on irrigated fields has no greater intrinsic merit than a complex and selective use of forage resources. Moreover, it is a timebased analysis which ignores the limitations of space and distance. In an anxiety to promote the idea of progression and development, anti-Malthusians take no account of the sublety of a culture which may incorporate all these 'stages' in one system of farming and also involves itself in animal husbandry as well. Nor does it take account of the ways in which a diet is built up of both *preferred* and *reserve* staple crop types (see figure 1.1), the more susceptible cereal (e.g. maize) being backed by one which will sustain a community through drought or a crop failure (e.g. cassava, or the upland rice complementing the swamp rice species). Nor is it possible to demonstrate the use of a surplus cereal or a tree crop to yield a fermented beverage, without taking account of the significance of local brews which form an essential part of labour exchange arrangements in many if not most societies in Africa.

So our aim in the first chapter is to present a model of the relationships between subsistence and exchange, adaptation and ecology, continuity and intervention. In the next four chapters we examine the ways in which processes of transformation involve an understanding of this often complex and subtle interplay of factors. Such changes sometimes involved significant shifts in established practices, both in terms of production and exchange relations, which required new technology. It has, in these cases, altered proportions of land, labour and capital. In other instances, however, the older technology and systems of landuse have been retained although new forms of control and ownership have been established. The two situations are not mutually exclusive and may co-exist even within the same rural communities.

During the century 1830–1930 African agriculture, largely but not exclusively in the West, underwent a phenomenal expansion which took two forms. First there was the emergence of peasant farmers and small commodity producers creating significant changes in economic response throughout the tropical zone. The crops of this 'cash crop revolution' (Tosh, 1980), coffee, cocoa, cotton, groundnuts, palm oil (E_2 in figure 1.1) were still integrated with the food economies based on grain and tuber cultivation. Even though it was increasingly orientated towards external markets in Europe and dependent on the merchant capital and trading expertise of Europeans operating under the umbrella of colonial rule, production remained essentially in the hands of rural Africans. Throughout the period of modern development West Africans have generally continued to control the means of their production. But development planning and state control often involve an increasing dimension of outside interference in the mechanisms of this activity. The most obvious changes which have involved a high level of external intervention have been in East, Central and Southern Africa where Europeans developed settler or plantation economies and alienated large tracts of land using wage labour and industrial methods of merchandizing. But even in these areas, recent political developments mean that the changes have been more piecemeal, with the new interventionist activity of independent states spatially juxtaposed with the introduction of more traditional peasant modes of adaptation.

So while we find it convenient to compare the long-term introduction of the first commercial crops (and the rather slow change in social and economic relations of production that the growing of such crops induced in western Africa) with the more rapid and traumatic confrontation between 'modes of production' which took place in the eastern, central and southern parts of the continent, it tends to become a heuristic device. Intervention often means alienating land from customary use, whether by colonial power or independent state, and it has certainly become an accepted method of development planning. The ecological rupture that such alienation can produce, not to mention the social implications of such activity, may be seen as entirely justifiable in relation to the need to improve terms of trade, to feed a growing urban population or to satisfy political dogma, but may have long term ecological and social consequences. It is these regional and temporal contradictions and paradoxes that underpin our model of change. They have also led us through the structure of the book, in which at each point we have allowed the past enough room to impinge on the present.

In chapter 2 we look at the labour process which is still central to African farming, and in many instances exercises constraints upon farming practice and output. But one of the persistently underestimated aspects of rural economy and society is that households are fed, sustained and reproduced by incomes earned off-farm, sometimes in locations far removed from the village (chapter 3). The absence of men from households has both negative and positive implications; it may disrupt farming and place additional burdens on women thus contributing to the food production crisis, or it may provide valuable inputs and means of accumulation or even basic survival in rural areas. Often non-farm incomes are used to buy land, and the question of land rights and land accumulation is a contentious one, especially in those areas where land is becoming scarcer.

As we have indicated above, the alienation of land by Europeans in the past, the increasing commoditization of land in the present and the expropriation of land by the state makes the political economy of land a crucial area of concern, not least where the land issue has been an integral part of the struggle for African independence (chapter 4).

The impact of these developments on African societies was considerable – both expanding and reorientating existing markets and changing the nature of labour relations. The role of the male as forest clearer and hunter was transformed by a growing involvement in the production of these socially prestigious and economically necessary cashcrops and the development of mechanisms for marketing this produce (chapter 5).

Produce markets and the exchange of goods and services also form a significant part of rural life especially in Western Africa and are most obviously a point of intersection of rural and urban interests, as well as those of the peasant and the state.

At the same time, again especially in West Africa, where Islam did not constrain female participation in trade, women also took on new roles as traders in the burgeoning market-place, both permanent and periodic, which catered for this expansion in activity. Many Africans were drawn into a wider economy which relied on labour being transferred from one sector and one region to another. This developing class of small commodity producers and migrant labourers was soon linked with the development of an urban population with its connections to the world economy. Here then was a situation where domestic producers were growing substantial amounts of export crops and incorporating new crops into the regimes of their farming structure, some of which required the use of migrant labour drawn from areas with poor or no potential for commercial crops. In some areas export crop production pre-dated colonial rule, but eventually increased levels of production and labour migration were underwritten by increased monetization and new forms of taxation and control. But in general, apart from some plantations, European intervention was indirect and West African farmers controlled production and were employers of other Africans. Another area of 'intersection' is that of pastoralism and animal herding (chapter 6). Pastoralists occupy areas which have been affected by climatic disturbance and, in addition, they suffer disruption of their coping mechanisms due to the intervention of the nation-state, and a bias towards urban and rural sedentary interests.

In chapter 7 we confront the issue of intervention by settlers and colonial administrators. Some of these interactions involved the work of conscience:

the benign and committed work of colonial civil servants, scientific officers, missionaries and teachers who acted as cultural brokers. Other changes were less benign, involving expropriation and exploitation which precipitated moments of crisis, reaction and resistance from African peoples. These were not exclusively the product of competition for land, but were most manifest in areas of European settlement in East and Central Africa. They took the form of land alienation by those acting on behalf of colonial powers intent on the furtherance of industrial capital through the exploitation of mineral resources. Land was also alienated for capitalist farming enterprises by settlers and African expansion was curtailed by strictly imposed protectionist quotas. The scene was set for separate development in these regions in which commercial agricultural expansion was in the hands of Europeans. Potential African producers were forced, by a combination of poll tax and vigorous recruitment, to enter the European economy instead and at a different point: as low wage labourers for European estates, plantations and mining corporations. This form of expropriation is of wider significance because it is the context which became part of the strategy of state intervention through large-scale estate and scheme enterprises throughout tropical Africa largely, though not exclusively, in the post-colonial period.

The most striking and sudden transformations have also occurred where the state has intervened in the shape of marketing boards, development schemes, or socialist reconstructions of post-colonial states. Development schemes often physically transform environments through the building of dams, land consolidation and the replacement of small intercropped farms by larger monocropped ones (chapter 8). New forms of control and new techniques have been implemented in order to increase relative surpluses from labour as the state has attempted to gain greater control over agricultural surplus. Yet such schemes have often sought to introduce highly complex technological packages to peoples who are either peasant farmers or small commodity household producers. Results have been disappointing if not disastrous and objectives have rarely been achieved. Many development plans have been the means of recirculating state monies, of advancing particular interests, of deepening capitalist relations of production, of controlling markets and cementing political alliances and allegiances.

In contrast to development schemes and projects, there have been attempts to make more thoroughgoing reconstructions of society, usually on socialist lines. Such attempts have been prominent in Eastern and Southern Africa where the struggle for independence has been prolonged and where guerrilla warfare has raised political consciousness and material expectations to higher levels than in countries where independence was achieved with less effort and where power fell to elites reared within the colonial system. In the 1980s, both types of intervention – state capitalism and socialist reconstruction – have had to contend with external intervention via the International Monetary Fund (IMF) and the conditions it imposes on loans and debt repayments.

The issue of Euro-American theorizing on changes in African economy and society and what current development planning policies really mean, is taken up in our final chapter (chapter 9). Here we emphasize the ways in which a good deal of energy has been spent in explaining Africa's past in general and imperialism in particular. Much of this debate is wrapped up in identifying the significance of capitalist penetration: parasitic or partial, constructive or destructive, benign or malevolent. At the same time the whole nature of planned intervention is held in question. For African politicians, depending on country and circumstances, development plans can be viewed either cynically as platforms for election and the acquisition of power for themselves and the alliance of interests they represent or more altruistically as the means of grappling with post-independence problems of providing adequate incomes and basic needs.

Given the wide array of farming systems and forms of production and reproduction, what is the future direction and development of African agricultural and rural society in general? Is there an inexorable and necessary deepening of capitalist relations of production as *both* orthodox Marxists and liberal economists believe? For those espousing a materialist view of history it is certainly a necessary prelude to socialist reconstruction. Is the lack of autonomy of African states so great (because of their dependency on the world capitalist systems) that they will remain impotent unless they break free and reconstruct their societies on revolutionary socialist lines? Is there a third option, where the real revolution and further improvement in the lives of rural Africans lies within their own societies and especially within their own systems of agriculture and indigenous knowledge? The populists believe that rural Africans have a remarkable ability to cope with adverse economic and environmental circumstance: that the peasantry is robust and resilient and given more sympathetic treatment by development authorities has the potential to feed itself and develop its inherent capacities for innovation. Others think this rather simplistic. In fact there remains a level of debate between populist writers (Richards, 1985; Dumont, 1966; Wilkinson, 1973; Schumacher, 1974) and Marxist scholars (like Watts, 1983; Kitching, 1982) on whether or not relations between factors of production and exchange have gone too far to allow for such a benign view of prospective rural autonomies.

Few, if any, deny the sophistication of the cultivation techniques used by African farmers, or their resourcefulness when faced with variations in the natural, economic and political climates. Despite rising food imports, it is still true that the bulk of foodstuffs are produced by domestic groups, or small-holder farmers scattered throughout the countryside. But two questions can be asked. First, are these innovative, adaptive systems breaking down, or have they broken down, as they have been transformed by external influences to such a degree that they can no longer provide surpluses for export and for urban markets, as well as for domestic consumption? Second, is this the root of the agricultural crisis in Africa, or is it the case that given the right approach by developers and government agencies (or market forces) indigenous production and landuse systems not only have the resilience but the potential to raise levels of productivity and create surpluses? Such a view is predicated not on introduced technology and foreign plant and crop species, but on incorporating the existing expertise of farmers and herders into policies of development and rural change. Or as Richards (1983) has argued, is there a potential for an indigenous agricultural revolution? If this is the case then the agricultural crisis thus lies with the transfer of inappropriate technology and misguided state intervention. These two arguments, the one of deterioration of food production systems beyond a point of recovery, the other of the potential for coping and improvement, can also be applied to animal herding (chapter 6). Also these arguments about the potential or otherwise of African production systems are particularly pertinent to those arid and semi-arid environments which have suffered from drought, desertification and food shortages. Are droughts and famines the result of systems of production which have been pushed beyond the point where they can cope with variable climates?

Despite any possible indirect spread effects of development schemes, on present evidence we do not feel that significant change is going to be brought about by some 'one-shot adjustment' or 'technical fix' whatever the ideological underpinnings of development schemes may be. Development projects are not going to resolve overnight the inequalities in access to resources, opportunities and the basic means of subsistence. Nor does it seem likely that populist/ecological models of transformation can do more than indicate some sensible constraints and opportunities. As in the past, changes and improvements are likely to be slow, erratic and patchy. One of the aims of this book is to try to focus some attention on the real nature of rural Africa and the forces of change which exist both in the past and today, in the hope that this might provide clues to the formulation of policies and strategies for the future.

As we have already noted above, a good deal not only of practical but also of ideological input has derived from European and North American experience of problems and may be seen by recipients as a parcel of strategies for the management and control of the Third World by the First. At the same time, African scholars have been conspicuous by their relative silence in this debate. It is possible to view this as evidence that Africans themselves regard all this pontification (including this book) as further evidence of continued cultural paternalism. From the admittedly limited published evidence on this subject, it seems very likely that African theories of development and change may eventually be very different from those generated by outsiders.

1

Systems of Production and Landuse Management

We turn our attention first to the elements of African rural production and landuse systems, and identify a wide range of operations which extend from foraging to commercial crop production. African farmers are adept at using a diverse range of ecological niches for foodstaples, to which have been added the demands of export crops. Furthermore, landuse systems are not mutually exclusive and any one household or rural community may embrace several methods of production and landuse. Our analysis begins with four broadly interdependent generalizations.

First, all truly indigenous systems are built on the cornerstone of a sophisticated knowledge of the local environment, both its opportunities and constraints. Knowledge of the 'foraging' opportunities (what a local environment can yield through hunting and collecting), is a primary requirement for most rural settlements in Africa. To this must be added the knowledge of the rainfall and temperature regimes, the quality of seasonal variation in farming opportunities and the capacities of each of the soil types and conditions of slope. In the equatorial zones farmers have to cope with excess water and cloud, while in the savanna moisture conservation or supplementation (irrigation) are primary issues. It is in intermediate zones – drier forest and wetter savannas – that landuse management is at its most complex and requires the integration of upland and lowland (wetland) cultivation systems. Secondly, many West African settlements if not obviously mobile are still built on the premise that site migration is at least possible, if not probable in the foreseeable future. The shift from temporary, or relatively temporary, to permanent settlement as newer building materials are substituted for mud, wattle and straw is therefore critical in any rural system. Thirdly, associated with this is the tendency of all African rural systems to be centred on the operation of an effective set of socio-economic linkages which extend well beyond the immediate family, both in terms of the need for labour and for social and political security. Indeed, despite the changes referred to above it is still possible to view the rural settlement, its form and function, as more of a manifestation of the organization of domestic groups than of the built environment. Fourthly, it will be clear that all these elements come together in the manipulation of the local resource base and the sharing of its product. At its most basic expression this conjunction of environmental management, settlement and domestic organization, is seen in the growing, gathering and eventually in the preparation and consumption of food. It is the arrangements for preparing and sharing food and drink on a regular basis which help to define the 'traditional' currents of co-operation and obligation in domestic groups, the pattern and form of community and its settlement and the basic mix of activities in the social and economic relations of a rural system.

From these starting points then we can define the main components of the traditional economy and society and associate these with the introduction of exchange-based activities either by indigenous commoditization or by foreign intervention. The building blocks of this process provide us with a taxonomy of incremental change. They are identified in relation to parameters such as intensity of cultivation, population density, exchange and markets, interventionist strategies and ecological balance (see figure 1.1).

FORAGING: THE ART OF ENVIRONMENTAL MANAGEMENT

Most African rural diets consist of four main elements: the protein and 'garnish' collected from the bush (fish, fowl, game, insects, wild plants, roots, nuts and berries); a main starch staple (millet, rice, yams, maize, cassava, sorghums); a locally brewed beverage (palm wine, millet or maize beer); and protein from small domestic animals. But the first principle of African diet is an effective manipulation of the forage resources of an environment. Not the least important point of departure in this process is the collection of firewood. Firewood is of crucial importance in the lives of most rural Africans. The diminishing or impoverished stock of suitable timber in areas of increasing population density is causing considerable concern, not least to the women who have further to go to collect their headloads of firewood.

The products of hunting and gathering even in quite complex close settled regions of permanent cultivation, play an important part in the local economy, especially in times of crisis or need. Clearly it is most significant amongst those who practise hunting and gathering or shifting cultivation as their mode of life. A strong case has been made for the view that hunting and gathering societies and shifting cultivators achieve an ecologically well-adjusted low-level ecological equilibrium. It was hunting and gathering which traditionally sustained African people, especially when they were moving into new environments from desert fringes to savanna and from

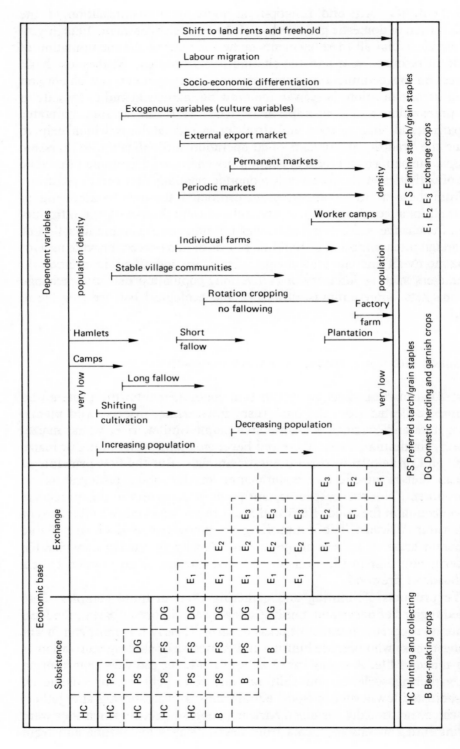

Figure 1.1 A taxonomic model for African agriculture

Source: author

savanna to forests. It is fashionable to decry hunter-gatherers as primitive when in fact they represent a richly adaptive response to an environment which is not open to more intensive use. The most frequently quoted examples of this mode of production are the Kalahari bushmen and the Congo pigmies. Sahlins (1974) was able to use work by Lee and DeVore (1976) and Lee (1979) in the Kalahari to demonstrate that, given a low population density and natural mechanisms of population adjustment through high infant mortality and the relationship between breastfeeding, low body weight and reduced ovulation, the life of the !Kung is not excessively harsh compared with the urban poor. The rhythms and cycles of hunting and gathering in an apparently hostile environment did not involve an average of more than a few hours of food gathering in a day. This leaves a good deal of time for social interaction, ritual and storytelling. Nor is there any doubt that the largely vegetarian diet is rich, varied and well suited to the human metabolism (table 1.2). Such observations are even truer, perhaps, of the forest peoples where the environment is richer (Turnbull, 1961, 1976), but in general the use and nutritional value of leaves and plants is underperceived and underenumerated by those agencies interested in local food supplies.

If such systems were so successful, what then promoted change? It was probably shifts in the pattern of resource use, prompted by climatic changes, or the need for food surpluses related to changing economic and political systems, or the introduction of a new technology which caused increases in the population. This meant that, for the most part, foraging was eventually supplanted in importance by the more arduous cultivation of a staple cereal, though, as we have already indicated, foraging continued to be of vital importance in the economy. For example, Scudder (1962) and Colson (1971) provide a rich documentation of foraging based on the economy of the Gwembe Tonga in southern Zambia, a shifting cultivation system which incorporated as many as 250 species of wild plants, animals and insects. Similar studies by Richards (1961), Miracle (1967), Lee (1979), and Lee and DeVore (1976) make the same point. In these systems, *shifting cultivation* is only part of the system in which foraging is an equal partner.

SHIFTING CULTIVATION

Shifting cultivation is also associated with very low population density and involves the movement of cultivated plots over a well-defined territory and a less frequent but important movement of dwellinghouses to accommodate changes in agricultural location (figure 1.2). This system is predominantly practised in humid and semihumid areas of Central Africa (Peters, 1950; Allan, 1949, 1965). In its use of large areas of land per unit of population, it is in some ways comparable to pastoralism. Large or small circle plots are

Table 1.1   Composition of some major San wild foods

Common name	Mongongo nut	Mongongo fruit	Baobab fruit and nut
San name	//"×a	//"×a	≠m
Botanical name	Ricinodendron rantanenii		Adansonia digitata
Season of use	year round	Apr-Nov	May-Sept
Composition in g/100 g eaten			
Moisture	4.2	13.4	5.2
Ash	4.0	5.7	7.3
Protein	28.3	6.6	14.3
Fat	58.4	0.6	13.9
Fiber	1.5	3.5	10.7
Carbohydrates	3.7	70.2	51.4
K calories	654	312	338
Composition in mg/100 g eaten			
Ca	249	89.6	272
Mg	500	195	630
Fe	2.07	0.74	9.51
Cu	1.90	0.45	2.47
Na	2.0	1.01	76.3
K	686.6	1760	4173
P	704	46.0	1166
Zn	4.09	1.39	6.96
B-Carotene	–	0	–
Thiamin	0.127	–	–
Riboflavin	0.139	0.113	–
Nicotinic Acid	–	0.121	–
Vitamin C	0.57	8.51	–

Source: cited in Lee and DeVore, 1976.

cleared and piled with the branches of trees. This wood is burnt and in the accumulated nitrogenous ash a wide variety of garden plants are intercropped. All the basic elements of the diet, and all the constituents of the stockpot can be found in each garden patch, as a risk-reducing *mélange*.

Settlements associated with this regime are small and scattered. Trees are allowed to regenerate for up to 20 years before land is revisited and small kin groups make a slow progression over the landscape occupying new ground every three or four years. Work cycles are responsive to, and activated by, seasonal changes and particularly the short rainy season. The

most interesting feature of this form of subsistence, which is still a significant adaptation in sparsely populated woody savanna areas in East and
Central Africa in particular, is that at its most developed it in many ways
represents a sophistication which remains a part of more ostensibly mature
farming systems. Such intimate knowledge of local plants is now the basis
of a developing interest in African traditional medicines promoted by
medical schools throughout Africa. Moreover, a rich alternative technology
which is associated with an adaptive use of the products of an environment
and re-cycled introduced items may now comprise at least part of the
populist strategy for rural development in many African countries. (Schumacher, 1974; Richards, 1985).

FALLOW ROTATION

If hunting and gathering and shifting cultivation were the basis of all
successful rural economic systems and still comprise an important part of
the subsistence ethos, the development of the 'transition' to bush-fallow
rotation systems and permanent cultivation is deemed by some to be the
most significant change to affect African rural life, enough, as we have
argued in the Introduction, whether or not this is the product of population
pressures remains a moot point. Probably the most widespread cultivation
system in tropical Africa is *rotational bush-fallowing*, where between one-
third and two-thirds of the land is cultivated each year. Farmland is made
by cutting forest, bush or grassland and firing vegetation in a fashion
similar to shifting cultivation. Landholdings and farms are usually clearly
defined in fallow systems and the main settlements are fixed (figure 1.2) or
move only within the compass of a fixed site (Morgan and Pugh, 1969). The
area of fallow comprises self-sown plants, grasses and shrubs on land
formerly under crops. Fallows change in character according to the number
of years they are left undisturbed, and as use increases so the number of
plant species is diminished, a process which is accelerated where soils and
slopes are unsatisfactory. Fallowing can support between 50 and 600
persons per square mile, according to the nature of soils and rainfall
regimes, but when the demand for land is heavy as population rises, so
fallows are shortened, often to dangerous levels and regeneration gives way
to soil erosion and reduced yields.
   A distinction can be made between woody-fallows and grassy-fallows; the
former are restricted to humid areas where moist conditions after harvesting allow the seeds of shrubs and trees to re-establish themselves, or where
root stocks are left to regenerate. Larger trees may be left uncut, which may
include economic species such as oil-palm. Clearing of woody-fallows can
be heavy, labour intensive work whereas in grassy-fallows with dry conditions after harvesting, clearing of land needs only pulling, cutting and

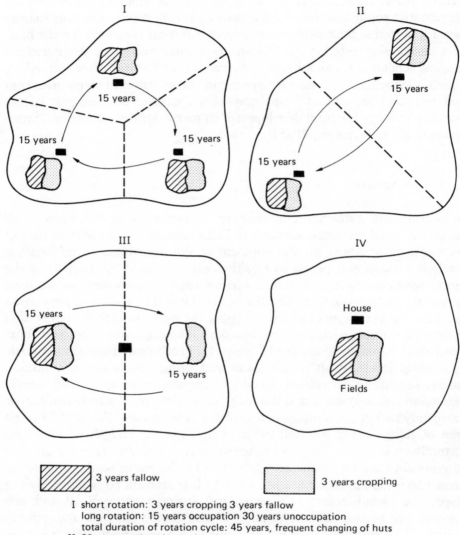

I short rotation: 3 years cropping 3 years fallow
   long rotation: 15 years occupation 30 years unoccupation
   total duration of rotation cycle: 45 years, frequent changing of huts
II 30 years semi-stationary housing
III 30 years stationary housing
IV 3 years cropping, 3 years fallow

Figure 1.2 Shortening rotations and stabilizing settlements
Source: after Baum, 1968, in Ruthenberg, 1980

burning of grass. Grassy-fallows are naturally associated with savanna and the cultivation of guinea corn, millets, maize, wheat and *fonio*, whereas woody-fallows in the humid forest zones are used for the cultivation of plantain and rootcrops such as yams and cassava, although in some areas such as the western Guinea zone of West Africa, rice (upland and swamp) is the dominant foodstaple. In such areas fallow rotation and permanent cultivation can be combined.

In Sierra Leone, for example, many farms cultivate upland rice and swamp rice based on a huge repertoire of local species and races (Richards, 1983, 1985). It is for this reason that Richards believes that in the intermediate ecological zones of tropical Africa it is particularly dangerous to label cultivation systems as extensive or intensive, and we must construct our generalizations with this proviso in mind.

All fallow cultivators make use of crop mixtures, rotations and successions. Crop mixtures (intercropping) allow a high density of plants per unit area by combining plants which make different demands on soil and maximize the use of nutrients. They also spread the labour of planting, weeding and harvesting, or by close planting reduce the area which needs to be weeded. Crop mixtures do not give as high yields per unit area as pure stands, but they do offer some protection for the soil against heavy rainfall, reduce risks and maximize returns for labour. African cultivators have a subtle understanding of the micro-environment and place crops on the top of mounds and ridges, on the sides, or in the furrow as best fits their physical requirements (see figure 1.3). Ridging is also a method of protecting soil and in tropical Africa in general it is the physical properties of soils which are most at risk. Successions usually consist of planting one crop after the other to spread the amount of labour required, as well as phasing the establishment of crops according to the amount of moisture available. Crop rotations extend the period of cultivation before abandoning a farm to fallow. For example, upland rice farms may be planted in the second year with cassava which grows as a 'reserve' crop on depleted soil, and it may even be left in the ground into the fallow period to be lifted later as a further insurance against the failure of rice crops.

PERMANENT CULTIVATION

When fallows last for no more than three or four years, the distinction between the amounts of land in use and in fallow virtually disappears. Land may be held in short or longer fallow rotations in the same community and cropping may be adapted to these regimes, but despite the caveats outlined earlier regarding a simple relationship between population density and permanent cultivation, there is no doubt that in densely settled areas of both West and Central Africa short fallows may comprise no more than the

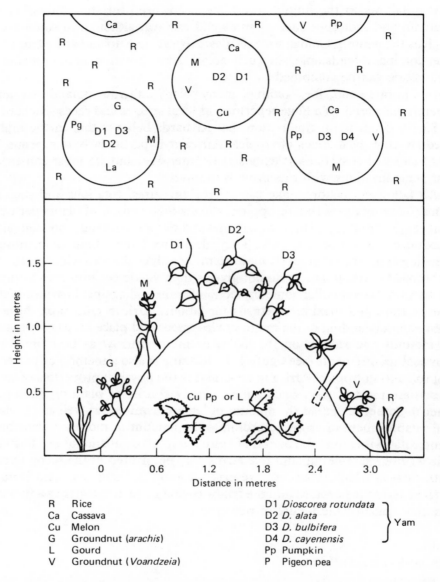

Figure 1.3 Spatial distribution of crops on mounds in Abakaliki, Anambra State, Nigeria
Source: after Okigbo, 1978, in Ruthenberg, 1980

dry season (if there is one) and result in annual cultivation and permanent fields.

Annual cultivation is not geographically widespread in tropical Africa, but it does occur associated with conspicuous islands of high population density, notably in Nigeria, parts of Malawi and Uganda, which now contains between one-fifth and one quarter of the continent's population. For example, in the Igbo area of eastern Nigeria (Anambra and Imo States) rural population densities of up to 1000 per square mile (400 km) are not uncommon, occuring within the forest and southern Guinea savanna zones. Settlement is scattered, partly because of the acephalous nature of Igbo social and political institutions and partly because of the disintegration of nucleated settlements as population has increased and landholding become individuated and subject to sale. Here annual cultivation and permanent fields are common and the indigenous yam has been replaced by cassava as intensification has increased. High and sustained outputs of foodstaple for consumption and sale have been managed by growing a large variety of cultigens, up to 30–40 species on half a hectare. The natural forest has been largely replaced by oil-palm, the traditional cashcrop of this area.

High population densities and permanent field systems are also features of northern Nigeria, especially in what have become known as the Kano and Sokoto close-settled zones. Located in the drier savanna with a mean annual rainfall of between 33 and 27 inches (846 and 694 mm) and light sandy soils, the close-settled zones have become intensively cultivated by the application of animal dung, of the contents of old latrines and of compound sweepings in the densely settled rural areas. The major towns of Hausaland, Kano, Katsina and Zaria have long established urban histories and up to British rule were city-states controlled by their Emirs and other officials. Sokoto founded by the Fulani was established in the nineteenth century and became the centre of the Sokoto Caliphate, which was the largest and most populous state in nineteenth-century Africa prior to the establishment of colonial rule.

The highly centralized state of the Hausa-Fulani with their systems of taxation, tribute and servitude has led to high levels of urbanism and zones of intensive upland cultivation where the annual cultivation of millets, guinea corn, cowpeas, groundnuts and cotton takes place within the limited wet season of seven months. The dry season is in effect the short fallow period and in many places fields are grazed over by the transhumant herds of Fulani cattle. In those parts of northern Nigeria adjacent to the Niger, Sokoto-Rima and Kano rivers, the floodlands (*fadama*) are cultivated, which means that continuous or permanent cultivation is possible. Rice is grown in the wet season followed by crops of onions, tobacco and vegetables in the dry season using simple irrigation or floodland retreat techniques. Similar areas of continuous cultivation occur in the middle Niger, and along the margins of the Senegal river. But even in areas where annual and continuous cultivation are practised, farmers still continue with foraging, a practice which may assume greater significance in periods of crop failure or drought. Also, fallowing is often mixed with annual cultivation where the demands on land are less.

Areas such as northern Nigeria demonstrate the wide range of cultivation systems possible in Africa and the flexibility with which they are practised in response to specific environmental and economic circumstances. Figure 1.4 shows a sample of landuse from northern Nigeria where annual and continuous cultivation are carried out together with foraging and cattle grazing.

DOMESTIC ANIMALS

Particular attention will be given later (chapter 6) to pastoral economies and their frequently uneasy relationship with settled agriculture, but the significance of smaller domestic animals in the lives of agricultural peoples is considerable and like forage resources often underestimated by researchers and development agencies. Small domestic animals such as sheep, goats and chickens are important sources of protein throughout rural Africa. Small domestic animals require low capital and management inputs and they are not restricted by trypanosomiasis, yet they are rarely mentioned in accounts of farming systems (Okali and Sumberg, 1986). Goats in particular are an important source of meat and are used in a variety of ceremonies. Furthermore, like pigs and chickens, goats can be kept around the compound and fed on waste and integrated with the food processing activities of women. The neglect of small domestic animals has to some extent been recognized now by the setting-up of the International Livestock Centre of Africa which is currently evaluating methods of improving sheep and goat production systems. One of the problems of keeping small animals is that as population density rises and landuse is intensified, grazing becomes more restricted, which means more intensive feed and management systems are required.

A TAXONOMY OF RURAL PRODUCTION SYSTEMS

We have attempted to incorporate these elements into a taxonomy of both structure and process. It is (see figure 1.1) a taxonomy which is constituted from the building blocks of African rural production systems rather than from some implicit statement about the virtues of increasing the intensity of exploitation and productivity per man hour.

Hunting and Collecting (HC):   the product of the local environment (trees, shrubs, herbs, roots, medicinal plants, fish, fowl, game and insects) which

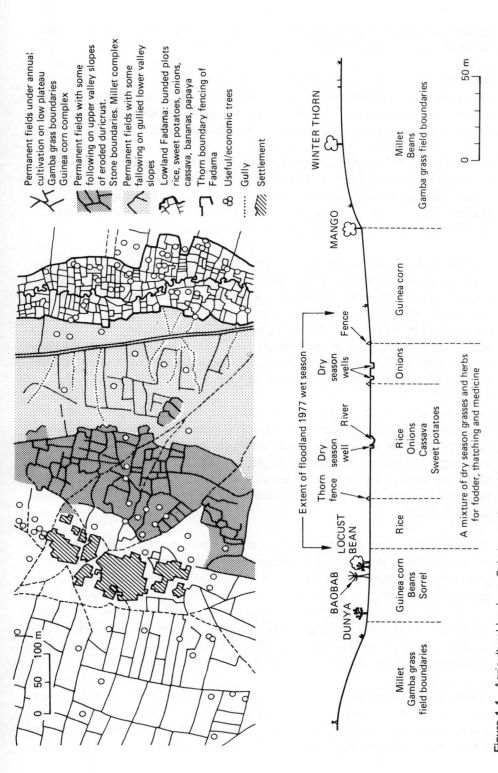

Figure 1.4 Agricultural landuse, Sokoto, northwest Nigeria, 1979
Source: author

Permanent fields under annual cultivation on low plateau
Gamba grass boundaries
Guinea corn complex

Permanent fields with some following on upper valley slopes of eroded duricrust.
Stone boundaries. Millet complex

Permanent fields with some fallowing on gullied lower valley slopes

Lowland Fadama: bunded plots rice, sweet potatoes, onions, cassava, bananas, papaya

Thorn boundary fencing of Fadama

Useful/economic trees

Gully

Settlement

Extent of floodland 1977 wet season

WINTER THORN

MANGO

Millet
Beans
Gamba grass field boundaries

Guinea corn

Dry season wells

Fence

River

Dry season well

Onions

Rice
Onions
Cassava
Sweet potatoes

Thorn fence

LOCUST BEAN

Rice

A mixture of dry season grasses and herbs for fodder, thatching and medicine

BAOBAB
DUNYA

Guinea corn
Beans
Sorrel

Millet
Gamba grass field boundaries

0   50 m

0   50   100 m

can become increasingly important in times of crop failure and shortage, but may also in particular circumstances become exchange items.

Preferred staple (PS):   the cereal which in farming economies provides the basic preference carbohydrate bulk food (yams, finger millet, maize, rice, cassava) which can be expanded into commodity production (and withdrawn from it) as the supply situation and prices dictate.

Famine staple (FS):   the carbohydrate staples grown as standby or secondary crops should the primary staple fail. Some, like cassava, are left in the ground during the dry season. Others occur where environmental conditions allow a distinction between dry-land and wet-land crops and the deployment of an alternatives such as upland swamp rice.

Garnish and amenity crops (DG):   grown principally as garnish for the stockpot or as a protein supplement. The list is long but would include peppers, sweet potatoes, eggplants, groundnuts and various fruit trees. Amenity crops include textile and fabric crops – raffia, palm and cotton – oil producing palms and fruit crops, many of which become exchange items. In this category we would also include small domestic animals – sheep, goats and chickens – which are important items of protein supplements and also used in a wide range of rituals.

Local exchange (E_1):   crops which form the basis of simple commodity exchange within and between local communities. These include the fortuitous supplies of foodstuffs, local alcoholic beverage crops which were sometimes a product of surplus staple put down to fermentation (maize, finger millet) or a by-product of another crop (oil-palm) or the products of favoured localized resources circulating within the smaller-scale periodic market system.

Regional commodity exchange (E_2):   crops entering the pre-colonial economy associated with the development of indigenous merchant capital; primarily cash crops for export or for regional and urban markets beyond the confines of the local market system (palm oil, cotton, tobacco, kola, onions, copra, salt, foodstaples). However, as we have noted, all food exchange crops have a variable involvement, especially in regional commodity exchange, in that they are subject to withdrawal when subsistence needs intervene in times of shortage following a bad harvest.

International commodity exchange (E_3):   crops associated with the penetration of foreign merchant capital (petty commodity production) and state–industrial capital (plantations, estates and large-scale commercial farms) geared to international markets (cotton, cocoa, coffee, groundnuts, sisal, sugar). The introduction of these crops, as part of existing systems or to replace them, has important repercussions on the organization of farm labour, and on systems of marketing, the development of off-farm incomes, labour migration, the scale of enterprise and changing rights to land. The question of the shifts of emphasis from E_1 to E_2 and then to E_3 and their significance for domestic production and its social relations will be the principal subject of this book.

All the elements discussed in this chapter and in the introduction seem to imply incremental process and it is perfectly posssible to use this as a device to identify the process of incorporation as one in which eventually commoditization dominates as much as it does in the affluent farming regions of the world. There are certainly regions where considerable progress has been made towards this objective and we spend some time in discussing the frequently complex land and labour relations which have developed in such circumstances in early chapters of this book. The extreme position in this projection, as we show in our model, is of the landscape of fully mechanized large-scale capital intensive agribusiness units which employ a landless wage labour force with labour costs reduced to a minimum in the effort to produce maximum output at lowest costs. But as we shall see later, tropical Africa has many examples of schemes and enterprises which have had this aim in mind both in the colonial period and since, yet very few have succeeded and completely removed peasant farmers from their means of production.

Another interpretation of our model is possible. In dividing the elements which constitute African rural production systems into building blocks, we have also stressed the inter-relationship between these elements. One element cannot be seen as replacing another in the march of progress. So our 'taxonomic process' also contains statements about the possible ecological implications of interventionist strategies which lead inexorably towards something close to monoculture.

CONCLUSION

With such warnings in mind, it is tempting to suggest that the different levels of development associated with colonial rule, and their superimposition on the different economies and traditions of subject peoples, when combined with different ecologies, make both structuralist and populist positions (outlined in chapter 9) tenable, given a degree of geographic and historic specificity. For example, one can justifiably point to situations where foraging and food collecting on traditional lines produces nutritional levels which are far superior to the vegetable farming which development agencies introduce to improve African cultivation systems and levels of well-being. On the other hand it is true that where African farmers have the practical knowledge to implement useful systems of intercropping, crop relays and ridging, there is no guarantee that all households within rural communities are actually able, or have the means, to implement these techniques. Recent work in northern Nigeria suggests that in villages the ability to hire sufficient labour – always a potential constraint but more so given the lure of alternative non-farm employment – is often the key to the implementation of sound indigenous practice. In fact, those households with reliable non-farm incomes may be far better equipped to use traditional methods than to resort to new inputs such as ox-ploughs and fertilizers. It is in this area of social differentiation and non-farm incomes and off-farm work that the populist view often fails to embrace the relationships of rural communities and urban sectors, industry and other classes both within and outside the rural milieu.

We have remarked upon the heterogeneity of rural settings in our introduction and this will become apparent throughout the next few chapters. With reference to our incremental schema of elements of rural production it is worth re-emphasizing that it is often the case that one community or one household may embrace several production systems, and that their reproduction may depend on several economic systems. In other words they straddle the urban and rural systems, the agricultural and industrial, the subsistence and the commercial; they use family labour and hired labour, communal land and freehold land. But has there, or is there occurring an irreversible shift towards the commoditization of production and a breakdown or replacement of indigenous systems of production? We believe that this shift is a differential one across space and time; some portions of the African rural community have moved further in this direction and at a greater speed than others. The post-independence experiences of countries vary; one should not expect to find exact similarities in rural systems on the urban peripheries and in remoter rural areas, and one should expect Nigeria, Zimbabwe and Sierra Leone to have different trajectories of change and development, given their ecologies, populations and histories.

The forces of the international economy may be pervasive throughout Africa and colonial rule was almost universal, but it was the variations in the impact of external forces and the differing levels of resistance which shaped African rural economy and society.

2

Farm Labour: Mobilization, Management and Control

INTRODUCTION

The mobilization, management and control of farm labour in Africa has traditionally revolved around systems of kinship and descent, chieftaincy, public office and servitude. Unlike Europe and Latin America, access to labour not land was the basis of economic and political power in a continent where population densities were low and the concept of ownership rather different. Surplus labour was appropriated by heads of lineages and households from wives, juniors and slaves and by states and polities through various forms of tribute. Labour supply was maintained by an emphasis on biological reproduction, and subordination.

From the nineteenth century onwards the penetration of European merchant capital, the development of new export crops and the settlement of Europeans led to significant changes in farming and to land tenure, which were accentuated or underwritten by colonial rule. New crops created new demands for labour which were only partially satisfied by the internal resources of commercial crop zones. Labour was also drawn from areas with little immediate economic potential of their own, and migrant labour systems became well established by the 1920s. There was also forced labour (for example the notorious concession system in Belgian Congo) but this declined by the 1930s.

Changing labour relations required new kinds of work contracts and methods of payment; these were (and still are) varied and not mutually exclusive. They include piecework, contract and day labour for wages, or a mixture of food and wages, while share-contracts are another means of employing farm workers. By the early twentieth century wage labour was becoming widespread (although it had existed earlier) and was part of a general commoditization of the African economy and the appearance of capitalist relations of production, which found expression in the household economies of Nigeria as well as the plantations and estates of Kenya and

Uganda. Yet the new class of wage labourers was the product of a highly individual balance of political forces rather than simply the working of an inexorable economic logic. Notwithstanding the importance of plantation and estate workers in some areas, the majority of agricultural wage labourers are employed by small commodity producers and it is in this often unenumerated sector that one finds the most diverse labour relations and modes of payment (Swindell, 1985). Furthermore, even though the small commodity producer may hire workers he still relies on inputs from his family and kin. The domestic group, although greatly transformed, still remains the core of much African farming, whether for foodstaples or export crops.

This chapter develops a number of these issues beginning with the supply of farm labour, its seasonal deployment and changes associated with commercial cropping. The issue of women's increasingly crucial role in agriculture is given special attention. A principal theme in the chapter is the organization of farm labour within domestic groups and the conditions under which they recruit extra household labour. Non-household labour takes several forms, including labour co-operation, share-contracts and hired wage labour. Other forms of organization like plantation and migrant labour are discussed in other chapters.

LABOUR SUPPLY

Africa has a relatively small population with average population densities of around 12 per square kilometre compared with 72 in Asia although there are 'islands' of higher population density, for example, in Nigeria; around the shores of Lake Victoria in Uganda and Kenya; and Ruwanda-Burundi, where densities can exceed 250 per square kilometre. But for the most part villages may number no more than a few hundred people, or in East and Central Africa comprise groups of scattered homesteads only technically termed villages. Misconceptions about the nature of African farming, demography and rural settlements in the 1950s assured the adoption of development models largely based on Indian experience, which were built around shifting surplus labour from the traditional sector (agriculture) into an expanded modern sector characterized by industry.

Helleiner (1966) suggested this Indian model was not applicable to the African situation and an alternative three-stage model was proposed. In the first stage, land is in surplus and labour is the limiting factor to increased production. In the second stage, population increases where labour and land are balanced. Finally in the third stage, labour is in surplus and land is the limiting factor. However, all three stages may be observed within one country or region. For example, the shift from land to labour shortage can be seen with increasing distance around some of the larger African towns;

close by the city there is considerable competition for land whereas in remoter areas labour is in short supply especially when aggravated by urban migration.

The availability of surplus labour for hire is also influenced by the ability of many domestic groups to reproduce themselves with only partial or limited recourse to waged employment. Continued access to land has proved to be an important factor in limiting the creation of a class of agricultural or industrial wage labourers. On the other hand there is considerable competition for what labour is available. In the twentieth century competition for wage labour has come from the colonial and independent state, non-indigenous enterprises, large-scale white settler enterprises and indigenous employers.

A poor labour supply may not be a sufficient reason for limited agricultural production, but it does exacerbate the problems farmers face when they have to mobilize enough labour within what can be a very short growing season, when large amounts of work have to be done at very specific points in the cultivation cycle. Uneven workloads and seasonal deployment are issues of great practical importance to the African peasant farmer, and it is to these that we now turn our attention.

SEASONAL FARMING AND THE DEPLOYMENT OF FARM LABOUR

As temperatures are generally high enough throughout tropical Africa to sustain plant growth all the year round, it is the amount, duration, incidence and reliability of rainfall which are the crucial factors for the agriculturalist. Therefore, the length of growing season is closely related to seasonal rainfall and agriculture is confined to the wet season, unless water control systems are available to allow farming to continue throughout the dry season. Rainfed agriculture is the norm in tropical Africa although there are enclaves of perennial cultivation associated either with modern irrigation schemes or indigenous floodland cultivation, for example along the Niger and Senegal rivers, which are frequently integrated with highly seasonal regimes. The labour requirements of each system may demand special adjustments.

When farming is restricted to the wet season, then it means there is an uneven spread of farm workloads and it is the *flow*, not just the *stock* of labour which is important. Also, during the farming season labour inputs can vary significantly from day to day and the length of the working day may therefore depend on both the arduousness of the task and its urgency. Some jobs, such as clearing land, are both arduous and urgent if farms are to be ready for the coming of the rains, while other jobs, such as weeding, are primarily a matter purely of urgency. It is for all these reasons that bottlenecks in the supply of labour can be a major problem. Time is also absorbed in travelling to and from the fields, although this is much more a feature of nucleated zones of West Africa than the more scattered settlement pattern of East and Central Africa. In all these circumstances, the timing of specific operations is always critical in that they need to be carried out over relatively short periods of maximum input to achieve good yields. African farmers spend between 500 and 2135 hours per year on farm work compared with an average of 3000 hours for their Asian counterparts, but the working days are squeezed into a limited growing season which has crucial peaks of activity (Cleave, 1974).

The fluctuating demand for farm labour means that its marginal productivity can be very high at certain times and numerous studies have shown that markedly improved returns can result from quite small additional applications of labour, for example during weeding and harvesting. Therefore one of the objectives of many farmers is an adequate strategy for coping with these structural and geographical imperfections in the system of supply and demand for farm labour. Studies undertaken in Senegal and The Gambia, for example, have shown the wide differences in returns from groundnuts planted in the early and late season. In Senegal it has been estimated that for every day that planting is delayed there is a consequent 2 per cent fall in yield, while Haswell's work in Genieri in The Gambia showed yields of 663 lbs per acre on early-planted, well-weeded plots, compared with 304 lbs from late-sown and little-weeded plots, (Tourtre, 1954; Haswell, 1953). However, Haswell found that even for the later-planted crop, adequate and correctly timed weeding substantially improved the yields of groundnuts. Groundnuts are integrated with other crops, which means farmwork is phased throughout the growing season in response to the number of crops grown and their specific requirements.

THE MARKET ECONOMY AND THE SEASONAL DEPLOYMENT OF LABOUR

The successful cultivation of cashcrops, at least in the first instance, is intimately related to their integration into an established complex of food crops (see chapter 1). The viability and effects of commercial cultivation are part of the argument about whether or not there was a nineteenth-century 'cashcrop revolution'. Today the issue is relevant in the context of state involvement in the modernizing of agriculture, or in relation to farmers who are entering new urban markets. As long as the majority of farmers use labour intensive methods, and when, either in whole or in part, the reproduction of the labour force depends upon the production of food staples, then a satisfactory allocation of labour between food and non-food crops is of paramount importance to survival.

It has been argued that the introduction of cashcrops such as cotton and groundnuts into savanna regions has presented greater difficulties than the introduction of cocoa, coffee, rubber and palm oil in the forests (Tosh, 1980). The assumption is that in areas of higher regular rainfall in the humid zones there has been a successful integration of tree and food crops into a regime which previously relied on bush-fallow agriculture and was already furnished with zones of forest (often around settlements) for tree and bush products. Indeed, in some ways this was a natural extension of integrated foraging activities which are a normal part of the human ecology of African rural life (see chapter 1). But the introduction of a cashcrop can disturb the equilibrium of labour needs. It is certainly true that the wet season is more limited in the savannas, whereas in the forests the growing season is much longer and the labour peaks for tree crops and foodstaples exhibit some complementarity. But a great deal depends on the type of food crop grown. In Ghana, for example, the combination of cocoa with plantain and cocoa with yams gives a good measure of complementarity, as the emphasis on foodstaples comes from February to June, while July to January is when the chief inputs on cocoa are needed (Beckett, cited in Cleave, 1974). However, when rice is grown there is a considerable clash between harvesting this crop and cocoa planting and weeding.

Villages in Nigeria where yams and maize are grown have rather a better degree of integration, and better still when cassava is the main crop as the labour inputs are smaller and regularly spaced throughout the year (Galletti, cited in Cleave, 1974). But in all cases cocoa generates the greatest seasonal fluctuation in labour demand, and the extent to which seasonality can be modified appears to vary greatly with the complementarity of food and cashcrops, with grains giving the least flexibility. Since cocoa was introduced there is evidence of a shift to those foodstaples (such as cassava) which reduce clashes and this is particularly important for those farmers who cannot afford much hired labour.

The chief commercial crops grown in the savannas are cotton and groundnuts, which have to be cultivated with food crops such as sorghum, millets and maize in a growing season which may be as little as six months. Compared with forests the shorter growing session in savannas is an added problem when growing food and cashcrops, and the degree of flexibility may be less, especially in the range of alternative food crops. Cotton is particularly demanding of labour and requires correctly timed planting at regular intervals, periodic thinning, constant weeding and rapid and careful harvesting. Observations from Tanzania (Sukumuland) show that 600 man hours per acre are required for cotton compared with 380 for sorghum and there is *simultaneous* competition for these inputs over a relatively limited growing season (Von Rotenhen, 1968).

An example of seasonal labour use from Uganda can be used to demonstrate the deployment of labour over the season and the problems farmers have in combining food staple with cotton (see figure 2.1). In January and February rainfall is very low, but in March the rains begin and land has to

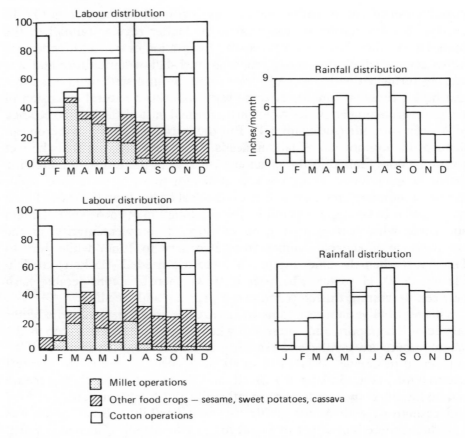

Figure 2.1   Seasonal distribution of labour, cotton farms, northern Uganda
Source: modified from histograms supplied by M. Hall, cited in Cleave (1974: 87).

be prepared for millet while sweet potato mounds are dug and the land is made ready for cotton. By May the first weeding of millet is done and cotton has been planted and last year's cassava is harvested to break the hungry season. But the peak labour demand is in July when cotton planting has to be finished, early millet harvested, groundnuts weeded, and sesame beds prepared. Cotton picking begins in December and runs on to January and although hours are long, work is lighter. Looking at the distribution of work throughout the year it might appear that there is a complementarity between the major foodstaple, millet and the chief cashcrop, cotton; the peak labour inputs for millet is March–April when work on cotton is minimal. But this complementarity is achieved through a reorganization of cropping to avoid conflicting labour demands. The planting of cotton is spread over May–July which is not the way to get the best yields of cotton. Similar problems associated with the combination of cotton and foodcrops have been reported by Bassett (1988) in Ivory Coast. The responses of peasant farmers to labour bottlenecks include the mobilization of labour from outside the household, increased use of women's labour, changing cropping patterns and, among better-off households, the use of ploughs and herbicides. In addition the dominance of cotton in Ivory Coast has led to crop neglect and reorganization of culturally prescribed farming practices and festivals.

There are of course those farmers who have access to sufficient family labour, or more importantly, who can hire it and so treat both crops in the best manner possible, giving them better yields and ultimately higher incomes (and more opportunity to hire labour). The potential conflict between subsistence risk and commercial profit is clearly rationalized by eliding the potential of a food crop to serve as a cashcrop (or vice versa) whenever surpluses allow. It is a strategy which is an expression of a well-integrated indigenous response of the kind we refer to in chapter 1, (E_1 – E_2). Where the dominant cash crop does not serve as a food crop as well and where the labour demands of crops such as cotton prove disruptive of farming schedules, there is considerable evidence of farmers growing alternative food crops, or increasing the output of what had been formerly subsidiary famine staple (FS) crops. Cassava, for example, has undergone a remarkable expansion and diffusion in the past 50 years and part of its present prominence as a good crop is its adaptability to a wide range of soil and rainfall conditions and particularly the low labour inputs it requires. Its main advantage is that it can be left or stored in the ground from one season to another and used in this way it can be an insurance against main crop failure, or shortages arising from poor weather or insufficient labour. After the compulsory introduction of cotton production in Obangui in 1926, for example, cassava production was rapidly expanded. A similar situation existed in the labour deficient areas of rural Zambia depleted of males by the mining economy, the Oriental Province of the former Belgian Congo and the Zande district of Sudan (Jones, 1959). It has been estimated that some 48 per cent of the crop area of tropical Africa now contains some cassava. What is clear is that the shift towards new commercial food and non-food crops has involved changing the internal division of labour in many production communities. One of the most notable features of this change has been the increasing role of women as the principal suppliers of food in rural households.

FARMWORK AND GENDER

The sexual division of labour is a basic principle in the organization of farmwork and variations in the amount and type of work undertaken by men and women is of considerable importance. Development planners interested in the introduction of new cropping systems have frequently ignored or misunderstood gender roles in the production process and the social and symbolic relationships which may underpin them. Social relations are created as well as economic ones when a wife either becomes a paid farmhand and/or ceases to tend food crops. However, the allocation of work according to age has not received as much attention as the sexual division of labour, perhaps because western-orientated observers are accustomed to thinking of children and the elderly as insignificant members of the workforce. Division of labour may of course be related to both age and sex, for example only older women may do certain farm jobs, or have farms of their own. In Sierra Leone women have swamp rice farms, but only when they are middle-aged and past the point of rearing their last child. The distribution and size of women's rice plots may also be different from those of men, for example in The Gambia on unirrigated swamps, women's plots are smaller and closer to the compound, as this reduces the time travelling to their fields, as farming has to be integrated with a wide range of domestic duties within the household.

The subject of women as farmworkers has attracted a good deal of attention over the past 20 years and also the current interest in household studies and household economy has highlighted the issue of gender and how differences in power, resource access and labour allocation between men and women have a fundamental effect on patterns of production and demographic change. There is now a widely held belief that women provide the bulk of agricultural labour in tropical Africa; a contribution of 60–70 per cent of total labour input is commonly quoted. This belief in part dates from Boserup's work in 1970, but a more careful reading shows that in fact she pointed out that the percentage of farm labour provided by women is 9 per cent in Nigeria, 29 per cent in Senegal and 56 per cent in Cameroon (Boserup, 1970). Since the 1970s a number of village and household surveys also suggest that there is considerable variability.

The whole question of women as farm labourers, the amount of domestic work they do, their access to and control of resources must be placed within the context of the social and economic differentiation within rural communities, and the kinds of households in which they live and work. In Zambia, Kumar (1985) found that women's share of farm work amounted to 45 per cent in male-headed households, but rose to 83 per cent in female-headed ones; in polyganous households it was 51 per cent. This is a well-developed response to a long period of male out-migration in response to demands for the mining industry of the Copperbelt and Southern Africa. In The Gambia, Webb (1988) found variations within a relatively small region around Georgetown; in Georgetown female labour accounted for some 56 per cent of the total and dropped to 35 per cent in surrounding villages – the difference being accounted for by the greater involvement of men in non-farm work in Georgetown which underlines the importance of outward male migration from rural areas either daily, seasonally or for longer periods.

None of the above reservations are intended to diminish the importance of women as farmworkers nor suggest that a significant change in their contribution has not occurred during the colonial and post-colonial periods. Indeed it is intimately connected with agricultural innovation. The sexual division of labour within farming groups can be radically altered by the introduction of new crops as the demand for labour rises either in general, or at particular points in the cultivation cycle. Also, patterns of marriage and reproduction may be influenced by new farming practices, together with the opportunities for non-farm work which favour men. It is necessary, therefore, to look at how the reallocation of male and female labour occurs within domestic groups as they become producers for local and international markets.

Haswell's work in the Gambian village of Genieri spanning the period 1950–60 is one of the few long term studies of the changing role of women. As the size of production units shrank and population remained relatively stable within the village, women began to enter adult production at an earlier age and leave it later. Women now have lengthening careers associated with the shift to swamp rice production in an economy where the cost of replacing home-grown with imported rice is very costly; thus the roles and place of women in Mandinka society have changed. Also, the production of groundnuts (the staple cashcrop of The Gambia) has been achieved indirectly through women working longer on subsistence crops, which has increased their independence and the amount of bridewealth demanded for those women skilled in swamp rice farming. Also, divorce rates have increased in the 25–35 years age group, a time when women's rice farming potential is at its greatest (Haswell, 1953; 1963).

More recent studies in The Gambia of the effects of introducing pump-irrigated rice have demonstrated that in the rice development projects men have assumed control over new technology and rice lands and have displaced women from their role as rice farmers (Dey, 1981). However, Webb (1988) has shown that this has meant a corresponding movement of women into the production of millet, sorghums and groundnuts (traditionally a male-dominated crop). But because of the demand on labour by irrigated rice farming, men have had to contribute more time and there has been a shift towards production on communal fields with less time spent on individual plots by both men and women.

Reports of changes in the division of labour and the role of women come from many parts of tropical Africa and we may conclude this section with examples from Kenya and Zambia. In East and Central Africa the presence of Europeans as settler-farmers and the development of industry and mining curtailed commercial farming by Africans, in favour of labour recruitment, which frequently disrupted traditional production relations (see chapter 7). In the pre-colonial economy of Kenya the economic spheres of men and women were autonomous and complementary. Land was vested in the patriclan, men assisted in cultivation and women exercised 'ownership' of the crops. In the colonial period land was alienated and concepts of individual ownership were introduced which have been reinforced since independence. In many places in Western Kenya there is a well-developed land market and increasing landlessness, as richer peasant farmers, school teachers, government officials and shopkeepers acquire land by purchase. The registration of land and the division of clan land into private plots has been to the advantage of men, with the position of women becoming more precarious. Also, men have become heavily involved in cashcrops and non-farm employment, with women providing increasing amounts of labour for both subsistence and cashcrops (Smock and Chapman, 1981; Mönsted, 1977). Policies of colonial taxation and labour recruitment drew men into the non-farm sector and many of them have become seasonal or permanent town dwellers.

The result is that men's contribution to farmwork has become marginal and they have been 'detached' from the household farming economy. There is now a division between male and female circuits of production and reproduction with many women responsible for growing sufficient food-stuffs to feed their families in the rural areas.

In Zambia, the migration of men into the copper mining areas had begun as early as 1906 and by the 1930s Audrey Richard's work on the Bemba pointed to the effects of male migration on the viability of the *citemene* system of rotational following (Richards, 1961). The lopping of tall trees prior to burning posed problems for households headed by women. Recent work by Moore and Vaughan (1987) has suggested that the problem is not simply one of male absenteeism. As well as doing a good deal of farm work, women spend a large amount of time on domestic chores, and this pre-cludes adequate diet and child-feeding. Female-headed households, in some cases, can resort to kin or beer-parties when they lack sufficient male labour, but this is dependent on the household's life cycle. Young newly-married women with many dependents do not have the ability to draw on extra-household labour through a wide range of kin as older women do. Households are not a homogenous category. The introduction of commer-cial maize cultivation and ox-ploughing schemes in Northern Zambia have involved women in more farm work, as they are required to engage in all aspects of cultivation and the amount of weeding increases as greater areas are cultivated. Moore and Vaughan (1987) have shown that child malnu-trition may actually be higher among commercial maize farmers, not because of an inadequate food supply, but because women in these house-holds have restricted amounts of time for food preparation and the rearing of small children.

DOMESTIC PRODUCTION AND FARM LABOUR

Age and sex are important principles in the organization of farmwork and impinge upon access and control of labour. But as we observed earlier, the majority of farming is carried out in the context of domestic groups which comprise sets of people socially bound together as they engage in basic acts of production and reproduction. In addition to the bonds of marriage, descent and kin play their part in welding together production units through acts of obligation and co-operation. Production units are agents of production whose dimensions and structure are determined both by the forces of production and the relations of production. Each unit is charac- terized by the way it combines the factors of production (land, labour, capital) in specific quantities and by the social relationships between the constituent parts of the unit. In other words, there are the technical problems of growing crops in a certain environment, by using particular cultivation systems, which are operated by sets of workers defined not only according to their size and composition, but by the forms of their co- operation. Once the co-operation of individuals is demanded by the job, then there must be control and organization of work and division of labour. The relations of production also determine how the produce is distributed as well as the structure of consumption units, although this does not mean that consumption and production units necessarily coincide.

Questions about who is working for whom and with whom and how the produce of labour is distributed lead to questions about associated forms of hierarchy and subordination as well as those about reciprocity and internal and external exchange. In the view of Meillassoux (1964, 1972) it is the investigation of economic relations which leads on to kinship, politics and ideology and how these play their part in the reproduction and continuation of domestic groups. The concept of production can be extended to include the production of people as well as goods and the control of the means of human reproduction (through the distribution of wives) may be of more importance than the control of the material means of production.

In their most expanded form, units of production and consumption comprise lineages and sub-lineages and for many anthropologists lineage and kinship as organizing principles are distinguishing features of pre- capitalist societies (Meillassoux, 1964). Lineage organization is probably strongest in areas where 'stateless' peoples predominate, whereas in pre- capitalist societies with a history of well-developed social division of labour and statehood, joint-families are more the norm. Although descent and kinship are powerful in binding groups together, there are contrary forces which lead to the splitting of groups. Lineages become segmented, and joint-families are susceptible to fission and cycles of development and decay. It seems that the shift towards smaller domestic groups centred on conjugal units is increasing in many parts of Africa. This can be associated

with three factors: the development of commercial farming, the individu-
ation of land holdings and the use of hired labour. It will be appreciated,
therefore, that questions about the size, composition, social structure and
dynamics of domestic groups are crucial to our understanding of agriculture and agrarian change. Such groups devise strategies (successful or
otherwise) to combat external pressures such as state invervention in the
rural sector, or make decisions about expanding or retrenching household
production.

But, the definition of these domestic groups, which comprise units of
production consumption and investment, is by no means easy: flexibility is
often more apparent than 'boundedness'. The nature of African familial
relations is contentious and recent critiques have been levelled at the notion
of the group or household as a social actor or unitary whole which denies
the existence of a number of sub-units which may reach down to matrifocal
ones (see Guyer and Peters, 1987). Lineage or joint-production may be
strongly represented in the efforts to produce foodstaples, but may be
disolved completely or partially where commercial crops are concerned.
For example, among the sedentary Fula of Senegambia the compound
(*galle*) may comprise a conjugal unit of a man, his wives and their children,
or it may be much larger, and comprise a complex unit of joint-family, built
around a father and sons, or a set of brothers (Pelissier, 1966). The whole of
the compound joins together under the direction of the head of the family
to cultivate common fields for basic foodstaples such as maize, guinea corn
and millet, which go into a common granary. Maize is grown in an infield
(*bambey*) close by the village and out-fields (*marou*) are used for the other
staples. In addition to collective cultivation, adult males and older females,
depending on their status, have individual plots (*kamangnan*), which are
cultivated by them and their immediate families who form sub-units within
the compound. These plots are commonly used for groundnuts, although
they may be intercropped with some millet and guinea corn. All members
of the compound work for three or four days on the common fields, the rest
of the time they devote to their own plots. At peak periods reciprocal
arrangements exist within the compound, but the proceeds of groundnut
sales primarily accrue to the plot holders, who may also decide to hire
additional labour. Thus households can be areas of divergent as well as
convergent interest.

The size and composition of domestic groups is a major factor in their
ability to mobilize and co-ordinate farm labour for successful production;
too many children, or too few men, may seriously impair agricultural
potential. Yet domestic groups are not static, they pass through a developmental cycle, as well as being affected by longer term shifts from complex
groups to simpler ones. The life cycle of the groups is therefore an
important concept; Fortes (1958), compared the domestic group to a living
organism experiencing a cycle of change whereby there is growth, dissol-

ution and replacement of the original unit, by one or more units of the same kind. The developmental cycles of domestic groups are reflected in their age-sex composition, which in turn gives rise to different dependency ratios (producers related to consumers) between the most active, less-active and non-active members. If one adds to the developmental cycle the incidence of death, illness and absence, then the domestic group is inherently unstable and may require external supplies of labour. Such additions to the labour force can be critical even if they amount to no more than a few days of help. This is because, as we have observed, the timing and rapid completion of certain jobs are vital ingredients of successful farming. This is equally true of farmers who have a negligible interest in producing surpluses for sale.

Clearly the size of a domestic group is not just a question of stages in a cycle of growth; the maximal or optimal size a group attains differs over time and space. For example, in parts of northern Nigeria, The Gambia and Senegal, many dwelling units, or compounds rarely comprise more than a minimal extended family household of a married couple, their offspring and old folk, who form one farming unit. Upon marriage sons leave to set up their own farming households and compounds, while daughters move to those of their husbands. Although the development cycle still obtains, it is operating from a lower base-line than in large compounds, which at some stage comprise multiple family households.

THE CHANGING STRUCTURE OF DOMESTIC PRODUCTION

The introduction of new commercial crops and the increase in non-farm employment have been influential in eroding production relations based on extended groups, leading to a radical alteration in the size and composition of farming households. The demise of large complex units and their replacement in whole or part by simpler conjugal based groups, sometimes (or in some regions often) headed by women, is a crucial issue in the organization of farm labour, which is part of the crisis facing many agricultural producers in Africa at the present time. Therefore, it is important that we look at the causes for the emergence of smaller farming households and how they are reproduced.

A good example of the transformation of agrarian households can be found in the studies of the Hausa-Fulani in northern Nigeria, who have attracted the attention of several researchers interested in the nature and structure of agricultural production and the changes which have occurred over the past 50 years (Buntjer, 1973; Goddard, 1973; Hill, 1972, 1977; Norman, 1972; Goddard *et al*, 1971; Shenton and Lenihan, 1981; Smith, 1955; Wallace, 1979). The household production unit among the Hausa (*gandu; gandaye*) is ideally any combination of a senior male (*mai gida*) along with his married and unmarried sons and brothers, and their sons and clients, wives and children, who comprise a joint consumption-production unit. This household form has much in common with those of the Fula described earlier, and similarly they can be arranged around paternal or fraternal relationships. Like the Fula, work is traditionally organized communally on three days for the cultivation of crops grown for subsistence and taxes, while the remaining days adult males work on their own farms.

Work arrangements and eating arrangements are fluid and consumption and production units are not necessarily coterminous. The important attribute of the *gandu* is that the head has sets of obligations and responsibilities which are matched by the subordinates. Traditionally the head organizes land, tools, payment of taxes, arranges marriages, naming ceremonies and represents the household in the village community. Although internal arrangements for work and consumption are varied, the head is responsible for the reproduction of the household and its continuance. One advantage of such extended units is that they comprise several nuclear families who are at different points in their life cycles and when they experience adverse dependency ratios the larger household acts as a buffer and labour can be internally redistributed. The roots of *gandu* lie in the pre-colonial society when many domestic groups were much larger as they included slaves who added considerably to the labour force at the disposal of the *mai gida*.

Even if we discount the effect of the development cycle in domestic groups, and that men in their lifetimes may experience different types of household organization, there seems to be a good deal of evidence for the decline in the three-generational type of domestic grouping based on the close kinship of adult males. There is some consensus among several authors that now about one-in-five production units are based on fathers who have at least one dependent son who works with him and about one-in-ten where brothers co-operate at least for a limited period, although it rarely survives the marriage of one of them.

Wallace (1979) stresses that the nature of co-operation between men is very varied; sometimes it lasts just for the wet season; sometimes for a few days and while most unmarried sons will work for their fathers, it may be for a limited number of hours as their time is constrained by their other work as craftworkers, traders or wage labourers. It would appear that what is happening is that the old split-time system of three days on communal farms and four on one's own has shifted so that the emphasis is now either on one's own farms related to a conjugal household, or to some non-farm job; the communal element of working with fathers and brothers has become vestigal, although it may strengthen in times of crises or need. We have then the skeletal remains of the *gandu* systems, with kin still loosely connected in productive tasks and the facility remains to call on kin-based labour at particular times and to give security to aged parents as they become infirm. But the underpinnings of mutual responsibility have gone and Goddard (1973) has proposed there are three types of *gandu*: the traditional type where the head is controlling a composite unit of production and reproduction, a modified type where each man pays his own taxes and thirdly where conjugal production units have individual farms and responsibility for taxes and marriage dues, but they co-reside in a compound organized by a senior male who acts rather in the capacity of farm manager and intermediary between the compound and the village. One can add a fourth type, where co-residence has disappeared but labour is still redistributed among fathers and brothers as the need arises. It can be legitimately asked whether such arrangements merit the term *gandu*, especially as labour is frequently hired by individual farming units within the compound.

Shenton and Lenihan (1981) give a graphic account of the processes of change within *gandaye* in northern Nigeria as the pre-colonial cotton industry was reorganized and expanded by the British in the early twentieth century. The British Cotton Growers Association were given monopoly buying rights in 1905 and the company used agents as buyers, paying them commission. Competition among buyers led to the use of a cash-advance system for farmers, who responded to this incentive as they needed increased amounts of cash to take advantage of the increased availability of local and imported consumer goods and to pay their taxes in British coinage. Perhaps more significantly cash payments affected the cycle of social reproduction as bridewealth became a transaction which needed not just calabashes, local cloth and grain, but such things as enamel pots and sums of cash.

The development of cotton growing affected not only the level of economic well-being among *gandaye* but brought about changes in their internal structure. Although it may be difficult to measure the decline in size of *gandaye* it is possible to chart the changing obligations and rights of members, which began to erode such farming households. Heads of *gandaye* provided tools, marriage expenses, personal plots of land and paid taxes. Subordinates provided labour on communal farms but kept the produce of their own plots and whatever they earned from non-farm work which was especially important in the dry season. Under the conditions brought about by cotton farming and cash-advance systems, there emerged a group of heads who could no longer meet their obligations and accordingly reduced them. Taxes were paid from personal plots, or from non-farm jobs; the *gandu* was decentralized and while the men might be grouped together for the purposes of organizing farming, the patterns of distribution and consumption were individualized. Under these conditions the extended household system was weakened and the conjugal or nuclear family became the focus of production and consumption.

The nature of domestic groups, the variations they display from one area to another and the different ways they develop, emphasize the difficulty of conceptualizing this social and economic entity which is central to rural life in Africa. But as Guyer and Peters (1987) suggest, households should be considered as both 'units' and 'processes' and one needs to generate principles and processes that explain variety rather than resorting to typologies. Some believe there should be an emphasis on bargaining, negotiating and contracting or on transaction and exchange, as a means of incorporating individuals and groups within one analytical framework. Domestic groups are also arenas of conflict which reflect larger social, economic and political issues, such as the introduction of new techniques by development agencies (see chapter 8). Yet it would seem that an emphasis on the organization of production and consumption within and among groups is essential and is especially manifest in the manner in which labour surpluses are appropriated. Furthermore, it is necessary to understand the conditions under which groups are reproduced and when circumstances change so as to inhibit or transform their reproduction.

NON-HOUSEHOLD LABOUR

It will be apparent that for a variety of reasons the domestic group or farming household is often unable to meet all its labour requirements from within its ranks. The developmental cycle, absence, fortuitous illness, and premature death all take their toll, while the possible decline in larger extended groups and the demands made by new crops mean that non-household labour has to be recruited in some form or other. In some cases either male or female members may be able to request assistance from their natal households and in their turn reciprocate as required. Indeed while the focus on intra-household relations is both informative and healthy, it is always necessary to appreciate the linkages and interaction among households. But if households are not able to rely on descent or kinship when labour bottlenecks arise then other methods are available which range from labour co-operation through share-contracting to hiring wage labourers. We shall briefly discuss each of these in turn.

Labour co-operation: labour exchange and work groups

Although labour co-operation does not preclude the use of kinsmen or family it frequently cuts across familial ties. The various forms of labour co-operation allow the mobilization of labour which may be required to do small jobs as a matter of urgency, or big jobs such as bush clearing. Groups of different sizes are involved and they can be either age or sex specific and used for a variety of agricultural tasks (Moore, 1975).

A distinction can be made between exchange and festive labour based on the degree of reciprocity. Exchange labour usually comprises a small number of households combined on an understanding of strict reciprocity with no payment other than the provision of meals and drinks. Kinship, affinal ties or merely friendship are the means of bringing labour together. Festive labour is usually organized on an *ad hoc* basis for a specific task and comprises a large number of workers who are called by a farmer who will pay them in drink and food, often on a fairly lavish scale. In East and Central Africa they are frequently referred to as 'beer parties'.

Festive work groups are widespread throughout tropical Africa although they have undergone a relative decline compared with labour exchange; also they may have been transformed into hired gang labour. Festive groups were often a means whereby 'big-men' in villages could appropriate surplus labour from others because they alone had the means to feed such large numbers of workers. Despite the principle of 'come-one-come-all' and a disregard for the marginal productivity of labour, such groups are the means whereby chiefs, rulers, functionaries and traders could secure large and immediate supplies of labour for their farms. Among labour-exchange groups on the other hand there is the tendency for the members to be of the same approximate social status.

Festive work groups may evolve into capitalist forms of surplus labour extraction when the element of social obligation becomes replaced as poorer farmers require extra cash and the 'caller' assumes greater control by paying wages. In many villages, especially where cashcropping has taken hold, one can find gang labour which comprises groups of men or youths who hire themselves out on a daily or piece-work contract basis. Furthermore, on the periphery of large towns this is the means whereby rural entrepreneurs engage the urban unemployed or underemployed in farm work. The complement of this is that such arrangements allow many poorer urban migrants to survive in the town between jobs, or their agricultural wages are just part of a series of day jobs on which they rely for food and rent.

Share-contracts

Like exchange labour and work groups, share-contracts can be the means whereby domestic groups extricate themselves from labour shortages arising from demographic imbalance within the group. But share-contracting is also the means whereby both landlords and tenants have been brought into the market economy, especially for the production of export crops. Robertson (1987) has argued that the widespread development and persistence of share-cropping stems from the inherent instability of domestic groups combined with the economic uncertainty of national and international environments within which they are located. Usually share-contracts are seen by liberal economists as inert and inefficient and by radicals as repressive and exploitative. Both agree that the demise of share-contracting is inevitable. However, there is a good deal of evidence in Africa that share-contracts can be innovative and help redistribute wealth and re-sources. Compared with wages and rents they spread risks, something which might be analogous to the traditional practice of intercropping referred to in chapter 1.

Share-contracts, however, do have an element of ambiguity. The gains may shift from tenant to landlord over a farming season or over a much longer period of time. Time is of the essence in understanding these contracts and Robertson (1987) distinguishes between the level of pro-ductive relations which he calls *ontogenetic* where the terms between parties and their bargaining status varies within the internal demands of the household, compared with *phylogenetic* where contracts as a 'species' are transformed slowly in response to structural adjustments of markets, land–labour ratios and such things as world recessions.

In many contractual situations the landlord's chief concern is access to additional labour while the tenant may be after land in a specific location, for example, suited to export crop production. In Africa the general shortage of labour often puts the tenant in a good bargaining position, quite unlike Latin America or India, where 'seigneurial' systems put the tenant at a disadvantage. But in Africa when land values increase, for example in the vicinity of towns and when the price of labour is bid-up, then share-conracts may give way to wage labour and rents. However, it would be unwise to see share-contracting simply as part of some unilinear shift from domestic farming to wage labour and rents (*vide* the Bosrupian schema of land intensification).

While share-cropping is not exclusively associated with export crop production it has played a significant role in the development of crops such as groundnuts (Senegambia), cotton (Sudan) and perhaps above all in coffee and cocoa production (Ivory Coast and Ghana).

In Ghana early cocoa farms were developed using annual contract workers, but soon the *abusa* system became widely used, where the worker received one third of the cocoa crop together with a piece of land from his host on which to grow food. Since the early twentieth century, the relative importance of share-cropping, annual contract and daily wage labour has fluctuated. For example, after 1946 when farmers became increasingly devious over the payment of contracts, the more experienced workers opted for the *abusa* system, especially as they, as well as their landlords, thus benefited from the rising price of cocoa on the world market. Employers responded by trying to increase the supplies of contract workers from the north of Ghana and beyond by using recruitment agents and by tightening up the *abusa* contracts. From the 1950s onwards the shortage of labour due to increased demands from the state sector, the timber industry and urban employers, encouraged the adoption of daily wage labour and piece-rate systems. The falling prices of cocoa further undercut the share-cropping system although it has not yet fully eliminated it (Van Hear, 1982).

Hired labour

Hired labour is becoming more common as greater differentiation of wealth and income occurs as the rural sector is increasingly commoditized and integrated into national and international economies. Where crops such as cocoa, coffee, cotton and groundnuts are grown for export, hired labour and migrant workers have a relatively long history. In this respect there are differences between West and East-Central Africa, as the former has an economy where the sale of export crops and foodstaples in local markets has experienced greater development. But hired labour is also used when farmers are primarily growing foodstaples for consumption, or local sale, and hiring may be a function of the absence of male members of the farming household who are working elsewhere. In such cases remittances from paid jobs are used to take on extra workers.

In more densely populated parts of Nigeria, hired labour is used by many farmers, although there is a relatively small class of landless labourers, but a growing one of 'land poor'. Workers are usually hired for short periods of time and paid by the hour or by the job on a contract basis. These workers usually come from poorer households with less land, or from those with surplus labour. In three village studies near Zaria, some 19 per cent of labour came from outside domestic groups; households used this labour throughout the year, matching their own monthly labour inputs on wet season upland farms and on irrigated lowland farms in the dry season (Norman, 1972). Many domestic groups had members working in off-farm employment, which noticeably continued throughout the year, even at the peak labour seasons of June and July.

The proximity of towns to villages is an important factor in generating off-farm employment in the formal and informal sectors, and the location of villages and their accessibility to urban produce and labour markets is a significant component in farming patterns and organization of farm labour (chapter 3). In the urban periphery of Sokoto in north-west Nigeria there are villages where every household hired some labour for assistance with farmwork (Sutherland, 1985). But there are also households within villages where there has been considerable accumulation of land, where wage labour is employed continuously throughout the farming season. The high proportion of hired workers is a function of household members being employed in the city (or further afield) and the need to either replace lost members, or where accumulation is taking place, of hiring workers for expanded production financed by non-farm income (see chapter 4).

Similar patterns have been reported in Kenya where Nairobi exerts a powerful influence on its rural hinterland. Kitching (1980) gives estimates for the 1970s of 311 000 landless, or land poor workers employed by other African smallholders. Another 178 589 men were employed by larger capitalist farmers, yet these wage labourers commonly retained plots back home which were cultivated by their wives and families. Kitching makes the point that so often the opposition of capital and labour is far from clear-cut in Africa. Those who are wage labourers may still have land on which they produce food and possibly surpluses for the market. More importantly, those who are *employees* in the formal or informal sectors are also *employers*, at least of a limited number of temporary labourers on their home farms. Quite clearly an African agricultural wage labour force is in the making, but it is very patchy and incomplete. Possibly on plantations and estates the distinction between capitalist employer and labourer is more distinct, but concepts of proletarianization do need handling with some care and include not only consideration of the mobilization of labour, but how it is managed and controlled. The exploitation of labour in its fullest sense is not about relative rates of pay or hours of work, but about the ability of the buyer of labour to exert influence on the manner in which that labour is reproduced.

Do farmers have any options other than hiring when faced with difficulties of funding labour? There is the possibility of farmers adopting new techniques such as a move towards more mechanized farming, which does not necessarily mean large-scale mechanization, but the use of ox-ploughs. This means that instead of expanding the labour supply (for example by using migrants) or of getting existing labour to work harder or for longer (appropriating an absolute surplus), they can turn to investment in machinery and raise labour productivity (appropriating a relative surplus). Ploughs can reduce the amount of time spent in preparing the land for planting and weeders can also be used with ox-plough equipment. But ploughs are chiefly an option in grassland areas, and even here ploughs do not necessarily offset the problems of harvest labour; it may lead to a greater labour demand at this period, if larger areas are cultivated as a result of plough cultivation. This partial mechanization of agriculture has led to a number of problems where it has been developed and has actually raised the demand for labour at specific points in the cultivation cycle (Iliya, 1988).

Another option – and one which is widespread among African farmers – is the combination of different farming or cropping systems such that the labour inputs achieve a better spread while maintaining necessary levels of production, or even improving them. An example from an investigation by Karimu and Richards (1985) in Sierra Leone illustrates this kind of strategy. In Northern Sierra Leone the median family unit of 8–9 requires about 90 bushels of rice per year, which can be obtained from upland rice by 3 members who between them can manage a maximum of 80 hours per month. Swamp rice can also be grown by sowing seed broadcast on unimproved wet-lands (local swamp) or on improved swamp where a considerable degree of water control has been combined with transplanting techniques. The latter system gives the best returns per acre, but is extremely demanding of labour. Because only one or two varieties of rice can be grown on improved swamps the harvest labour peak is accentuated, whereas on upland farms several varieties of rice are grown and this produces phased harvesting. The solution to the dilemma of better yields and limited labour resources has been solved by many family units by using their maximum labour inputs of 80 hours to grow two-thirds upland and one-third local swamp rice.

SUMMARY

In this chapter we have looked at the mobilization and management of farm labour and the problems encountered by domestic-based production units. Seasonal farming is widespread in tropical Africa and puts an emphasis on the stock and flow of labour. Timing is frequently of the essence in successful farming and in areas of low population density labour is a limiting factor. But it is evident that even in areas of high population density, the use of extra-family labour is not uncommon. As we have seen, the influence of kin is declining and domestic groups are becoming much smaller. Consequently their demography and morbidity plays a large part in creating shortages of labour and the need for redistribution within and between rural communities. But differentiation within the rural community is not exclusively a matter of the internal demography of their constituent domestic groups, but of differences in wealth and access to resources. Nor are villages discrete units and external factors influence patterns of farming. Alternative opportunities for employment attract men away from the countryside into towns, or agricultural areas which are better developed. Absentees are replaced by women doing more farmwork, by the redistribution of local labour, or by long distance labour migrants. The use of hired labour is quite widespread in areas of commercial crop cultivation, as well as around large towns and reflects the regional differentiation of African economies and the emergence of small as well as larger capitalist farmers. Non-farm incomes and off-farm employment is an integral part of socio-economic differentiation in villages and is important to the supply of farm labour and a fuller understanding of the rural economy. It is to this non-farm sector that we now turn.

3

Migration, Non-Farm and Off-Farm Incomes

Although a majority of rural households are engaged in farming, they are also increasingly shaped by a range of economic activities which lie beyond the agricultural sphere. The nature and tempo of rural life is influenced by the presence of small industries, commercial and trading enterprises which serve local needs as well as providing sources of household income. Non-farm income may thus derive from businesses located *within* the community and carried out within households. On the other hand, off-farm employment *outside* the local community rather than self-employment within it is also an important source of household and personal income. This might mean daily commuting into a nearby town, or it might mean becoming a migrant worker in a more favoured agricultural area, working on a plantation, in a factory in one of the larger towns, or in a mine. In this manner the rural economy is linked to that of other areas and with the national or international capitalist economy. Thus migration in all its forms makes an urban–rural dichotomy crudely simplistic. In those parts of Africa where spatial integration is more advanced, backward and forward linkages between small rural industries, together with trading, forge economic and social links in many directions, as well as integrating sets of villages into local and regional economies.

Off-farm and non-farm incomes are vital components in the reproduction of rural households but many have gone well down the dangerous road towards dependence on these sources of income, which render them economically and socially vulnerable. In this respect the retention of farmland by the household is crucial. The engagement in non-farm and off-farm work gives rise to a number of ambiguities. Men are removed from the household, often with severe implications for the role of women in both social and economic terms, but at the same time extra work can provide male migrants with much needed income for payment of taxes, provision of school fees or agricultural *inputs* (purchase of fertilisers, pesticides, farm equipment). Also, the engagement of rural households in non-farm work, especially where migration is involved, is evidence of the way in which they now participate in different economies and social situations. In many instances access to incomes from non-farm and off-farm employment is now the key to socio-economic differentiation within villages and may parallel, challenge or reinforce traditional means of differentiation. For some, non-farm and off-farm work are in reality the means of survival in the rural areas. For others they are the route to successful accumulation, investment in land and the ability to hire substantial amounts of farm labour.

In this chapter we look at some of the chief characteristics of non-farm and off-farm employment and the issues they raise. The first part of the chapter examines non-farm employment within the rural areas, beginning with a historical and descriptive profile. The second part of the chapter looks at off-farm employment, which usually means waged or salaried employment in the industrial, commercial or agricultural sectors. In both parts we try to answer some of the questions posed by the impact of non-farm and off-farm work on the household economy and their role in transforming rural areas.

NON-FARM WORK: AN HISTORICAL PERSPECTIVE

In association with the pre-colonial empires, the trans-Saharan and coastal trading networks eventually produced regions of urbanization and industrialization from which emerged an indigenous industrial and service sector of some complexity. In West Africa, crafts and small-scale industries grew in association with specific castes and classes of worker, although the differentiation is nothing like the complex caste structure found in India. For example, in Senegambia, caste is primarily associated with particular occupations which reinforce their occupational solidarity by endogamous marriages. The Wolof and the Fula ethnic groups have strong systems of functional specialization, with five categories of clearly defined occupational caste groups: fishermen, weavers, woodworkers, blacksmiths and musicians. Sometimes these castes amalgamated or were extended by the addition of sub-groups. For example potters were added as the new skill developed. These occupational castes are still recognized in Senegambia and they are particularly strong in the middle Senegal valley (Curtin, 1975).

Further east among the Hausa of Northern Nigeria there is a long history of industry and trading and the occupational status of particular trades is an important element of social stratification. Within the commoner class (*talakawa*) of the Hausa there is a comprehensive range of occupations which are ranked in order of status: *mallams* (koranic teachers), the bigger traders and merchants are placed at the top; butchers, praise-singers, drummers, porters, domestic servants and poorer farmers at the bottom. But the great majority of Hausa craftsmen, traders and farmers belong to the middle class (Smith, 1959). Although there might be a general consensus about the status of the highest and lowest, opinions vary about the placement of those in the middle classes.

Some impressions of the range of non-farm activities in Hausaland can be gained from the listings of occupations made by the early colonial administrators, for the purpose of tax assessments. Table 3.1 shows the occupations recorded during 1911 and 1948 for districts of Sokoto Province in Northern Nigeria and gives some idea of the diversity of non-farm occupations in the immediate pre-colonial and colonial period. The occupational structures are not very different for the two periods and up to about 1950 small-scale industrialists and craftsmen formed the bulk of the industrial sector in Nigeria. It was only after 1950 that the modern large-scale sector began to develop. In Nigeria during the 1970s there emerged a significant large-scale manufacturing and service sector as a result of the oil-boom, but in other smaller West African countries crafts and domestic manufacturing tend to be the norm. For example in Sierra Leone it was estimated in 1975 that 78.3 per cent of those employed in industry were in the small-scale sector located in rural areas, with only 7.5 per cent in urban areas. Both in terms of employment and the number of establishments, small-scale industries are dominant in Sierra Leone, with an emphasis on their dispersal among the smaller centres of population (Chuta and Liedholm, 1975).

Credit is often generated to finance these ventures by systems of informal reinforced reciprocity networks. The most well-integrated of these are to be found in Cameroon where credit rings have wide social and political functions beyond the generation of venture capital. In East and Central Africa the situation is rather different as indigenous crafts and trading did not experience the same levels of pre-colonial development as West Africa. Also in the colonial period, the permanent settlement of Europeans put the emphasis on the development of large-scale mining and ancillary industry (chapter 8). However, a burgeoning development of very small-scale petty trade in small manufactured items absorbed the remitted earnings of miners whose families remained in rural areas. African inexperience in handling the long distance urban and metropolitan focus of the activity meant that all but the most petty trade by pedlars was dominated by Asian trading concerns. The Indian store became an increasingly significant part of the life of much of the region and was not without significance in West Africa. However, since the 1960s Asian capital has been diverted from commercial enterprises into industries such as engineering, which were formerly owned by Europeans. Many of these Asian entrepreneurs were from this trading sector now increasingly overtaken by Africans. Many still have connections and capital in Punjabi towns. On the other hand, most Africans now engaged in small-scale industry and crafts have only first generation experience, and little experience of raising capital. In much of East Africa there was little labour specialization prior to colonial rule, and

Table 3.1 Occupations in the Home District, 1911 and Gumbi District, 1948, Sokoto Province, Northern Nigeria

Occupation	Home 1911	Gumbi 1948
Barbers	532	138
Blacksmiths	259	47
Brokers	223	–
Builders	–	154
Butchers	522	221
Dyers	351	104
Fishermen	–	229
Leatherworkers	133	43
Malams (religious teachers)	–	215
Middlemen	–	86
Tailors	545	–
Tanners	329	–
Traders	1105	570
Weavers	3634	600
Others	–	2655
	7633	5062
Total Population	130 846	18 103

Source: Sokoto Home District Assessment, 1911, Sokoto History Bureau HIS/9; Gumbi District Assessment, 1948, Sokoto History Bureau Acc 24 Sok/93/8/24.

what there was – such as iron working – came close to collapse afterwards (King, 1979). In such countries as Kenya, Zambia and Botswana it is difficult to speak of traditional industries and even those employed as professional workers are first or second generation. The whole character of non-farm and off-farm employment in this region is dominated by migrant wage labour and a relatively long-term commitment to urban employment. Rural credit for all the activities which involve the generation of any activity which is clearly focused in rural areas remains a problem. Incentives to return even from urban unemployment to a situation of rural poverty are not great. Only a very considerable change in prices for rural produce, perhaps along the lines suggested by Lipton (1977), is likely to change this situation.

One of the problems in understanding the rural non-farm sector is a general ignorance of its nature and lack of data on backward and forward linkages with farming and other industries. The majority of non-farm enterprises are domestic-based and as with agriculture it is important to understand the workings of the household production unit and the under-lying productive relationships. Most rural industries and services are in varying degrees combined with farming, and therefore household needs are satisfied by a diversity of occupational practices. This raises a number of questions. If the primary occupation is farming, are non-farm jobs a means of satisfying extra needs such as luxuries or tax payments, or are they an integral part of subsistence? What exactly are the jobs and trades undertaken, and how much do they contribute to total income? Is money reinvested in farming or non-farm activities? Under conditions of multiple employment how much labour is primarily engaged in non-farm activities, what is the nature of the jobs and their linkages with other sectors of the economy, and what form do they take? At a more general level the demand for labour and its allocations depends on seasonal workloads, production techniques, age, sex, health and labour mobility. Labour mobility is an important aspect of less developed economies and both local farm and non-farm employers may have to compete for labour which is attracted or forced into other regions where opportunities and rewards are greater. Therefore, non-farm work may involve local or long distance migration, and seasonal or periodic absences from home.

The character of non-farm industry and employment and the relations of production which sustain them are of course more than local issues and they cannot be studied in isolation; levels of technology, culture and relations with national and international market forces are often of paramount importance. Furthermore, there are important spatial differences in rural non-farm employment. The proximity of towns and market-places exert an influence on both the character and dynamics of rural industries and services compared with areas at a distance from main centres.

The proportion of farm work and non-farm work varies along a spectrum which at one end one finds farmers occasionally or seasonally engaged in some other pursuit and at the other end one finds off-farm work dominating the rural household who continue farming largely by hiring labour. The amount of non-farm work and the income generated may be the means of economic and social differentiation among rural communities and this is an important aspect of their structure and characterization.

Although the importance of the small-scale sector in the rural economy is now generally recognized, information about its structure and dynamics is still meagre. It is not easy to construct an accurate descriptive profile of non-farm work, because people frequently combine farming with other occupations and which job is the most important economically is not easy to determine. Also switching from one job to another may involve a move from one place to another. Itinerant craftsmen and traders are a well-established part of rural life and increasingly people move away from their villages either seasonally or daily to take up non-farm employment.

RURAL NON-FARM EMPLOYMENT: A DESCRIPTIVE PROFILE

Although the list of occupations shown in table 3.1 gives some idea of the diversity of employment and the degree of specialization found in villages in Northern Nigeria, contemporary observations from many parts of Africa show a similar diversity in rural areas. The number of activities is large and there are various ways of categorizing them, but one method which has been used for comparative purposes is the International Labour Offices Standard Classification of Occupation. On this basis non-farm occupations are sub-divided as follows:

1 professional, technical and administrative;
2 sales workers (traders);
3 miners and quarrymen;
4 transport and communications workers;
5 craftsmen and production process workers;
6 service workers.
   (ILO 1970)

Of these six categories, the two most important ones in tropical Africa are craftsmen and production process workers(5) and sales workers(2): these two dominate the non-farm sector, and probably account for 70 per cent of all such employment.

Craftsmen and production process workers comprise a large number of manufacturing occupations, and include food processing (for example, the conversion of cassava to flour and starchy paste), extracting palm and groundnut oil and brewing beer from maize and millets. Also, the conversion of hides and skins – tanning and leather working – and of cotton and cloths – spinning, weaving, dyeing and tailoring. Iron smelting, once a basic industry, is now virtually extinct, but blacksmithing flourishes and relies on imported materials or the recycling of scrap material, notably from wrecked cars and lorries. Other aspects of 'recycling' includes the use of tyres for footwear, well-buckets and old tins converted into lamps, funnels and water containers. Improvization of this kind is one of the striking features of this activity. African craftsmen draw on a strong tradition of innovation which often characterizes rural societies in transition when access to replacement is limited or costly. It is a tradition on which intermediate technologists build in suggesting strategies for development initiatives.

Craft work includes woodworking, especially the production of pestles and mortars for use in food preparation, together with a number of jobs which use local vegetable matter such as palms, grasses, gourds and crop residues (for example, guinea-corn stalks) for the production of mats, bags, fences, thatching, ropes and cane-work. Clay-working had a longer history than iron working, although local pottery is one craft industry which has probably suffered a good deal from the use of imported metal and more recently plastic holloware.

Trading is a widespread activity in Africa and even in small villages one may find permanent or at least part-time traders (chapter 5). However, there is some evidence to suggest that despite the ubiquitous trader, it is craft and small-scale independent industrial workers who are now more important in many rural areas. Frequently these jobs have been differentiated by sex. For example, among the Yoruba in Nigeria the majority of traders are women, whereas craft and industrial jobs are dominated by men. On the other hand in Uganda and elsewhere in Muslim East Africa male participation in all types of non-farm work is twice that of women.

In recent years the industrial service sector has changed in many parts of Africa as new opportunities have arisen for those who can repair watches, bicycles, radios and cars, as well as for those providing rural taxi and lorry services. These workers are more likely to be found in the larger villages which often contain permanent rural markets and reflect changing patterns of consumption and the expansion of transport. The larger villages have also seen the appearance of government and public employees such as teachers and dispensers, whom form a salaried class of village dwellers.

Although comprehensive data on the rural non-farm sector do not exist, available figures give the impression that the numbers involved are considerable and that the employees are occupied with varying degrees of commitment. In 1970 an ILO report on rural Western Nigeria showed that 27 per cent of employed males had their primary occupation in the rural non-farm sector, while a similar study in Uganda gave a corresponding figure of 20 per cent. As we shall see later, significantly higher proportions have been recorded more recently in Nigeria on the edge of towns. Those who are held to have their primary source of income from non-farm activities may of course do some farming on a seasonal, part-time, or occasional basis. For example, 8 per cent migrant groundnut farmers in the Gambia during 1974–5 were in fact small businessmen, principally traders and tailors, who were farming during the wet season when business was slack as a means of accumulating capital for either stock, cloth, or in some cases the purchase of a sewing machine (Swindell, 1981).

The proportion of rural dwellers involved in non-farm employment becomes even more striking when one adds those farmers who are engaged in crafts, industry and services on a *secondary* basis. In the Western Nigeria survey referred to above, another 14 per cent of men were secondarily employed in the non-farm sector, which pushed the overall percentage to 41 per cent. However, there are seasonal variations and especially in those areas with long dry seasons, such as the savannas, where non-farm employment is maximized when cultivation has virtually ceased. A study of villages in Zaria Province, Northern Nigeria, indicated that men spent 79 per cent of their time in February on non-farm work and only 27 per cent in August (Norman, 1972).

However, another survey carried out in Soba near Zaria by Schultz (1976) presents rather a different picture. Although the men in this village were concerned with non-farm work on a *secondary* basis, 40 per cent had secondary occupations which they carried on throughout the year. Even in the smaller villages investigated around Soba there was a higher proportion of employment in the all-year-round category. This perspective on non-farm employment suggests that farmers had little interest in non-farm work as a primary occupation but that there was a shift from the seasonal pattern of working towards the maintenance of their non-farm activities throughout the year. Schultz's survey was carried out some five years later than Norman's and may reflect rising levels of demand for goods and services in the rural sector as the Nigerian economy expanded during the oil-boom: the problem as we observed earlier is the lack of comprehensive data on what is happening in the rural non-farm sector.

From data that are available, it is apparent that the time spent on farming in combination with non-farm work, or vice versa, covers a wide spectrum of possibilities and practices. We have already mentioned that crafts, industries and services may be either a primary or secondary source of income for rural dwellers, as well as the possible seasonal fluctuations in non-farm activities. But there is another subset of workers located in villages, who are occupied on a full-time basis. These workers may comprise a small sector of salaried public officials and state employees whose presence reflects the changing patterns of economic and social life in rural areas, as government institutions such as schools and dispensaries have become established in the larger villages. In a household survey of sample villages in Bunyole county, Uganda, only 4 per cent had formal sector jobs as their primary occupation, but half of these were working in primary and secondary education (Mwima-Mudeenya, 1978).

Although salaried workers such as these are unequivocally in the permanent non-farm sector, they may still have farmland which they cultivate in the evenings and weekends, or more likely they rely on hired farm labour. In addition to public sector employees many larger villages have small-scale businessmen and shop-owners who have little interest in farming, except through the use of family members or of hired labour. There is no doubt then that it is not always easy to draw the line between primary and secondary, seasonal and permanent employment in the rural non-farm sector, especially as so little information is available about the financial returns and the relative importance of different occupations; and it is no easy matter to enumerate employment accurately and calculate investment in non-farm enterprises. What is clear is that it is very significant and manifests itself in cash income and improvement in the rural environment. Indeed cash income is most obviously apparent in the improved appearance and stability of the rural houses of Africa, with increasing reliance on zinc roofing and breeze-block walls.

SPATIAL DISTRIBUTION OF RURAL NON-FARM WORK

So far we have discussed the type of non-farm businesses and employment, as well as seasonal variations, but there is also a spatial dimension, not only on a regional basis, but also related to the distribution and size and quality of rural settlements. It seems fairly certain that the amount and type of non-farm activity tends to vary directly with the population size of rural settlements and their location, especially their proximity to larger urban centres and major roads. The ILO survey of Western Nigeria (1970) found that in villages with fewer than 500 inhabitants only 31 per cent of males were engaged in non-farm activities, while in the villages between 1450 and 2600 inhabitants, 73 per cent were involved in such work. Schultz's findings in Soba in 1976 confirmed this pattern, as in the largest central village of Soba only 28 per cent of males had no secondary occupation while in the smaller satellite villages, 51 per cent had no secondary employment.

The size of rural settlements seems not only to influence occupational type and structure, but also the size of the firms. The survey of small-scale industry in Sierra Leone (Chuta and Liedholm, 1975) found that for all small-scale industries the average size of firms by employees (including proprietors) was 1.9 workers per firm; this figure fell to 1.6 for settlements below 2000 inhabitants and rose to 2.3 in villages of between 2000 and 5000 inhabitants. Furthermore, the dominance of tailoring was further accentuated in the localities with over 2000 inhabitants, where on average half of the enterprises were engaged in this activity.

The occupational structure of villages may also be influenced by their location close to large or medium-sized towns. In the Sudanic zone of West Africa there is evidence of the disappearance of traditional crafts and industrial processing, notably spinning, dyeing and weaving, as these industries have been centralized in the towns, or have been replaced by cheap imported cloth sold in the large town markets. On the other hand the service sector in the village on the urban periphery (e.g. barbers and butchers) seems to have been maintained or even expanded with the dispersion of retail traders from the towns who have set up business in surrounding villages, providing local services rather on the lines of sub-urban general stores in Western cities. For example, Schultz (1976) found that in Soba district non-farming permanent businessmen were generally in-migrants, who had come into the larger villages via the nearby town of Zaria.

Villages in urban peripheries and hinterlands have particularly high levels of local non-farm employment and poorer peasant farmers have become dependent on the 'formal' and 'informal' sectors of nearby towns for their incomes to the extent that their farms have become subsidiary parts of the sustenance and reproduction of their households. On the other hand better-off small commodity producers have also become involved in urban employment and trading, but at the same time maintain their farms by using hired labour, often producing foodstuffs for the urban market. In a study of two villages near Kano in Nigeria, Amerena (1982) found that 31 and 34 per cent of farmers participated in non-farm occupations in both the wet and dry seasons, but between 64.9 and 90 per cent of them considered non-farm work as their chief source of cash income. These farmers had become semi-proletarians who relied on younger members and wives to run their farms, while the 'big-men' of the village hired-in wage labour. The study of the British type of 'Pay As You Earn' (PAYE) tax returns for the two villages (Amarena, 1982) showed that up to 34 per cent of males in some villages were employed in the 'formal' large-scale commercial and industrial sector of Kano. It was also apparent that participation in all non-farm activities had been given a significant boost by the drought which extended from the late 1960s into the mid-1970s.

Although the majority who live and move within the rural–urban fringes have access to land, irrespective of whether they are primarily urban or rural dwellers, there is an increasing number of landless workers, or land poor households, in the vicinity of urban settlements. The pressure on land around large African towns can be acute and may originate from within the urban salariat and trading community who are interested in land speculation and building, as well as from rural 'big-men', farmers and traders who wish to increase their landholdings to take advantage of the urban market for foodstaples (Cohen, 1976). The result is that small farmers may be squeezed and sell land and they are especially vulnerable if the household is at a point in its developmental cycle where there is an adverse dependency ratio. If this is combined with illness, debt, or bad harvests then the sale of land may become inevitable. Around Kano, the majority of the now proletarianized villages are dependent on urban employment. Landless or land poor workers from non-viable farming households move between town and countryside in response to daily or seasonal opportunities for work. It is these kinds of workers who may be mobilized as gang labour on the bigger farms in the rural areas, as well as forming the nucleus of a permanent wage labour force in the town.

HOUSEHOLD INCOME DERIVED FROM FARM AND NON-FARM WORK

If information about the general nature and operation of the non-farm sector is not particularly abundant, there is even less about the allocation of labour between farm and non-farm activities and the relative amounts of income generated within households. If many households still satisfy their main needs by the production of most of their basic foodstuffs together with the sale of surpluses and by growing a cashcrop specifically for the market, there are also increasing numbers for whom this is not possible. In some cases, the household possesses special skills which divert it from agriculture. Here members may engage in crafts, trade, small-scale industry, or become migrant workers. But the relationships between farm and non-farm activities (and income produced) is not constant, especially when non-farm work is of secondary importance. Poor harvests, low prices, environmental hazards and the developmental cycles of family groups may force at one time more and at another time fewer workers into the non-farm sector.

The household survey carried out in Uganda by Mwima-Mudeenya in 1978 attempted to measure returns from different activities, although it was confined to cash incomes and excludes subsistence. Analyses of total household income have been attempted using imputed income for subsistence farming, and apparently runs at about 30 per cent. But in the Ugandan study this was not attempted and cash incomes were identified as being derived from one or more of four sources: cash from the sales of cotton and increasingly maize and rice; poultry and livestock; wage employment; other non-farm activities. The 11 sampled villages in Bunyole County, Uganda, showed 32 per cent of cash income by household came from sales of cashcrops, 32 per cent from wages earned in the formal and informal sectors, 25 per cent from non-farm activities carried out in the household and 11 per cent from livestock and poultry. These average figures hide large variations from village to village for example the non-farm sector income ranged from 15 per cent to 64 per cent while in the village which was the administrative centre of Bunyole County, wage earning accounted for 61 per cent of household incomes.

The general impression from the Ugandan survey was of the declining importance of agricultural produce as a source of income, as wage earning became more important and it appears the non-farm sector still has potential for expansion. The rural economy from the colonial period onwards was increasingly tied to external market forces associated with cotton cultivation and this led to higher levels of monetization and the demand for new manufactured goods procured either locally or imported. In the 1970s with declining prices of cotton, there appears to have been a shift to wage earning and petty commodity production to maintain cash incomes.

The amount and sources of household income is provided by the various economic surveys of Kenya, which have been analysed by Kitching (1980). Tables 3.2 and 3.3 show gross earnings for households in Central Province (which includes Nairobi) and Nyanza province, which lies on the western border of Kenya. A comparison of the two areas shows that the proportion of cash receipts derived from wages and salaries (earnings) was higher in Central Province for all income groups (except the richest) and reflects the employment opportunities available in Nairobi, together with casual employment on other smallholdings in an area where commercial agriculture was well developed. On the other hand, income coming from remittances is much higher in Nyanza Province, which reflects a less well developed

Table 3.2   Household cash income in Nyanza Province, 1970: gross terms

| Income group (shillings) | Household Gross Cash Income (%) | | | |
	Earnings	Remittances	Trade & Business	Agriculture
1 300–599	14.2	24.7	2.8	39.7
2 600–999	14.4	19.4	7.6	35.5
3 1000–1499	16.3	11.8	10.1	43.9
4 1500–1999	14.8	15.7	6.7	43.1
5 2000–2999	18.0	14.1	9.5	45.7
6 3000+	46.6	11.6	16.5	17.3

Source: cited in Kitching, 1980.

Table 3.3   Percentage of household cash income from different sources according to income group, Central Province

Income group (shillings)	Wages or salaries ('services')	Remittances	Trade & business
1 50–1000	32.2	19.3	4.6
2 1001–1500	33.1	17.4	8.8
3 1501–2000	26.5	10.5	9.5
4 2001–2500	35.6	6.4	12.2
5 2501–3500	29.1	6.4	13.0
6 3501–5000	32.5	4.6	12.0
7 5000+	32.1	2.2	25.2

Source: cited in Kitching, 1980.

commercialization of agriculture and the prevalence of long distance migration. The proportion of gross household cash coming from trade and business is lower in all income groups in Nyanza Province which Kitching suggests is again related to levels of commercialization and marketed surpluses in agriculture.

But despite these differences there is a marked similarity between the two provinces inasmuch as the farm/non-farm structure of cash incomes are alike. At all income levels non-farm sources are more important than farming, something which is especially apparent in the richest and poorest households. The poorest households derived between 56 and 60 per cent of their gross incomes from off-farm activities, while for the richest households in Nyanza this could be as much as 83 per cent. In Nyanza low returns from commercialized production made it rational for the richest households to direct their labour power into off-farm employment, mainly higher paid wage and salaried jobs which their access to education made available. In addition, business and trade were important, and it was this factor which made their income double that of any other group. At the other end of the income scale in Central Province the opposite forces were at work. Higher population densities forced poorer households to market as much of their total output as possible and supplement household incomes by casual work for better-off farmers, or by taking jobs in nearby Nairobi.

The household profiles from Kenya emphasize the importance of off-farm work and associated income, which appear to be far more important than has often been imagined. The findings of the various economic surveys suggest that there is considerable geographical, as well as social differentiation of household off-farm employment. Furthermore, they substantiate the need for continuing surveys of this kind in as many countries as possible, if governments and planners are to make any sense of the rural sector.

THE ORGANIZATION OF THE NON-FARM SECTOR

So far nothing has been said about the organization of businesses and employment in the small-scale industrial service sector, nor of how one might define small-scale. The distinction between small-scale and large-scale enterprises can be arbitrarily defined according to the number of employees and the amount of capital invested. For example it has been held that small firms employ less than 50 workers. On the other hand there are definitions such as 'informal' and 'formal' sector industry which have been applied to separate out the large-scale from the small-scale operations. One distinction which has been offered between formal and informal is based essentially on wage earning (formal sector) and self-employment (informal sector) (see Hart, 1973). However the distinction advanced by Wallace (1972) suggests the difference lies in the structure within which they operate. For example a manual worker digging wells on a government farm is in a formal job, enumerated, and earning the statutory government minimum wage, but someone digging wells for a small cashcrop farmer who has no security of tenure, or way of ensuring that he gets paid is in informal employment. Davies (1979) believes that the definition must rest on the recognition of different modes of production. The formal sector is based on highly developed social productive forces; the informal sector is not, as both its means of production and its techniques of production are non-capital-intensive. On the other hand in the formal sector, the means of production are privately owned by a small class of proprietors and the business is operated by workers for the benefit of that owning class. In the informal sector the means of production are generally owned by those who operate them and unlike the formal sector the division of labour is rudimentary and horizontal rather than vertical.

In terms of employment rural non-farm enterprises are small and frequently comprise only the proprietor and one or two workers who may be either drawn from his family, or paid labourers or apprentices. Apprentices appear to be the commonest form of additional labour, especially in the newer industries such as vehicle repair, radio and watch-repairing. In Sierra Leone the workforce of small informal sector enterprises was made up of 41 per cent proprietors, 42 per cent apprentices and 17 per cent hired labourers. In Nigeria the proportion of apprentices is probably much higher. Certainly the apprenticeship system is the chief means of developing technical and entrepreneurial skills and although those who are primarily interested in non-farm employment have a higher level of formal education than farmers, success depends more on managerial and technical ability.

The amount of physical capital is limited in both rural and urban informal sector enterprises. Businesses are commonly housed in temporary buildings constructed of mud, thatch and corrugated iron. The use of machinery tends to be minimal and concentrated in certain industries (for example tailoring) and less used in the smaller villages. The use of power-driven machinery is even more limited and found chiefly in urban-based enterprises. An important question is the efficiency with which these small establishments combine labour and capital and again data are very poor. In 1962 Kilby estimated that in Eastern Nigeria small industries were capitalized at about the rate of £100 per worker, whereas in the large-scale formal sector it was more like £3000. More recently in Sierra Leone which has a much weaker economic structure, estimates based on tailoring indicated that small businesses had about £35 per worker invested compared with large-scale establishments where it was about £2600 per worker (Chuta and Liedholm, 1975). Among tukolor weavers in Senegal, Dilley (1986) found that it cost about £50 to set up a business (equivalent to 50–100 days' profit) and the majority of this sum was invested in imported yarn. Such a sum is considerable and in the absence of capital for starting up, a weaver may initially be employed by a cloth trader or have to find a patron.

NON-FARM ENTERPRISES AND THE EXTERNAL ECONOMY

The size of production units, the supply of capital and labour are important attributes of the organization of businesses in the small-scale sector, but it is also necessary to consider the influence of local and international market forces and the demand for the products of rural crafts, industries and services. The demand for these products and services is an integral part of the growth of the agricultural sector and dependent on farm prices and income, which underline the need to keep in mind the complex relationships between the agricultural and rural non-farm sectors. The introduction of cashcrops and new agricultural practices have in many cases increased the demand for rurally produced consumer goods and services, associated with rising incomes within the farming community. On the other hand the demand for rurally produced agricultural inputs and the opportunities for processing outputs are possibilities which arise from both forward and backward linkages in the agricultural sector. In The Gambia and Senegal the spread of groundnut cultivation has promoted the introduction of ox-ploughs, and wheeled tool-bars manufactured by local blacksmiths. In Nigeria the development of small petrol-powered grinding machines has been a recent innovation which allows millet and guinea corn to be quickly ground, as well as pulping tomatoes to produce paste either for domestic use or sale in local markets. Tomato paste processing has been so successful that the attempts of an international company to introduce large-scale tomato processing plants in Zaria failed because of the competitive and widely distributed village grinderies!

Nonetheless, it is true that if circumstances raise the opportunity costs of rural non-farm labour then the competitive position of rurally produced goods may be undermined by cheaper imports from the urban centres or imported goods from external sources. In the latter case there have been some countries such as Nigeria which have experienced a dramatic decrease in rural spinning, dyeing and weaving as a result of cheaply produced cloth with a wide range of designs either from indigenous mills such as those in Kaduna or imported. The cost of handspun and woven cloth is such that it is now virtually a luxury item and a status symbol for the well-to-do. On the other hand local weaving using imported yarns has continued while tailoring of imported cloth is a ubiquitous business in both urban and rural areas.

One of the effects of an increased use of imported yarns for weaving has been a shift of weavers away from the countryside into urban centres. In Senegal, Dilley (1986) has shown that as local cotton production has declined, village weavers can no longer afford time-absorbing trips into towns to buy imported yarns, so they relocate in larger towns such as Dakar and Diourbel or become itinerant weavers moving among a number of towns. The move out of the rural areas has removed weavers from a network of patron/client relations into the money economy, yet they have not entirely severed their links with the villages. Weavers still return to their homes to cultivate farms, which is not highly disruptive for their trade as the wet season is generally a slack period when demand for cloth is at its lowest.

There has been a fairly widespread acceptance that as economic development proceeds and the indigenous economy has been penetrated by the world capitalist economy, rural crafts and industries have declined in the face of substitutes either imported or produced locally in the larger urban centres. However, there are alternative views and evidence to the contrary, and in Kenya it was reported that wage employment in rural non-farm activities, including trading, increased by 45 per cent between 1967 and 1970. Perhaps this should come as no surprise in the light of King's remarks about the recent growth of the small-scale industrial sector in East Africa being a matter of no more than two generations (King, 1979). But even in West Africa it has been asserted for example, that among the Yoruba, craft industries such as textiles were generally confined to the towns until the beginning of the twentieth century (Bray, 1969). While this may be true of some industries in Nigeria, there were other types of non-farm employment in rural areas which already existed in the pre-colonial period.

In West Africa internal trade not only survived colonialism but it was expanded from the 1930s onwards with the growth of population, the spread of new transport networks, the reduction of internal costs of transport and rising *per capita* incomes not only in the towns, but also in the wealthier export crop producing regions (Hopkins, 1973). Our detailed knowledge of the dynamics and changes in crafts, industries and services during the twentieth century is no better than the state of our present knowledge about their structure and operation and, in the absence of adequate data, theories of decline or expansion have yet to be fully tested (O'Hear, 1986).

Although some traditional industries may have *relatively* declined, there is no reason to assume that they have *quantitatively* declined and their levels of output may remain as high as they were in pre-colonial times. But it seems fairly safe to assume that expansion, decline, adaptation and the emergence of new enterprises and occupations in the rural non-farm sector proceeded simultaneously but differentially over time and space and that there was no wholesale liquidation of local industry. Indeed a more pertinent question is why on the one hand it has survived and adapted so well in areas where pre-colonial industry and trade flourished, and on the other why the small-scale informal sector has developed where hitherto it had little place in the local economy.

The reasons for survival and expansion in the small-scale sector are several. First, some products are protected by the need for specific locations close to their market and by low overheads. For example, the production of pots and holloware continues in rural areas because of cheap local raw materials and high transport costs, but this is less true of those larger villages on main roads and those on the periphery of towns where imported plastic holloware and the use of recycled tin-ware have undercut local crafts and industries.

The demand for local goods and services provided by the informal sector is enhanced for reasons of economy. Local producers compete favourably with small-scale businessmen by avoiding overhead costs and taxes, by paying government minimum wages and by using cheap family or apprentice labour (Davies 1979). Moreover, some products continue to sell in competition with cheaper imported or urban-produced goods, because of consumer preference and because some traditional crafts survive as they exploit particular niches. For example some local cloths have a particular prestige value. Some industries have survived and prospered by employing new techniques and this has been particularly important in the case of tailoring, where the local production of clothes was advanced by the use of the sewing machine. The introduction of the sewing machine must rank along with the introduction of the lorry in the transformation of both urban and rural life in tropical Africa. Sewing machines have led to a cut in production costs and an increase in output. Finally, some industries and services are the product of new consumer patterns, for example, the use of radios, watches, bicycles and the increasing consumption of wheat-bread.

It has been suggested that the role of the informal sector and its continuance can be explained by the informal workers themselves rather than the demand for the goods and services they produce. One argument has been that small-scale informal activities are a transitional stage in the development of a permanent wage labour force, while the formal sector is incapable of providing enough jobs and agriculture is failing to support the population because of its underdevelopment. Therefore the small-scale informal sector is seen as occupied by labourers and business people who are simply wage-labourers 'in waiting'. This may be an oversimplified view and ignores the stratification which exists in the informal sector and the fact that there are many who have no wish, or intention, of seeking employment in the large-scale formal sector. It is only in the urban areas that the argument may have some validity where the absence of jobs is more important than the professed desire of workers to remain in the informal sector.

An alternative to the workers 'in waiting' argument is that many in the informal sector are incipient capitalists, or petty commodity producers (Davies, 1979). Work goes on in this sector because it gives a viable income for the small entrepreneur and is the means of capital accumulation. But as in the case of potential formal sector workers, all of those in the informal small-scale sector cannot be viewed as incipient capitalists, and many are vulnerable to competition from industrial capital. Nevertheless, in the rural areas the combination of farming and non-farming occupations may be the best or only strategy for household reproduction in the face of low incomes derived from either farming or non-farm employment and the low level of labour specialization.

The need to reproduce domestic groups, or the desire to improve income levels may be achieved not only by engaging in domestic industry or trading, but also by taking up wage employment in the formal or informal sectors in areas beyond the local community. Seasonal and permanent labour migration by one or more members of a household may be necessary processes, well entrenched in less developed countries and sub-Saharan

Africa certainly provides many instances of these forms of regional and international movements of labour.

MIGRANT LABOUR AND THE RURAL ECONOMY

The search for jobs may mean no more than short-distance movements into neighbouring villages or towns, lasting for a day or two, or it may involve long-distance migration lasting for a season, a year, or more. For example some rural dwellers take up employment either in local villages, or become agricultural labourers for small farmers or in areas of specialized farming where crops are grown for either local or export markets. These rural to rural movements comprise the hired workers which we discussed in chapter 2. Rural dwellers may also move into towns (rural to urban movements) to become employed in the small-scale informal sector, or take up formal sector jobs in commercial organizations, government institutions, industry and mining. Mining employment is frequently found in distinctive enclaves of economic development and under highly regulated arrangements. The methods of recruiting migrant workers and their contractual agreements vary enormously. A West African migrant cocoa farmer may use indigenous organizations to facilitate his movements and may be employed as a share-cropper or hired labourer. On the other hand migrant workers in East and Central Africa obtain jobs in mines and factories through recruitment agencies and are subject to the stringent controls and the intrinsic variability of modern sector wage employment.

The search for jobs which are frequently seasonal or semi-permanent leads to a higly mobile labour-force: for example each year three to four million rural dwellers in tropical Africa leave their villages for varied periods of time to take up work in towns, villages, plantations and industrial enclaves. The high level of mobility reflects imperfect specialization of labour in the African economy, as well as regional inequalities in resource endowments and differential economic development. Alternatively it can be seen as the result of an historically structured process of underdevelopment, associated with the penetration of the world capitalist system, which has created labour 'reserves'. In particular, the articulation of a 'modes-of-production' thesis sees migrant labour initiated by policies of colonial taxation and monetization with wage rates kept low because the reproduction of households in the sending areas is sustained by those left behind who work the family farms (see chapter 9).

Quite clearly migrant workers and the income they do or do not provide is an important element in the rural economy right across tropical Africa. Arguments about the impact of migration are plentiful and include the belief that it is responsible for the deterioration of rural life, that it undercuts rural progress or at its best it staves off rural starvation. Alternatively there are those who point to its role in promoting accumulation in rural areas, its importance in developing class relations and the emergence of a *petite bourgeoisie*. One is inclined to agree with Stichter (1985) that there is no simple inverse relationship between labour exports and the decline of the peasant economy, although there might be upper limits beyond which a given number of absentees from an area for an extended period of time causes severe dislocation. The effects of male absence varies according to population density, land availability, ecological conditions, types of crop, farm technology, social division of labour and socio-economic differentiation as well as fluctuation in market prices and wages.

Within tropical Africa it is possible to discern three general types of migration. First where migration co-exists with subsistence farming such as among the Mossi of Burkina Faso and the Mambwe of Zambia. In the past the Mambwe and other northern groups in Zambia have been classic circulatory labour migrants between their home areas and the Zambian Copperbelt (though permanent migration is now increasingly common), while the Mossi continue to move seasonally from their savanna homelands at the rate of some 200 000 a year into the cocoa-growing areas of Ivory Coast and Ghana. Most return home, although each year some remain which constitutes a longer-term drain on manpower from Mossi villages. A second type of migration is where it co-exists with cashcrop cultivation, for example among theKikuyu, the cocoa areas of south-western Nigeria and within the Senegambian groundnut basin. Here local farmers employ not only longer-distance migrant workers, but substantial numbers of local farm labourers who circulate among local villages. Thirdly, there are those areas where migrant labour has become the primary overriding source of household income and where farming has become a peripheral activity, these areas would include the labour reserves of black Southern Africa, although there are individual households in this category scattered across Africa.

Geographically a distinction might also be made between West Africa and East, Central and Southern Africa. In the former, local and long-distance migration has been marked by a wide range of contractual arrangements, a lack of formal recruiting agencies and the employment of Africans by African entrepreneurs in both the town and the countryside. There are exceptions, notably the state as employer and mining areas in Ghana, Nigeria, Liberia and Sierra Leone. But in East, Central and Southern Africa the alienation of land by Europeans, the substantial plantation estate and mining sectors set up by Europeans and subsequently maintained in the post-independence period have given a different aspect to migration. In the last chapter we noted that substantial male absences from rural areas have exacerbated the workloads of women in East and Central Africa where the absence of males may reach 40 and even 50 per cent of village populations. There was a brief period in Southern Rhodesia and Kenya from about 1890 to the 1920s when peasant proprietors responded to the colonial market for food in towns and mines, which led to increased stability and prosperity in the rural areas. But this was curtailed by the demand for farm and mine labour by Europeans, the imposition of produce quotas with the subsequent shifting of rural men into wage labour.

In Kenya in 1924 some 1715 settler farmers were employing 87 000 African workers, while in 1920 the arrival of the Brooke Bond Tea Corporation initiated the plantation sector. About the same time Unilever opened its oil-palm plantation in the Congo and later added plantations in Uganda, Tanzania and Malawi. In Tanzania the plantation workforce of former German East Africa numbered some 4000–5000 in 1900–1, but by 1980 the total wage employment stood at 607 730 (cited in Sender and Smith, 1986). In Zimbabwe earliest figures for wage employment refer only to the mining industry which by 1906 was employing 19 800 wage workers. By 1982 the wage labour force had increased to 1 042 600 with women accounting for over 25 per cent of wage labour in the 'commercial' agricultural sector. Sender and Smith (1986) have argued that from the late 1930s and 1950s onwards improvements in working conditions have occurred in the capitalist mining and industrial sectors as a result of employers' requirements and pressure from organized labour. The result has been a stabilization of the workforce. Employees no longer require limited consumption goods bought by wages acquired through temporary employment. They now often desire a greater range of social goods such as schooling which means more permanent employment. Also, differentiation in rural areas has increased the number of landless and land poor who are dependent on wage labour.

Increased socio–economic differentiation in the rural areas arising from non-farm and off-farm employment either locally or further afield is an issue of some importance in the transformation of rural Africa. There are many variations on this theme, but Kenya provides interesting relatively well-documented examples which show the levels of non-farm income among households and its effects. We have already referred to the amount and sources of household income provided by the various economic surveys of Kenya, where employment in the better non-farm jobs such as clerks, artisans, minor government employees have been an important element in producing what Kitching (1980) describes as a *petite bourgeoisie*. Non-farm employment has been achieved through investment in education which initially favoured chiefs and their clients, and in turn surplus income has been invested in commercial farming such as coffee growing. Thus a process of 'straddling' or double participation in the wage sector and rural commodity production has emerged, a process which is widespread in Africa and an integral part of rural change and development (see Iliffe,

Table 3.4   Occupational structure of African households in Kenya, 1970

Category	Definition	No. employed 1969–70
1	Agricultural employment for a male, 'home plot' retained for wife and children	178 589
1a	Non-agricultural employment for a male, 'home plot' retained for wife and children	466 264
		644 853
2	Squatter agricultural employment, 'home plot' on hiring farm	44 647
3	Higher-paid non-agricultural employment, usually in urban areas, wife and children dependent on wage earnings alone	120 000
4	Employment of the landless or 'poor peasants' by other smallholders	311 000

Source: Kitching, 1980

1983) in the town and commercial agriculture in the villages. Kitching argues that employment in the state sector is the route to accumulation and the access to state revenues. The problem has been how to maintain and expand the state wages bill, which principally derived from taxes, borrowing and earnings from the state marketing boards. In this last respect, Kitching represents the state as merchant capital.

The upshot of non-farm employment especially in the state sector is that better-off peasants have bought land from the poorer ones who have become more involved in the labour market. But while this has led to increased socio–economic differentiation in the rural areas, the picture is a complex one. Table 3.4 shows the occupational structure of African households in Kenya in 1970 which vividly illustrates the heterogeneity of the labour situation. First, there are peasants who work for capitalist farmers leaving their wives to work the family plot. Second, there are other peasants who work for capitalist farmers, who are given land and are joined by their families thus giving up rights to land at home. Third, there are peasants who gain better-paid employment in industrial or state sectors and who become dependent on these incomes and give up their land. Fourth, there are the land poor or landless who work for neighbouring farmers, who may well be the wife of a farmer in the first category. As Kitching points out, employment in the fourth category is made possible by that in the first; there is no mutually exclusive category for the source of surplus labour and for the appropriator of surplus labour. Moreover, there is no clear polarity between capital and labour; the man employed in the capitalist manufacturing sector is also an employer on his home farm. This particular scenario is not confined to Kenya. For example it is very apparent in Nigeria in the hinterlands of the state capitals where urban employment is the route to rural prosperity, as well as in the older established export crop areas. Low's book on household economics produces evidence from Swaziland where he suggests that urban wage labour combined with the preservation of communal rights to land farmed by women make migration a quite viable household strategy (Low, 1986), though its impact on social relations is another matter. Of more interest is the contention that the adoption of new agricultural techniques such as hybrid maize, ox-ploughing and tractor ploughing is not to increase food production but to save time. Development projects do not appear to produce the surpluses expected because if all household activities are taken into account, then off-farm work and farm work can be integrated to produce the most advantageous outcome. Furthermore, Low believes that the condition of the rural economy is largely produced by migration rather than the reverse.

THE POST-MIGRATION ECONOMY

So far little mention has been made of the importance of the mining industry and plantations as employers of labour. It was the mining and commercial farming sectors in the Republic of South Africa and Southern Rhodesia (now Zimbabwe) which depended so much on international migrant labour to supplement internal recruitment. The Republic of South Africa formerly relied heavily for indentured labour on the rural populations of Lesoto, Swaziland, Botswana and Zambia. At the same time Mozambique, Angola, Namibia and Malawi together accounted for one third of the Republic's industrial labour force. In Malawi in the early 1970s about 20 per cent of the male population was working abroad in any one year and in some rural areas it was as high as 75 per cent.

After independence many countries attempted to stop labour migration into the Republic but their efforts were inhibited by the continued dependence of their economies and the physical linkages through transport networks with the South African ports. Malawi in particular maintained labour migration through the presence of recruiting agencies from the Republic up until 1974 when a disastrous air-crash of returning migrants radically changed Malawi's attitudes. Many of the 300 000 labour migrants who subsequently returned were absorbed into the extension of agricultural estates and into the peasant sector of a country which environmentally offers a good resource base for agriculture.

Today the estate sector is alive and well in Malawi and has continued to expand with the closure of the traditional escape route from farm labour into wage employment in the Republic (Palmer, 1985). As in Mozambique, Lesotho and Zambia, once areas of labour shortage, have changed into areas where many compete for the limited jobs available. The plantation sector in Malawi began in the 1890s and not until recent times has there been an 'adequate supply' of labour so that employers can pick and choose, hire and fire.

The patterns of labour recruitment by the Republic have been changed largely by international policies, rather than by changes in management policies within the labour reserves (Taylor, 1982). Until the mid-1970s low wages had been maintained in the face of increased demands for labour simply by expanding the geographical size of the catchment area for migrants. However changing external relations and the fall of the Portuguese regimes in Angola and Mozambique finally made this strategy less and less secure. The rising price of gold allowed some increases in wages, and the mines began to recruit from the Bantustans within the Republic and to pursue a policy of 'internalization' of labour recruitment. In 1973 some 70 per cent of the mining labour force was foreign; by 1978 it had fallen to 45 per cent with about half of the foreign workers coming from Lesotho.

The effects on the countries formerly supplying labour have been problematic, as their economies have become integrated into the larger regional economy of Southern Africa which is dominated by white interests in the Republic. Reabsorption of labour in Malawi has not been difficult, albeit at pitifully low wages, but the difficulties for countries which have a poor environmental base such as Botswana, which includes the Kalahari Desert, have not been so happy. Although there has been a spectacular expansion of the Botswanan economy through the development of diamond and copper mining and beef exports, the effects have not been widespread throughout the rural sector. Mining in Botswana does not provide many jobs and about half the cattle are owned by 10 per cent of the population. Labour migration into the Republic, though on a reduced scale, remains important and many households combine activities which are rural and agriculturally based and those which are urban and industrially based. For many households, labour migration is not just a question of supplementing incomes, but an essential part of their maintenance and reproduction. In 1976 an average household income was made up of 14 per cent from crops, 33 per cent from the cattle and 53 per cent from mining. The Botswana government is now faced with having to try to create alternative sources of income and job opportunities on which so many rural households are dependent.

The post-migration economy is also apparent in Zambia as demonstrated by Pottier's investigation of Mambwe villages (Pottier, 1983). The decline of copper mining and the limited opportunities in the urban informal sector have disrupted the pattern of labour migration. Many Mambwe became dependent on imported consumer goods provided by wage labour yet neither they, nor the government, invested in agriculture in their home areas. Subsequently they have turned to filling niches as local traders and contraband traders, which have become viable options as government co-operatives have collapsed and imported goods have become scarce.

Apart from bean farming for the 'line-of-rail' markets, farming has deterio-rated and cassava, which needs lower labour inputs, has spread at the expense of millet.

SUMMARY

Despite the ILO employment surveys of the 1970s non-farm work and incomes generated outside farming remain relatively neglected areas of inquiry. Yet there is enough evidence to suggest that non-farm work and off-farm work employment have a profound effect on agriculture and the rural economy. The effects are clearly of a negative and positive kind and much depends on the type of employment, its location and rewards. Furthermore non-farm and off-farm jobs and incomes must be considered in the light of their effects on the production and reproduction of rural households.

As we have shown there are local industries, crafts and services operated from within villages, which are frequently integrated with farming and are difficult to evaluate. Some have argued that the 'informal' sector (both urban and rural) is subordinate to the interests of urban economies and subject to manipulation by merchant capital through the supply of raw materials and the organization of markets. But it is difficult to believe small industries and services will disappear in the face of an expanding capitalist (or state) sector. In capitalist countries small businesses flourish despite their 'dependence' and fill niches outside the large-scale sector, as well as displaying flexibility and innovation which ensures their survival.

In rural communities there are those who have relatively secure and well-paid employment in the industrial or more often the government sector. They either commute or become town-based migrants, yet they make contributions to their rural households which may involve land accumulation and investment in agricultural inputs. It must be conceded that investment also occurs in the education of young people in rural areas which usually promotes out-migration. Those rural households who have members with substantial non-farm jobs straddle rural and urban econ-omies and have been identified as *petite bourgeoisie* in the making. Good jobs, successful trading as well as the production of commercial crops are an important key to land accumulation and socio-economic differentiation in rural communities.

But as we have seen rural areas may contain significant numbers of poor migrant workers who find jobs on neighbour's farms, on plantations or in mines and factories. The rural areas in many parts of Africa are still little more than labour reserves of poorly-trained low grade manual workers with little job security. When these households also have little or no land, then they become increasingly dependent for their subsistence and reproduction on off-farm and non-farm jobs and thereby increasingly vulnerable. These people are a proletariat in the making, although as we have shown it is evident that the opposition of labour and capital in Africa is by no means clear. Above all African rural communities are heterogeneous comprising a whole range of wage earners, artisans, industrialists, land rich and land poor. A failure to seee how these sets of people intermesh socially and economically certainly diminishes our understanding of rural communities.

4

Land Rights, Land Markets and Expropriation

In previous chapters we have shown that indigenous agriculture varies a good deal within, as well as among, regions and countries. Bush-fallowing may co-exist with permanent field cultivation, while household labour is used in combination with work groups, share-contractors and wage labourers. We have also stressed the importance of non-farm and off-farm labour in shaping household production and reproduction and how non-farm incomes may be the source of investment in land. Although farm labour is still of central concern in the working of farming systems, it is becoming apparent that in many areas access to land is not as easy as it was in the past. The model of abundant land worked under an equitable system of corporate tenure adjusted to the size of domestic groups is now untenable. In many areas, land is becoming scarcer and private tenure, rents and leasing are now much more widespread than is often imagined. Even in those areas where corporate arrangements characterize land relations, they rarely exist in the form described by popular models (Cohen, 1980). In fact indigenous rights to farms and landholding are complex, and quite different systems may operate within one village or household. Rights to land and its product may differ if land is used for hunting and gathering, whereas on cultivated land they may differ according to whether crops are consumed within the household or sold in the market.

The land issue in Africa has been further complicated by the intervention of Europeans and the processes of decolonization which have varied significantly from one part of the continent to another. As we shall see in later chapters, in East and Southern Africa land was alienated by whites, Africans were pushed into reservations, or became squatters while land was also summarily expropriated by the state or on behalf of capitalist interests for plantations and mines. Land became an integral part of freedom struggles in Eastern and Southern Africa and it has become a sensitive political issue in subsequent efforts to bring about change and rural development. Elsewhere in post-colonial Africa state expropriation of land for rural development schemes has evoked different orders of resistance as well as favouring different class interests.

In Africa today one finds diverse and parallel systems of tenure and rights to farm, which include communal usufructary systems, loaning, pledging, different forms of labour renting associated with squatters and share-contractors, fixed rents, leasing, freehold purchase and land nationalization. These different forms of landholding and farming are rooted in different relations of production underwritten by religion, kinship and political authority, as well as varying with ecological circumstance. Like the labour process, land is not easily fitted into neat categories and there is no simple linear development over time and space. Yet the land and labour issues are connected. For example, where the landless and land poor are on the increase due to land accumulation and the strengthening of individual tenures, or where expropriation by the state is accelerating, then there is a tendency for proletarianization. On the other hand there are areas where communal landholding and household labour is still commonplace, although there is the impression that both are undergoing internal changes. Sender and Smith (1986) have suggested that the transformation of tenures can be basically divided into two categories; pressures from below and pressures from above. Pressures from above refer to state initiatives, the influence of large-scale foreign companies and colonial settlers; pressures from below embrace processes of rural differentiation and the *de facto* development of land markets resulting from social forces which operated more or less independently of the state. As Sender and Smith acknowledge, this is not a clear-cut distinction and as we suggested in the last chapter, a good deal of rural differentiation is predicated on access to the state wages bill, or other state revenues through trading and employment within the government sector. The differentiation that exists within much of rural Africa seems increasingly related to hiring labour and the means to purchase or rent land, and while the notion that rural differentiation is explicable in terms of demographic characteristics of households may still be valid in some instances, there are many others where the disparities in observed landholding is too great to be a function of household size and composition, as households of exactly the same size have widely differing landholdings. Also, when land becomes scarcer as population rises there is not necessarily enough land for the appropriate allocations, i.e. the system cannot reproduce the household-land relationship (Sender and Smith 1986).

The political attitudes to traditional patterns of tenure and rights to land alter with the prevailing wisdom concerning the nature and objectives of development. In the colonial period African rights were largely ignored or subverted to suit government or European interests. The modernization ethic of the 1960s and 1970s favoured the total abolition of traditional familial and communal patterns of landholdings, because they were seen as obstacles to mechanized agriculture which requires large uniform tracts of land. This position was equally maintained by those who believed land should be held by the state rather than a burgeoning class of capitalist farmers. But in the late 1970s and 1980s another shift is discernible coming from different quarters. First the populist view of agriculture has emphasized the inadequacies of large-scale intervention by the state and capitalist entrepreneurs, while recent IMF initiatives have eschewed the former but not the latter in the process of land accumulation, agrarian change and development.

Later in this book we shall examine the role of interventionist strategies, stimulated by both political motives and the growth of opportunity for the introduction of technological innovations (chapters 7 and 8). In this chapter we examine the different types of indigenous land rights and tenures which obtained in Africa, how they were affected by colonial rule and how land was alienated. We conclude with some comments on the redistribution of land in Southern and East Africa after independence.

COMMUNAL AND KIN-BASED LANDHOLDING

African villages frequently display a whole cluster of rights, claims, privileges and liabilities related to the ways in which inhabitants hold and work the land, or have access to it and its products. The nature of these rights is embedded in the particular relations of production. These 'traditional' rights of land are always underwritten by a complex palimpsest of social, political and religious factors. A persistent problem is how Africans, let alone non-Africans from different ethno-linguistic polities, understand the linguistic and legal concepts used in other areas. At a very general level, kin-based or communal land rights are frequently associated with peoples whose polities do not conform with modern concepts of boundary and ownership, where lineage forms a powerful base for the organization of society. Alternatively there are areas where Islamic concepts of landholding apply. So at one level there are Europeans and Africans familiar with European practice, who employ the terminology and legal concepts associated with capitalist relations of production; and at another, a range of alternative perceptions of non-capitalist societies which vary remarkably from one place to another.

Communal and kin-based systems of landholding were associated with areas where land was plentiful and where cultivation systems were of the relatively extensive type, such as shifting cultivation or rotational bush-fallow. Rights to land were derived from membership of a social or political group such as a chiefdom, a village or a lineage. Most frequently the link was between land and lineage. The genealogy of a group found its territoriality expressed in the land it needed and used. Under such circumstances, concepts of holding and using land rested on the timeless cyclical perpetuity of the relationships which bind particular groups to their land, relationships which embrace a cosmology which includes the living, the dead and those as yet unborn. Membership of a group secured the rights to land of an individual provided the necessary obligations to other members (past, present and future) were observed. Technically this security is inalienable in most traditional African societies, but an important difference from West European practice must be defined. This security does not necessarily have to be vested in a particular *piece of land* to which one has permanent or hereditary rights. Effective use was the criterion for the lineage, the family and the individual. Access to land was the key factor. Should it not be needed, then it must be returned to the common genealogical pool. The amount of land farmed by the village or lineage segment could vary within the limits agreed with neighbours, according to the size and needs of the groups and continued and full use was not a prerequisite for the maintenance of their claims to land (Biebuyk, 1963). The reader must be left to imagine for the moment the impact of a European concept of land acquisition and alienation caused by the flooding of a valley and the resettlement of its people for a major hydro-electric scheme.

At this point it is instructive to pay some attention to how 'land' may be conceptualized by different social groupings, a theme which has been developed most effectively by Bohannan (1963). It became an increasingly complicated feature of African life as to how these different perceptions could be peacefully and profitably resolved. Bohannan suggests that we need to question such terms as 'land', 'tenure' and 'rights' if we are to understand any system of land tenure. He further suggested that there are three general assumptions which underpin land tenure and it was the way people consolidate them which is important. First, people have some kind of representational 'map' of their country. Secondly, they have sets of concepts for speaking about and dealing with the relationship between themselves and 'things' and thirdly, the spatial aspect of their social organization has some sort of overt expression in both word and deed. Western peoples easily correlate (1) and (2) because they rely on grid-maps. Within these precise terms of reference people are assigned rights to specific pieces of earth (parcels) which maintain their integrity even when the owners change. People are related to these parcels of land through legal mechanisms such as 'rent', 'freehold' etc. On the other hand, many Africans easily correlate assumptions (1) and (3). Their 'map' was (and often still is) a spatial dimension of their social organization which is fluid and not related to specific parcels of land. The issue we are confronting here is that different peoples in different stages of economic and social development have a different 'geography' which expresses the 'man–man' and 'man–thing' relationships differently.

Among the Tiv of central Nigeria, Bohannan (1963) found that these people had a geography cast in the same image as that of their social organization. The idiom of genealogy and descent provided the basis not only for social groupings but also for territorial groupings. Starting from a minimal lineage there was a process of inclusion which continued until all Tiv were included both genealogically and spatially. But this 'map' of the territories of the Tiv was fluid and shifted around; Tiv people had rights to farms rather than to specific pieces of land in perpetuity. Men were related not to parcels of land, but to a temporary farm through their social relationships with their lineage and other Tiv. This is a situation which is common to many people who practise both shifting cultivation and rotational bush-fallow agriculture in which settlement sites migrate. It is this conception which one must set against European notions of land tenure, where they came into conflict with African values in the white settler regions of East and Central Africa. Many African leaders were duped into much more permanent alienations of land than their concept of ownership allowed. But this does not mean that, the notion of terrestrial boundaries lies outside the tradition of African peoples. Though areas of use and occupancy are not demarcated by survey, sets of landmarks are commonly used to identify the limits of a range of territory over which some hegemony is claimed. The Kikuyu for example had quite complicated 'maps' largely because they rested on two principles which did not coincide; in other words they had two 'maps'. The first comprised the 'lands' of individuals and of two-generation lineages, while the others were composed of 'ridges' which although they were also political units, often physically coincided with the interfluves of the fast flowing rivers which cut across the country. These were governed by a hierarchy of committees representing territorial sub-units. These political units of demarcation, had nothing to do with the exploitation of the land.

The Kikuyu have a clan system with sub-clans based on a group of agnates and each one had one or more 'estates' marked by trees, stones, streams etc. Rights to land were vested in membership of the sub-clan, although it was possible to make temporary grants to 'clients' who were not members. But a single 'estate' could be laid out in such a way that it crossed several ridges, and disputes were settled by the committee system. Thus we have a situation where land units did not correspond with political units, although parcels of land were carefully demarcated by terrestrial signs. So while the Kikuyu has a 'man–thing' unit rather like the European land parcel, he also has a 'man–man' unit which derived from membership of a unilineal descent group. As the grid-based map replaced the indigenous, ancestral one, the Kikuyu had relatively little difficulty in adapting to the new system. They already thought in terms of bounded parcels of land. It is therefore unsurprising that even before the onset of Mau Mau and the push for independence, the Kikuyu were demanding legal title deeds to their land.

The inequality of land ownership preoccupied the colonial administration in Kenya for many years, largely because they realized that the emergence of a smallholding agricultural economy, depended on adequate landholdings. Household incomes were related to the amount of land cultivated since the quick transition from a pastoral to an agricultural society had not allowed a tradition of intensive landuse to develop. Furthermore, the loss of labour power from peasant households to the cultivation of low yielding, low value cereals meant that household subsistence had to include income from off-farm employment. Also, the arrival of European settlers and capitalist farming introduced new concepts of exclusive landuse rather than use by the arrangement of interests. As population and pressure on land increased, lineages became more cohesive and self-conscious about their land and this phase was succeeded by another yet more individual one as population continued to rise and commercialization of agriculture increased. From the 1930s onwards clan control over households diminished as selling and renting land became widespread among household heads, clans and lineages. Household heads now turned from collective solidarity to ensure access to land, towards the colonial government and the issue of freehold titles. Until 1953 the colonial government was not sure whether to back this change, but afterwards it supported the issue of freeholds and the consolidation of land as some households began to expand their holdings (Kitching, 1980).

In the pre-colonial and early colonial period there was still a good deal of freedom for household heads as to how they used their allocation of land, while from the 1930s onwards, as more crops were grown for markets, the disposal of the product of land (even when it was vested in the community) was decided by household heads and individual members. But with the development of freeholds and land sales, land became irredeemable. This combined with rising population densities to produce conflict about ownership and how it was conceptualized. People wished to redeem land they had given out to clients or affines in return for a small present or tribute. Formerly the return of the 'present' was sufficient to redeem the land, but as land became scarce, those who had lent land claimed their clients had payed 'rent', whereas the other parties claimed they had 'purchased' the land; this conflict was exacerbated by the claimants being some generations distant from their ancestors who were the original contracting parties.

In areas where land acquired intrinsic value, from the 1920s onwards, chiefs, teachers, clerks, dispensers, traders and latterly politicians became land accumulators through the investment of surplus income and the information to which they were priveleged either by superior education, or contact with those in government. In the last chapter we referred to this as 'straddling' or 'double participation'. The extent and type of off-farm employment has become a pivotal element in determining the landholdings of many rural households, while in recent years the accumulation of land by the wealthy and influential has led to the collection and acquisition of land by those who have little interest in its immediate development, thereby reducing opportunities for others. But why do people sell their land? Usually because of distress and their inability to meet demands of subsistence and other expenses. Particularly difficult circumstances arise when harvest failure is coincident with the costs of weddings, funerals, school fees, taxes and adverse dependency ratios associated with the family developmental cycle. Kitching (1980) points out that in Kenya – and this is true for other parts of Africa – there are few money-lenders compared with Asia and while traders give deferred payment on goods, they do not always advance cash. Once a certain amount of land has been sold, then there is an increased risk to the household and further sales may be necessary. In Kenya many males tried to break this vicious circle by becoming migrant workers on plantations, mines, large farms and in towns. In Western Africa, the history of land expropriation has taken a different path.

LAND AND THE DEVELOPMENT OF COMMODITY PRODUCTION IN WEST AFRICA

The increased sales of land and the erosion of corporate land rights have been associated in a general way with the development of commodity production, the needs of expanding capitalism and the monetization of the economy. Also the rural dweller now has needs and aspirations which may conflict with communal values. But communal possession does not necessary imply communal use and may not be incompatible with production for the market. Communal possession of land may be the means whereby individual households have access to farmland, but household heads or individuals are the organizers of production and have the right to dispose of the product of their land as they wish. What has happened in many areas of commercial cultivation in West Africa when accompanied by increasing population density, is that the use of land has passed from lineages, to smaller descent groups and rights to land is vested in joint production and consumption units whose members then *inherit* rights to land. This process is usually signalled by the demarcation of 'family lands' and parcellization. The conjunction of traditional and modern usage is also to be found when the actual sale of land may take place only with the permission of the community in whom land is ultimately vested. Such a development is well illustrated by Lericollais's work in Sob a Sérèr village in Senegal where population densities are high and the commercial cultivation of groundnuts well developed. Figure 4.1 shows the allocation of lands by patrilineages which are made up of several households. But as Lericollais (1972) notes, the head of the lineage now only exercises a *moral* right, such as preventing sales of land, or reallocating land should a household head leave, but the effective control of land, its use and the disposal of its products now rests

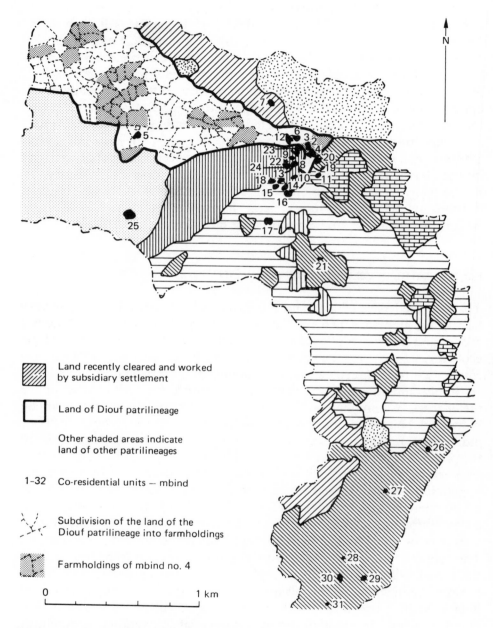

Figure 4.1 Apportionment of land by patrilineage, Sob, 1966
Source: after Lericollais, 1972

with the household who have rights to specific parcels of lineage land, which is passed on to their descendants.

The development of individual private property in land is also well illustrated by Clarke (1980) for the Yoruba of Nigeria where there have been important changes in access to land with the spread of cocoa cultivation. Two phases can be discerned: first the attempt by cultivators to retain or gain exclusive rights to and use of particular plots and second the allocation of plots of land by community members to migrant non-members who pay rent. The expansion of cocoa cultivation after 1915 entailed an expansion of the cultivated area and because cocoa is a permanent tree crop, bearing fruit from about the seventh to the fortieth year, it altered the nature of land occupation. Land was no longer farmed and then fallowed for a number of years, but it was occupied on a permanent basis. Furthermore the planting of trees meant that a producer had exclusive rights for a long period and unlike food crops, cocoa was always sold, which created new problems over the distribution of the product of the land.

Cocoa production became the means of access to goods, education and the accumulation of capital. As the industry expanded so competition for land grew and attempts were made to secure exclusive rights. Clarke makes the point that control of land and its product has shifted from lineages and extended families, towards household and individual household members who were the actual organizers of production. In this case the native courts set up by the colonial administration were used to secure the exclusive rights of individuals to specific pieces of land. The development of private property rights in this way did not in itself permit the owner to dispose of the land outside the community, but it did create the possibility that such a disposal could occur. We may infer from this that exclusive property rights and their inheritance may be compatible with a definite form of communal possession. Exclusive rights may be one form of distributing communal territory among members of a community and individual property rights creates only some of the conditions for the dissolution of community and kin-based systems. As Clarke shows, the development of cocoa farming was also associated with the even more refined practice of renting land.

The expansion of cocoa farms was limited by the amount of labour available within domestic groups and the distribution of effort between foodcrops and cocoa. After World War II the increasing importance of education gradually took young men away from farming and many no longer wished to continue as dependent agricultural labourers. Education, in addition to reducing the stock of labour, was also expensive and both problems had to be resolved by the heads of farming households. Wage labour was one possible solution to the decline in family labour, but expenditure on education demanded increased output and sales of cocoa. Higher wages might have extended the catchment for farm workers, but the expense and organizational problems led farmers to rent land. In 1948 migrants moved into the cocoa areas looking for uncultivated land, although few could afford to purchase it, even if community members had been willing to sell. The disposal of land under tenancy arrangements was therefore a compromise which suited both parties. Most tenants lived in semi-permanent villages while retaining houses in their areas of origin. Partial migration of this kind was made easier by British rule.

Alternatives to renting land, were share-cropping and temporary loans; the former usually to migrants and the latter to kinsmen, or friends. As Clarke (1980) is at some pains to argue, the individual ownership and disposal of land can and does take place without land being a saleable commodity, while the development of a specific market in land rights, namely tenancy, was part of the development of cocoa growing among the Yoruba as it evolved after World War II.

The disposal of land acquired through traditional systems of tenure, other than through sales, was and is now probably much more widespread in Africa than is often admitted. Given the fluctuating size of domestic groups, the lack of an effective land rights administration and lineages which are subject to fission and decay, there needs to be sufficient mobility in the transmission of land, just as there is for labour. Gifts, loans, pledging and labour-rent are means whereby land is redistributed to outsiders within communities where access to land is primarily by means of membership of a social group and where control is vested in its elders and the larger community. What really constitutes a turning point is when land is disposed of and is *irredeemable*, for example through sale and the establishment of freeholds.

Sales of land although often covert are now commonplace throughout Africa, especially in commercial farming areas and on the peripheries of towns. Although these sales are frequently associated with increased levels of commoditization and monetization subsequent to the arrival of the colonial powers, they were not unknown in some parts of West Africa before this time. Robertson (1987) has noted that in both Ghana and Sudan, land rents pre-date the systems of share-cropping which became an integral part of cocoa and cotton production. In northern Nigeria it is asserted that sales of land were taking place in the late nineteenth century, while the British administration recorded the renting of farmland on the periphery of Kano in 1903–4. In general, the Hausa-Fulani emirates were operating systems of land tenure partly based on concepts of communal ownership and partly on Islamic law which recognizes individual inherited tenure.

After the British took control of northern Nigeria a number of attempts were made to come to terms with landholding and tenure, which culminated in the Nigerian Land and Native Rights Ordnance of 1910. This ordnance declared the colonial state to be the ultimate owner of land but in practice existing systems of land allocation and control were continued or even strengthened. Shenton (1986) has argued that the 1910 ordnance was crucial to the way in which economy and society in northern Nigeria developed in the twentieth century. The 'nationalization' of land put a brake on land sales and retarded the emergence of a dispossessed wage labour force. This suited the interests of local and international merchant capital which preferred to secure its position by trading with myriad household producers. The blocking of industrial capital in the shape of plantations also satisfied the interests of the Muslim aristocracy with whom the British needed an accommodation in order to pursue the policy (and a cheap one at that) of indirect rule. Not that the 1910 ordnance stopped land sales. These probably increased in the 1930s and were certainly in evidence around Sokoto in the 1950s. However, the legislation did lay the foundations for the expropriation of land by the colonial, and more importantly, the post-colonial state in Nigeria.

The next step in land legislation was the 1962 Land Tenure Law, which recognized a distinction between customary rights (usually unregistered) and statutory rights (registered). The latter developed as new uses for land occurred, such as petrol stations or commercial warehousing and these statutory land rights were held on long government leases. An important attribute of statutory tenure (unlike customary tenure) is its acceptance as collateral which can be used to raise agricultural credit. It was during the colonial period that tracts of land were bought for government residential areas on the fringes of towns, while land used for schools and other institutions made in-roads into peripheral farm land.

In 1978 the Obasanjo military government introduced the Nigerian Land Use Decree, which in effect extended the system which had long obtained in the north, to the whole of the country. Land was vested in the state and administered by the governors of federal states, directly in the case of urban land, and through local government land use and allocation committees for rural land. The decree was hailed by some as an egalitarian measure, but others were less sanguine about its implications. Local governments were empowered to grant customary rights of occupancy for agricultural and grazing land with limits of 500 and 5000 hectares respectively without the consent of the governor. But this only applied to single grants; there was no limit to the number of grants which would be made, or the size if the governor gave permission. Far from being egalitarian, Francis (1984) suggests it was a means of legitimizing private interest through 'nationalization' and clientage between priveleged individuals and the state. The intervention of the state in land matters coincided with its interest in promoting certain groups and the development of large-scale mechanized farming on capitalist lines. However, so far the effects have been limited; large-scale farming requires expert management, capital investment often using scarce foreign currency and the mobilization of labour at rates which will compete with non-farm employment and self-employment.

It might be concluded from this evidence that colonial intervention in indigenous land rights might have actually retarded the development of capitalist production relations by supporting the concept of communal tenures and the transference of traditional authority to the colonial state. It may even have been the case that there was an element of inventing land systems or supporting traditional systems at a time when they were beginning to crumble. This phenomenon of inventing the past has recently been explored by Hosbawm and Ranger (1983). If this were the case in some West African territories, would this also be true of Central and Southern Africa?

THE LAND ISSUE IN CENTRAL AND SOUTHERN AFRICA

In Uganda a system akin to freehold tenures was introduced by the Uganda Agreement of 1900, which had far-reaching social and economic effects, not least on the emergence of large-scale African farming (Fortt, 1973). The civil disturbances in Buganda during the late nineteenth century led the British to negotiate a settlement in an attempt to bring stability to the region and to reduce the heavy costs borne by the British government in London. By granting private and official estates to the three regents and other leading chiefs and by making some 8000 square miles of land in what was virtually freehold tenure available for distribution among their followers, the British secured the accommodation they needed with local rulers to stabilize the region. In addition some 9000 acres of low-grade uncultivated and waste land was vested in the government as crown land.

The Uganda case was unique and elsewhere in Eastern, Central and Southern Africa the interest of white settlers or plantation owners became paramount. African entrepreneurial activity was reined back and again a case can be made that a developing African capitalism and market in land were subverted (chapter 8). In the Belgian Congo the notorious concessionaire system operated until it was abolished, while in areas more favourable to European settlement, land was alienated for commercial farming. In Kenya large tracts of land were acquired by Europeans in the White Highlands, where in 1924 1715 settlers employed 87 000 African labourers. Land shortages in the heavily populated Kikuyu areas of central Kenya forced many to become 'squatters' on white farms where they were allowed smallholdings in return for labour. By 1940 there was resistance from the Kikuyu which crystallized into the 1952 emergency. Subsequently, in the 1960s, financial assistance from the World Bank and the Colonial Development Corporation enabled Africans to purchase 1.0 million acres from Europeans, a process which continued with larger and more fertile tracts being accumulated by rich, prominent, successful Kenyans. Not only has there been the emergence of a *petite bourgeoisie* as described by Kitching (1980), but large-scale capitalist farmers as well. One of the ironies is that former squatters have been removed from the larger farms into the poorer areas and unequal land distribution has remained a feature of Kenya.

As for the plantation sector which effectively started with the arrival of the Brooke Bond Tea Company in 1920, it has survived independence and land redistribution. Despite the fact that 62 per cent of the coffee hectarage is in African hands, foreign plantations are still important and they, together with tea plantations, have retained more or less the same area as at independence. Plantations have in general become more capital intensive, especially in processing. Although the area owned by foreign companies has remained fixed, yet in 1968 10 000 acres of pineapple plantation were established on labour intensive lines which substantially eroded small-holder pineapple farming (Dinham and Hines, 1983).

In Kenya the land issue has been principally resolved in favour of small-holder farmers and a limited number of African and foreign large-scale capitalist farmers. In Zimbabwe the more recent conclusion to the war for independence makes the final direction and outcome of land redistribution more difficult to interpret. But as Ranger's analysis shows, an outcome to the land issue along the lines of what has happened in Kenya or Mozambique is unlikely (Ranger, 1986). In Zimbabwe there is popular peasant power born of struggle and the peasantry may well be a class in itself and not one in transition. The ex-combatants and peasants who supported the government have clearly articulated their demands for the peasantization of land and the recovery of what was lost. However the desire for land with no-one to 'boss them' or tell them what to grow runs counter to the government commitment to collectivization and socialist reconstruction (Ranger, 1986).

The inequitable distribution of land in Southern Rhodesia was entrenched in the fact that not only did the whites own half the cultivable area but they farmed the best land. In 1980 some 6000 whites owned farms which averaged 6000 acres in the ecologically superior highlands (figure 4.2, zones I and II), while 800 000 African farmers worked the poor drier sandier lowlands (zones IV and V). The allocation of land was set by the 1930 Land Apportionment Act which put aside some 29 million acres as Native Reserves and at the same time African rights to purchase land were removed, except in 7.5 million acres of what became known as 'Native Purchase Areas'; 49 million acres were reserved for the exclusive use of whites. The Native Purchase Areas although limited, contributed about one-third of the marketable output by black producers and these free-holders have become a sub-class prepared to defend their interests (Cheater, 1982). Today there are three categories of farmers: rural farmers who are the peasantry largely confined to the communal areas (former Native Reserves), small-scale commercial farmers, principally those who were on

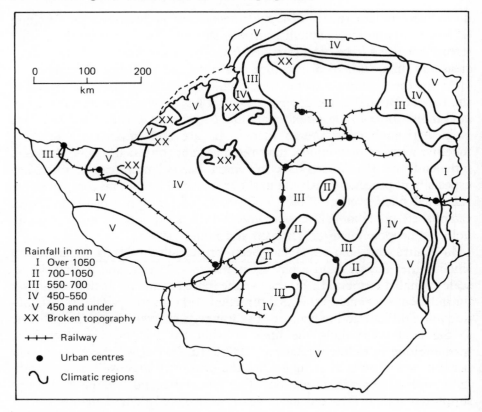

Figure 4.2   Agro-climatic regions, Southern Rhodesia
Source: after Federation of Rhodesia and Nyasaland Agro-Climatic Survey, 1961

the Native Purchase Areas and the large-scale commercial farmers both black and white. There is, however, the persistent problem of squatters which has proved a difficult issue for the government.

The colonial administration recognized several categories of squatters. First, there were those peasants who were already on the land purchased by the whites for farms and ranches. Second, Africans without land moved onto farms and were given land in lieu of wages. In 1980 it was estimated that there were between 50 000 and 60 000 squatters on white farms; the number on African ones was unknown. But in the Native Purchase Areas squatters were deemed to include anyone beyond the immediate family of the freeholders, such as kinsmen who were allowed onto farms in order to meet the severe labour shortages experienced by the small commercial farmers.

At the end of the liberation war new categories of squatters appeared as a result of the conflict. Many farmers who fled from their farms left them in the hands of 'caretakers', who have remained. Also, many farm labourers who lost their jobs on the farms stayed or returned as squatters, while those who became exiles or refugees in the war and lived in Mozambique and Zambia, have returned and joined those looking for land. Many jumped the gun at independence and moved from the crowded communal areas becoming squatters on erstwhile white farms. The situation has been particularly difficult for government resettlement schemes which have purchased land from white farmers and have had to contend with squatters already on the farms. The government have tried to deal with the squatter problem by recognizing those potential settlers with a genuine need for land. Those become part of a queuing system. Those who are merely trying to accumulate land were expected to return to their original farms.

Rural landlessness in Zimbabwe appears to be an increasingly common phenomenon and in surveys cited by Kinsey (1982), in some areas in south-east of the country 40 per cent of men aged between 16 and 30 had no land. Yet in the white-controlled area substantial amounts of farmland are unused. The response of the government to the needs of the landless, land poor and returning refugees has been to formulate and implement resettlement policies, especially in the unused or underutilized white areas. This is a complex process and involved the identification of settlers and the purchase of land from its present owners, using funds set up as part of the Lancaster House Agreement. The schemes are of two types; the 'intensive' and the 'accelerated'. The first involves village settlements with individual plots and communal grazing, or alternatively villages with a 'core' estate, while a different version is based on communal living on co-operative farms. The accelerated scheme on the other hand, is an emergency programme aimed at settling as many as possible using outlying commercial farms, with little or no provision of infrastructures.

Given the dimensions of the land problem vast strides have been made in a short time. In 18 months Zimbabwe had transferred land from whites to blacks in amounts which are only 10 per cent less than the Kenya government had transferred in 15 years as part of its smallholder scheme. However, farms in Kenya only averaged 12 ha in size whereas in Zimbabwe they are 60 to 70 ha. The difference is accounted for by soil and climate and also because substantial areas are included for pasturage and the assumption of the need for animal power.

Land resettlement has not been without its problems and contains several thorny issues. Not least is the breaking up of large commercial farms which reduced earnings not only from international markets and the related foreign exchange, but also domestic markets. In addition there has been a substantial loss of agricultural jobs in the large-scale capitalist sector, which has reduced income levels. Furthermore, the costs of resettlement are high and subject to inflation. As Kinsey (1982) remarks, 'If numbers are the criterion then resettlement has proceeded successfully, but if one looks at it in the longer terms of achieving the stated goals of "equity with growth", then there are a number of social and economic issues to be resolved'.

SUMMARY

The model of abundant land, worked under an equitable system of corporate tenure where allocation to households was adjusted according to their size, appears to have been seriously eroded in many parts of rural Africa. Nonetheless the heterogeneity of land rights, access and ownership still obtains within individual villages and households. But overall it seems difficult to escape the conclusion that the development of small commodity production and non-farm incomes has led to land accumulation and a growing market in land in rural areas. In addition, larger capitalist farmers are evident, especially near to the towns, while the alienation of land first by European settlers and latterly by state expropriation is another dimension of the land issue. In Southern and Central Africa land became an integral part of the struggle for independence, although this has not necessarily led to redistribution of land as white commercial farmers have been replaced by Africans. As land becomes scarcer in all parts of the continent and as the numbers of land poor and landless increase, so it will become an even more sensitive issue than at present and provide the backdrop to clashes of interests between classes, peasant farmers and the state.

5

Reciprocity, Exchange and Markets

INTRODUCTION

African rural societies have developed a richly varied and complex pattern of reciprocities, exchanges and interactions. Indeed it is tempting to suggest that no other culture has created such a range and subtlety of arrangements, alliances, obligations and chains of relationship both between groups and between individuals. While other societies develop rituals of formal exchange to high degrees of sophistication and leaven them with informal social activity, it is a particular skill of African societies to shape their elaborate informal exchange mechanisms by a minimum number of formal procedures. At the same time as such responses can seem outmoded (and there may appear to be something deeply anachronistic in these systems of interchange), there is no denying their vitality. Structurally they are often extremely stable, withstanding both social and political fluctuations.

While complex and diffuse systems of reciprocal interaction and exchange based on relationships among individuals, households and kinship groups are pervasive throughout tropical Africa, there are also sophisticated systems of market-place commodity trading which have been in operation for centuries. For example, the pre-colonial Mandinka and Hausa states of the western and central Sudan sustained local, regional and inter-regional trading in agricultural commodities, manufactured goods and animals which involved indigenous merchant capital, rulers and administrators located in major towns. Chains of patron–client relationships, brokerage and stranger settlements reached out into the rural areas and across regions. When the British conquered Kano in 1903 the city's traders included not only *kanawa* and other Hausa, but Jews and Arabs from North Africa and Yoruba from the south.

With the establishment of colonial rule the production of export crops and the importing of trade goods were expanded to embrace wider areas and greater numbers than hitherto – in some instances local traders and rulers were integrated into new commodity marketing systems, while in others new classes and institutions were required to market both export crops and food for the towns, mines and plantations. It was at this juncture that non-African traders such as the Lebanese, Syrians and Indians became important as traders, produce collectors and transport operators. Of particular importance was the introduction by governments of licensed buying agents for export crops and after World War II in British East and West Africa, the marketing boards. The latter were an expression of governments' need to control agricultural surpluses, and they continued into independence because they were a vital source of state revenue. In many countries foodstaples have also been brought within the realm of state marketing.

During the 1950s and 1960s governments and planners were unconcerned about local food trading and marketing as they perceived the established system was performing adequately. However, in the 1960s and 1970s rapid urbanization prompted the view that local markets were unreliable and inhibited in supplying foodstuffs to urban areas. It was held that traders were exploitative, a view at times held by colonial officials. The result was intervention in the food market in an attempt to secure urban supplies and to engineer more equitable conditions for rural producers. As many have argued, a better deal for producers usually does not mean attractive prices and not infrequently state intervention has led to the growth of blackmarkets and border trading.

The spectrum of exchange relations is a wide one in Africa but it is possible to discern a number of *foci* which derive from different production and exchange relations involving different social and geographic spaces. Seven foci are identified here. They are: the domestic group, kinship, patron–client relations, simple commodity circulation, petty commodity production, capitalist production and the state. The first two of these categories are oriented towards the simple reproduction of households primarily concerned with subsistence and together with the third are heavily influenced by concepts of reciprocity and redistribution. Categories five and six are the outcome of commodity production and involve marketplace trading, money and the appropriation of surplus value. They are also characterized by local and international merchant capital and exchange may take place over long distances requiring complex transportation networks and storage. Finally, the state may dominate exchange in specific areas and assume the role of merchant capital.

The foci of exchange outlined above are not intended as discrete categories and as with schema in chapter 1, there is no necessary unilinear development from one extreme to the other. While trends may be discernible there is often considerable simultaneity and overlapping of categories. In local rural markets there may be a hierarchy of trading relations where urban merchant capital operates both through a network of patron–client relations and through systems of kinship. We will now examine these mechanisms more closely.

RECIPROCITY AND REDISTRIBUTION

Most Africans know that they are only as secure as their patterns of alliances allow and that links at all these levels need to be constantly forged, re-forged, or reinforced by invoking obligations of debt and favour. In these circumstances success in the accumulation and manipulation of power and resources is often measurable against a temporal yardstick. Personal prestige and power is directly related to the time any individual or group can be expected to be kept waiting before an obligation to perform a service or pay a debt is realized. The result is often an elaborate process involving the accumulation of allies, to whom some further reciprocal obligation is then owed. By involving their own levels of reciprocity these allies bring pressure to bear in any conflict situation so that the conflicting interests are resolved. In some ways these grids of reciprocity and alliance may be seen as an extension of older systems of political alliance for the less peaceful resolution of conflicts.

Most exchanges of any kind are bound up with the process of giving (and receiving) favours and 'demonstrating' power. Roles are played with great energy and absorb large amounts of time. This is often infuriating for outsiders, whose exchange relations are now more stereotyped. At their most sophisticated, these exchanges and interactions extend across the whole field of human behaviour. Each action has its own clearly appreciated political, social and economic dimension. Even an apparently straight-forward exchange of goods or services can reflect much deeper ties of association involving kinship, marriage arrangements, other informal social liaisons, labour commitments, prestige, status and power alliances.

Social scientists who, by nature of background and training in a single discipline, concentrate on one dimension of this dynamic interactive process, miss much of the texture of this essentially holistic activity. Geographers, quite naturally, have been preoccupied with the physical manifestation of exchange in the rural markets. Few have paid much more than lip service to the dimensions referred to above, largely because they are only partly associated with the specific location of market-places. At the same time, anthropologists and ethnographers, political scientists and rural economists sometimes analyse the dimensions of this process which remain unconnected with the realities of space–time structuration which embrace the geographical study.

It is a mammoth task, well beyond the scope of this text, to attempt to bring these dimensions together in an account which satisfactorily embraces all forms of interaction but in the first part of this chapter an attempt will be made to explain the developing character of indigenous African exchange relations by first setting them in the context of the needs of simple household reproduction from which they all stem (see chapter 1) and exploring their subsequent ramifications and adaptations.

EXCHANGE RELATIONS IN A SUBSISTENCE CONTEXT

Exchange relations between subsistence societies and individuals within them are governed by three primary basic needs: to dispose of accidental or deliberate surplus production, to make good a temporary deficiency in the production system, to acquire spatially discrete essential resources (e.g. salt). As social systems develop power structures, exchange also expresses a need for familial or group security. By increasing labour inputs it is possible to create surpluses more regularly. Successful accumulation can be demonstrated by the possession of animals (cattle, sheep, goats) or treasured artefacts (fetishes, weapons, jewellery, cloth, gold, ivory). These possessions can then be redistributed to meet political requirements or 'demonstrated' to ensure alliances and allegiances.

In this phase in the development of what are often intrinsic rather than explicit class relations, the need for labour is clearly paramount. In male-dominated societies increasing female labour is one of the main means of accumulating a surplus. More wives means more land in cultivation and a larger surplus for exchange. Nonetheless, apart from royal households, there is a clear social and economic limit to the number of wives most men can support and this becomes an intensely localized intra-familial manifestation of accumulation.

Any further increases in wealth beyond the accumulation of more wives implies the manipulation of male labour. This can only be achieved by individuals by invoking reciprocal relations, reinforced by payments in kind, frequently through locally brewed alcohol (chapters 1 and 2). This has too severe limitations as a mode of expansion of influence by the larger-scale communal or ethnolinguistic politics and many groups resorted to a more negative form of 'reciprocal relationship', taking neighbouring weaker ethnic groups into some form of bondage. The simple expedient of raiding wives, cattle or grain stores of neighbouring groups was gradually reified as a form of feudal authority, sometimes embracing the idea of servitude and domestic slavery, by many ethnolinguistic groups throughout Africa who came in contact with weaker polities. While a number of these relationships were vigorously and persistently exploitative they frequently developed relatively benign characteristics. What is clear is that the systems of servitude which evolved from such interactions in parts of East and West Africa was often a more balanced system than the situation which developed from European contact. Slaves were fully incorporated into the social structure after a generation or two. At one level slaves gained status in host societies as they became established members of the group. At another, the stronger military power of certain tribes offered protection to weaker neighbours in exchange for labour services and goods. This was a common relationship between cattle or herding societies and the agricultural groups who were their neighbours.

Perhaps one of the best of many examples of this form of dominance is provided by the Zulu-Ngoni policy in South Central Africa. The eventual development of the Zulu nation and its control over neighbouring societies was the work of inspired leadership and organization through an autocracy but it had its roots in a social system developed out of the need to organize regular movement of homesteads *(Kraals)* to find new pastures for the growing herds of cattle which were the basis of chiefly power and authority. The relationship with more weakly organized agriculture groupings was cemented first by conquest then by marriage and then by economic interaction (Phiri, 1981). It was a pattern which extended throughout the middle and high veldt region from the Ngoni in the north-east to the Ndebele and Lozi in the centre and west with the main Zulu heartland in the south.

BALANCED RECIPROCITY

Often however, a more subtle level of interchange developed between groups. Alliances were and are formed which make exploitative relationships less likely to develop and the basis for such relationships is the gift. The gift, as Mauss (1970) was the first to identify, is a fundamental part of most trading relations, but in Africa it is deeply embedded in social and cultural life. It is of course a fundamental aspect of human nature to make appeasing or conciliatory gestures by giving a potential aggressor a gift or a chance to share in the social relations of consumption. Food and drink are proffered to strangers and also to those who have been asked for assistance in a particular task. This opens the way to reciprocal behaviour. Indeed the beginning of a good deal of subsequent exploitation on the part of European and Arab traders was their inability or unwillingness to read these conciliatory gestures. Gift exchanges cement relationships and make it easier to enter into other arrangements and contracts. Transformed subsequently by both indigenous and exogenous processes of more complex commercial relationships, these arrangements can degenerate into an intricate system of bribery and peculation. At its worst it is absorbed into the system of the modern state where none of the checks and balances of reciprocity (which control its operation at lower levels of interaction) come into play. Many of the new nations of Africa have learned to their cost that it is essential to their survival to begin to develop alternative moralities of the kind which led to successful commercial operations in the advanced economies.

Sometimes the disintegration of over-arching mechanisms of the state economy break down completely and it is at this point that the alternative, apparently more anarchic systems of trading relationships take over. In Ghana the collapse of cocoa prices has resulted in a quite successful development of these alternative mechanisms of distribution and exchange. At whatever level, this use of the gift to reinforce reciprocity is still an essential and sophisticated mechanism of mutual support. Amongst the peoples of the Cameroon, for example, the *djange* system of credit circulation is a well-structured form of social, political and economic freemasonry in which it is almost impossible (at least for an outsider) to disentangle the various elements of a web of relationships.

The principles of the *djange* system (Ardener, 1960) are the coming together of a group of men of similar status not related by kinship but by ethnolinguistic ties, for the purpose of raising capital for a specific need. A member of the group requests a loan. The purpose is considered by the group. If the request is accepted each member contributes to the fund until the required sum or amount is achieved. By his act of contribution the member earns his right, in strict rotation, to draw on the capital of the *djange* group for his own needs. In the past this need was of quite modest extent (the purchase of food supplies, the raising of a dowry, paying school fees). As the economy expanded this extended to much wider range of requests frequently involving the establishment of a business enterprise. The increased need for capital increased the size of contributions and the number in the group. These groups now also exist in an urban milieu and embrace a wider if informal range of social, political as well as economic functions. A *djange* meeting has become an entertainment as well as a business meeting. Membership of a *djange* group carries with it both considerable prestige and obligations.

The reciprocities engendered by gifting and loaning were further extended by barter relations. Items deemed to be of equivalent value were exchanged in elaborate trading relationships both within and between ethnic polities. Often these systems developed high levels of integration well before the development of a modern economy into which they have been incorporated in market-place trading.

COMMODITY EXCHANGE AND MARKET-PLACE TRADING

The market is a most vibrant manifestation of African rural life and it has attracted a good deal of academic attention both in terms of the spatio-temporal structure of marketing and social activity generated for and by the market-place and the processes of interchange for which the market is a focus.

The introduction of currency into trading relations led to a growing sophistication of the mechanisms of trading. It is at the level of the market-place that a full array of exchange relationships take place and the local market-place is in many ways the most sophisticated and most obvious manifestation of a vigorous rural society and economy.

The emergence of markets and market-place trading has been linked to political centralization and state formation. For example, it is argued that increased levels of welfare are possible through state formation and the development of markets (Bates, 1981). The state produces order and peace which allows comparative advantages to operate in production and the necessary exchanges of goods and services. The role of trade in Africa has been emphasized by numerous scholars and some have taken the view that African state systems are based on the extraction of gains from commerce (Coquery-Vidrovitch, 1976) and market-place trade. This neo-Marxian perspective sees the state not so much as a provider of collective advantage through trade, but as the means of promoting and protecting stratification and privilege through expropriation and the redistribution of wealth. It has also been contended that while decentralized lineage systems can facilitate trade, they are not as efficient as market-places in centralized systems, partly because of the danger of feuding and rivalry among lineages. There are examples of some lineage-based societies actually importing foreign traders to organize and control exchange; such was the case of the Ibibio in south-eastern Nigeria, who relied on the Aro to control and centralize trade in their area.

In some densely populated areas the casual and relatively informal exchanges between individuals and families were too frequent to be carried on in a piecemeal fashion and functional locations emerged in certain villages and at certain times when trade could be organized. Eventually the regularity and number of such interactions led to the emergence of space–time convergences of such activity. These unit areas of space were formally established as trading or market-places. Formalized exchange relations began to attract strangers and tokens of exchange (shells, iron bars, gold thread) complemented simple barter arrangements as credit arrangements were entered into.

A major distinction must be made between permanent markets and temporary or periodic markets. The latter are by far the most common. A large number of studies of periodic rural markets have attempted to explain the structure and function of market integration in terms of trading theory or the hierarchical ordering principles of central place theory.

The limitations of this approach are now well exposed. Part of the problem of typology arises from the desire to see a market system closely related to a central-place *settlement* hierarchy. But an important distinction must also be made between marketing activity and the towns in which such activity is focused. A market can and does exist without or outside the town. Trading relations are not bounded by the rigid structures of place.

Perhaps the best known example of this is the *sugi* in north Africa. Conflict and competition between towns forced traders to meet in neutral territory and these were soon institutionalized and developed as market-places. Similar developments have taken place throughout West Africa though not always for the same reasons.

Marvin Mikesell (1962) has written that 'the uniqueness of the *suq* in North Africa, derives from the fact that it is regarded as an institution, an event, and not as a feature of settlement'. There is evidence to suggest that this development is less unique than Mikesell realized. In areas of dispersed rural population elsewhere in Africa, such as the Bamenda region in Cameroon, market-places also developed spontaneously (Hollier, 1981).

In Nigeria, markets which attract large numbers of people and traders have appeared in bush areas which lie outside the control of district and market officials, and which frequently occur near borders. Border markets are a common phenomenon in contemporary Africa and reflect the post-independence fortunes of state import policies and the relative values of their currencies. Huge profits can be made in border trade through the exchange not only of goods, but also currency. The post-colonial period saw the creation of new sovereign states from large colonial blocs, which have created new possibilities for border traders.

Although the spatial ordering of rural market systems has been framed most frequently in terms of the central-place model, it is not the only analytical approach. Three alternative types of rural marketing arrangement have been identified: the dendritic-mercantile system, the solar marketing system and the network marketing system (see figure 5.1). In a more detailed review than is presented here, C. A. Smith (1976) has considered each as an irregular type, being appropriate primarily to inefficient and poorly developed and articulated patterns of peasant marketing. Perhaps for this reason, there are elements in these models which appear to have a more direct bearing on the precise structural relationship between markets in many African systems than does the central-place notion of commodity distribution.

Centre-periphery forces are especially prevalent within dendritic systems, with producers in the more remote rural areas seriously disadvantaged compared to those living close to the centre. Distribution channels are, by definition, particularly inefficient in that they only flow to and from the centre. In practice, exchange systems can exhibit two levels or organization. Locational patterns may express both central-place and mercantile ordering in varying degrees.

In spatial terms, there are some grounds for regarding solar marketing systems simply as truncated examples of the dendritic-mercantile model. Functions and structures, however, reveal important distinctions. Within solar systems, a network of markets is organized by a single articulating centre, producing a simple two-level hierarchy. In effect, a group of rural

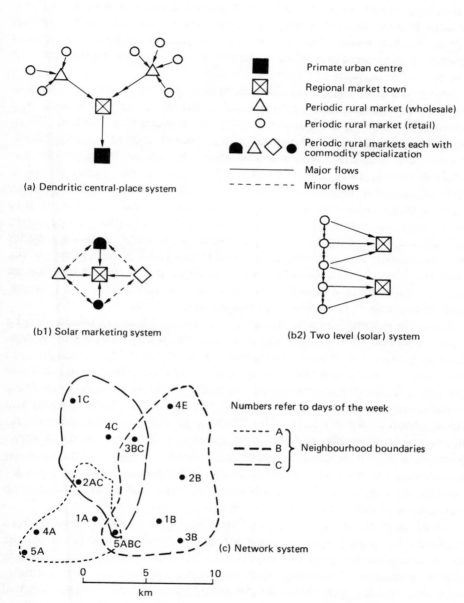

■ Primate urban centre

⊠ Regional market town

△ Periodic rural market (wholesale)

○ Periodic rural market (retail)

◐ △ ◇ ● Periodic rural markets each with commodity specialization

———— Major flows

------- Minor flows

(a) Dendritic central-place system

(b1) Solar marketing system

(b2) Two level (solar) system

Numbers refer to days of the week

------ A ⎫
— — — B ⎬ Neighbourhood boundaries
—・— C ⎭

(c) Network system

0   5   10
         km

Figure 5.1 Marketing systems
Source: Hollier, 1981

periodic markets, usually with specific commodity specializations, meet on different days and supply a single urban market or, as in a two-level system, perhaps two consuming centres. In these circumstances the urban hierarchy is restricted and characterized by the lack of intermediate market centres, though there may be some degree of horizontal interaction between adjacent rural markets.

Network marketing systems have been identified by a number of anthropologists and geographers working in West Africa, notably by Hodder and Ukwu (1969) among the Yoruba, and by Bohannan and Bohannan (1962), working amongst the Tiv of Nigeria, and the Konkomba of northern Ghana respectively. For the Tiv, socio-economic organization is defined by the neighbourhood, itself defined in terms of the people who share a complete cycle of the same markets. With a five-day week, there are five periodic markets that can be regarded as being both spatially and socially closest to each compound group. As one moves away from any market so one moves into an adjacent neighbourhood or cycle of markets. Although cycles overlap, there is a greater degree of social interaction between people of the same neighbourhood than between people sharing only one or two market days. In this way (see figure 5.1) a network of markets based on informal neighbourhoods is stretched out in chain-mail fashion.

In south-western Nigeria, the heavily populated and urbanized Yoruba region has one of the most sophisticated marketing systems in Africa. Hodder (1961), studying an area between Ibadan and Oyo, distinguished five types of market according to location and periodicity: urban daily markets (in the largest towns), urban night markets, rural daily markets (usually only for fresh produce and meat), rural periodic night markets and rural periodic day markets. The latter were the most widespread and important local markets, distributed evenly at distances of about seven miles with no village more than five miles distant. As we noted earlier the distribution did not correspond to a central-place hierarchy and markets are organized to serve the mutual advantage of rural buyers and sellers who have to travel and transport goods on foot.

These markets are also organized on a ring system where a ring forms a complete integrated sequence over a four-day week, which pre-dates the introduction of the seven-day week in the late nineteenth century. Such is the organization of the ring that successive markets are not normally adjacent, which represents a logical mutually-convenient organization of space and time with which to meet the demands of a rural population where daily markets would be too frequent, yet the four-day is sufficient to allow for problems of storage of produce and phased purchases. Such markets generate a huge movement of goods and people and it is not impossible, if necessary, for a woman to visit more than one market. Hodder's survey of the eight-day Akinyele ring showed most women visited two out of eight markets, with some attending five out of eight. Within the Akinyele ring some 10 000 people were on the move on any one day which represented 35 per cent of the total population.

Among the Yoruba, women are primarily concerned with rural marketing which in part reflects their relative economic independence and trading competence. In non-Muslim areas of West Africa women play a crucial role in the marketing process, and this is particularly true of Ghana and Nigeria, where the 'market mammies' have very considerable power and influence. In East Africa on the other hand, the Arab influence means that women are almost totally absent and a different atmosphere prevails. Female participation in West African market-place trade is crucial and in West Ghana and southern Nigeria their position is often of paramount importance in the structure of rural life.

It seems likely that by the late 1960s in some areas the system of periodic marketing was beginning to break down, as the essentially horizontal social and economic marketing mechanisms of the trading rings came increasingly under pressure from outside traders creating either solar or dendritic markets. So much so, that C. A. Smith (1976) has argued persuasively that 'viewed from the outside rather than internally, Tiv market rings in Nigeria appear to be the unstructured peripheral ends of a broader dendritic marketing system' and that 'in other words, the Tiv perceive and operate within a network system, although outsiders have created and operate within a dendritic system in the same places'.

This last point suggests that it is the perception and use of market-places that structures the degree of interaction within the marketing system as a whole. To categorize market systems, whether as central-place systems, or dendritic-mercantile systems or whatever, is therefore to mislead rather than to illuminate. The internal articulation and integration of market-places within a marketing system can be explained in several ways or dimensions according to the consciousness of the particular market users. More particularly, the nature of the relationship between a given spatial set of market locations can only be established when the precise character of the multitude of distribution channels is evaluated. For example, within any system, some foodstuffs destined for urban markets will be distributed through a simple two-level solar hierarchy. Other commodities may require a more redistributive (central-place) mechanism, while rural to rural flows may invoke quite different organizational forces, not covered by any of these models.

The inability to find marketing hierarchies elsewhere in Africa strictly constructed along the lines postulated by central-place theory is shown in work directed by W. O. Jones (1972). He identifies considerable differences in the marketing patterns of *specific commodities*. Furthermore, within any one rural market there is an internal differentiation where different spatial sectors are allocated to specific commodities, each with their own exchange system and clientele. Knowing a general system of markets and their hierarchies will not necessarily make it possible to describe the marketing of any one commodity, and because trading regions may be built up by aggregating individual commodities, studies of this development can be quite different from those arrived at by methods of anthropologists and geographers.

The root of the problem lies in the failure to uncover fully how market systems are integrated by the articulation of traders of both manufactured items and foodstuffs. In reality, it can be demonstrated that the two types of goods follow quite different patterns of distribution (Hollier 1981). Although the rural market may be the starting point for the upward flow of foodstuffs and the termination of the downward flow of manufactured items, the market towns between the top and the bottom of the size hierarchy may play a role in the distribution of manufactured items which is quite complicated. It is not the exact reverse of that for foodstuffs. The small scale retailer of manufactured items in a rural area is unable to travel to the source of the production or importation of those goods as his transport costs may be higher than his anticipated profit. Nor can he buy in sufficient bulk to offset these costs as his annual turnover is small. Even those traders from rural areas close to the centres of manufacturing industry may not be able to purchase from source as manufacturers or wholesalers often prefer to sell in bulk to a few large traders rather than to a large number of traders buying small amounts of cloth, clothing or footwear. As Hollier's work in Cameroon has shown, large scale traders of foodstuffs can travel direct to the rural markets of quite distant areas as their capital resources are sufficient to purchase in bulk, and large enough to subsume transport costs. Moreover, the scale of their operation is such that these traders commonly own a vehicle, or are able to charter a lorry at more competitive rates than those charged by the taxi operators in the public transport sector.

It seems important to assert therefore, that the successful identification of market hierarchies must depend not on the abstract, albeit theoretically satisfying considerations of size, function and spatial and temporal location, but ultimately on the travel patterns and marketing strategies of very different types of traders. Few attempts have been made to ask why traders operated in some markets and not in others or why some traders can eke out an existence in one market or set of markets when other market traders cannot (Hollier, 1981). In order to understand this phenomenon it is important to remember that many traders are in the market as buyers as well as sellers.

The northern Nigerian grain trade has a particularly sophisticated hierarchy of wholesalers and retailers and the social relations of grain marketing have been explored for one area in some detail by Clough (1981, 1985). Clough identifies three foci of the grain trade: merchant capital, the local ruling class and state governments. Urban merchants advance capital to inter-village wholesalers in November who quote rates slightly above the local price, which allows them to buy grain for themselves and their urban patrons in January and February. Grain is stored against price rises in the late dry season and when it is collected by urban merchants in July the price is twice that advanced in November. Inter-village wholesalers benefit in a number of ways through their clientage whith urban merchants. Advances allow participation in the grain harvest, they provide the wholesalers with money to buy and store their own grain, urban merchants pay a commission on grain stored for them, there is an acceptable level of cheating and finally the profits they make on grain trading in July (pre-harvest) are advanced to poor farmers as loans (*falle*) which are repaid at 100 per cent in kind at the November harvest. Thus urban merchant capital finances a cycle of accumulation for inter-village wholesalers, while urban merchants benefit from the storage-provided access to local markets. State governments are also purchasers from inter-village wholesalers and Clough quotes the example of one trader who in March had 1000 sacks in store for his urban patron, 500 for the local government and 250 for himself.

At the hamlet level, the inter-village trader has client-traders to whom money is advanced, to use their local networks for grain purchases. Post-harvest disposal of grain occurs when poor and medium farmers have insufficient cash to cover their expenses, especially if groundnut and cotton have not done so well. The post-harvest period is one when taxes are collected, marriages contracted, debts repayed, buildings repaired and consumer goods purchased. In contrast bigger farmers sell only in the late dry season when price rises have occured. Thus grain is stored by merchants across time, wholesales are periodized according to the relative wealth of farming households. Trading across time is very profitable compared with trading across space, where the price differential among rural periodic and urban markets is limited and is very competitive.

The grain trade operates through vertical clientage networks, kin groups and lateral associations of friendship. The ties are varied and flexible and may contain elements of redistribution. Clough makes the point that while surplus value is appropriated through commodity exchange, many rural traders deplete their capital resources through taking additional wives, going on the *haj*, distributing food at Muslim festivals, especially after *Ramadan*, making non-interest small loans (*rance*) and maintaining local koranic teachers. Wealth has to be continuously re-created and it is arguable that through redistribution some social stability is introduced into an otherwise exploitative system.

The heterogeneity of exchange relations in the Hausa grain market are a reminder that rural markets are places where wholesalers, retailers and local farmers buy and sell and are points of exchange for local and long-distance trade. They are also places where people converge for a variety of other reasons which may embrace buying and selling, but also include other motives which may be both social and political. Unquestionably the economic motive is uppermost, whether they are shrewd entrepreneurs or peasant farmers with a small windfall surplus to dispose of to discharge a debt. But the market also serves as a place to find one's social place in a wider context than the village. For the Mawri of Niger, visits to the market-place provide an opportunity to reassert the identity of a widely scattered group. Many are clearly there to enjoy themselves – to drink beer and to discuss events. Often political allegiances and marriage arrangements are re-affirmed or established in the market (Bohannan and Bohannan, 1962). It may also be the place where vital information is disseminated about a new vaccination programme, or a credit organization, or external aid activity, or a coming election. It is also the place where informal or formal letters and agreements can be drawn up between individuals using the services of a scribe or a 'lawyer'. Craftsmen of varying kinds flourish and it is possible to have clothes sewn, teeth extracted or leather sandals made. Indeed a whole range of ancillary services are provided depending on the scale of the market and local demand.

MARKETS, EXCHANGE AND THE MODERN STATE

The rural periodic market is an interesting and vital phenomenon, but is by no means universal in Africa, and as we have suggested may be best seen as the rural end of a hierarchy of markets and exchange relations which link rural and urban areas. Rural periodic markets are best developed in areas of high rural population density where historically urbanism and centralized state control required the extraction of surpluses from the countryside. Rural markets were also part of long-distance trade, but more importantly they served to feed the cities. The regional differences in feeding are well illustrated by the reaction of the colonial powers. In some instances such as south-west and northern Nigeria they encountered high degrees of urbanism and marketing system *in situ*, in other instances they created both new towns and the means of feeding them.

The feeding of Yaoundé, the capital of Cameroon, is a good example of setting up a marketing system *de novo* and has been admirably charted by Guyer (1987). In the pre-colonial period the local Beti, segmentary people, had no markets, therefore the Germans and French set out to construct a marketing system including a transport network, pricing mechanisms and the determination of the position of traders. Because Yaoundé was a white-collar town the policy objective was low producer prices amenable to government influence, which provoked a number of social and economic contradictions. In order to feed Yaoundé the French tapped in to the rich agricultural hinterland by creating local elites who could mediate relations between the state and the people; this was done by appointing chiefs who were given food supply quotas and the responsibility for the organization of new crops such as rice and cocoa. The result was corvée labour, restricted mobility of labour, village co-operative plots for new crops and the *indigénat* as a weapon of control.

When the *indigénat* was abolished in 1946 the power of chiefs collapsed but still there was no traditional marketing system. A new institution was developed by the French, the provident societies, which were used in French territories in Africa and Asia. These were really credit organizations and co-operatives organized under the bureaucratic umbrella of the state and the banking system. Membership was universal and compulsory and one particular society was given the task of provisioning Yaoundé. With decolonization the provident societies collapsed and a free market in the food trade developed, dominated by the Beti and the Bamaleke, but this was a system not controllable by Yaoundé's civil servants. Thus in 1972 as food costs rose, the state again intervened. Price controls appeared, which were seen by traders as a defence of class interests, but as producers would not sell, the emphasis was shifted to production and plantations and estates were set up together, which have failed as they have been undermined by the private sector. As Guyer points out, there has always been a gap between the Beti producers who occupy the Yaoundé hinterland and the consumers who occupy the city. Filling the gap on terms acceptable to government has proved difficult.

Even in areas where there were established systems of exchange, the colonial authorities and their successors found it necessary to institute or encourage alternative means of dealing with crop surpluses, especially crops grown for export. Merchant firms and traders were generally encouraged by colonial governments despite at times a conflict of interest, while the merchants themselves usually managed to resolve their own difficulties of competition by adopting pooling arrangements or amalgamations. Industrial capital in the metropoles also was interested in securing supplies of raw materials and a particularly illuminating example of the operations of industrial and merchant capital is that of the British Cotton Growers Association (BCGA).

In Nigeria and elsewhere the BCGA lobbied government for the development of colonial cotton production because of the declining supplies from America and deteriorating terms of trade. But in northern Nigeria the BCGA had to break into an existing market supplying a flourishing textile industry, as well as counter a number of other merchant firms engaged in general trading. In 1905 the BCGA pressed for, and was granted, monopoly buying rights. By 1916 the government only allowed the cultivation of Allen-type cotton which was of little use to local producers. The Allen-type was justified on grounds of higher yields, yet it was in fact more susceptible to boll-weevil.

Shenton and Lenihan (1981) have described the progress and effects of the BCGA in northern Nigeria and as they explain, it was the buying system which really clinched the success of the BCGA, as it was able to control the conditions of production and exchange. The buying agents for BCGA were the merchant firms, who in turn employed their own buying-agents in rural areas who worked on a commission basis. As competition developed among agents they used a system of advances to acquire farmers' cotton ahead of the harvests. They also made gifts to village heads for their co-operation. The advance system although frowned upon by the authorities attracted many farmers because taxes were collected before the cotton harvest, while imported consumer goods were increasingly being demanded for bridewealth, which was essential to household reproduction. When producer prices for cotton were high, the amount of labour required to raise money for goods was not excessive and up to 1924 cotton prices rose steadily. But with depression of the 1920s and 1930s many farmers found themselves in difficulties and in debt. It was at this point that those farmers who weathered the difficulties of the bad years began to hire increasing amounts of labour from less well-off neighbours, which contributed to increasing differentiation within rural communities.

The direct intervention of the state in produce marketing was most importantly accentuated over a wide range of produce during World War II and afterwards, through the establishment of marketing boards. The objectives of the marketing boards were the stabilization of producer prices and foreign exchange earnings, together with the reduction of interseasonal price movements. In addition, they were to assist agricultural research. Doubts about the validity of the boards were expressed by Bauer in 1954 who believed they did not stabilize prices or seasonal variations, rather they dampened producer incentives by paying them only a half or two-thirds of world prices of oil-palm, cocoa, coffee and cotton. Hopkins (1973) estimated that export crop producers in Ghana from 1947-61 lost 41 per cent, and in Nigeria producers lost 27 per cent of their potential gross incomes through marketing board taxes. Also, Williams (1985) points out that African producers after World War II were in effect paying for part of the UK's trade deficit with the US, as low producer prices reduced the colonies' demand for scarce imported dollar goods, while it channelled export crops into Britain and precluded US competition.

However, marketing boards were performing a function, but not the intended one. They became fiscal instruments for capturing and cheaply collecting an agricultural surplus to promote economic development (Helleiner, 1966). But very little of the development came the way of rural people. Urban interests took preference – in the shape of airlines, hotels, industrial estates and plantations. Furthermore, taxing the rural producer may well have reduced the rural demand for goods in favour of imported goods demanded by governments, bureaucrats and their clients which held back local industries. In Nigeria, Williams (1985) shows that once marketing boards were regionalized in 1954, they became the fiscal base for politicians on whom the control of regional economies had devolved. The boards' funds were used to pay for schools and roads, as well as for the private businesses of politicians and substantial amounts were syphoned off into party funds. In 1974 the federal government resumed control and in 1977 a return was made to the old commodity boards with the addition of new ones for grains, tubers and roots. In the 1970s the returns to farmers were slightly less in terms of purchasing power than in the depression years of the 1930s. Not surprisingly there was a shift by farmers into non-farm jobs which were increasing as the oil economy took off, as well as into other crops and border trading. The boards have not eliminated middlemen, or fluctuating prices, they have merely become the apex of the buying system and shaped it to suit the interests of ruling parties and local aristocracies and made themselves a means of consolidating patronage networks.

SUMMARY

Informal and semi-formal exchange is both varied and flexible within rural societies and reflects the ways in which agricultural surpluses are both created and circulated. The rural market is to some extent an indicator of the relative economic strength and vitality of rural communities and in addition it serves as a focus of social exchanges. But the rural market is also frequently the end of a chain of exchange where urban merchants and their clients offload rural produce as well as distribute imported or non-local goods. Over the past 30 to 40 years rural people have become increasingly affected by and vulnerable to, the intervention of the state, as it grapples with the problems of controlling agricultural surpluses, of feeding the cities or acquiring foreign exchange. In our next chapter we transfer our attention away from the rural agricultural sector to look at pastoralism. It will become apparent that here is another important sphere of rural life where the state has sought to engineer solutions to what it perceives as problem areas and people and has turned pastoral zones into adjuncts of the urban food market.

6

Nomads, Pastoralists and the Competition for Resources

INTRODUCTION

Drought, famine and desertification became widely discussed issues during the 1970s, giving rise to much academic debate, public concern, programmes of famine relief and international aid. Those primarily affected by these conditions are farmers and especially pastoralists living in the arid and semi-arid zones of tropical Africa. In many of these areas of low and variable rainfall, pastoralism alone or in some combination with cultivation is the only viable form of landuse. In this chapter we turn our attention to these pastoral peoples who live not only in areas which have been described as 'marginal' (usually by cultivators and outsiders) but who themselves have been socially and politically marginalized. Attitudes towards pastoralists display a polarity from the romantic idea of the free, noble nomad to the notion that nomadic pastoralists are an anachronism and if sedentarized could make an effective contribution to society by supplying urban markets with meat products.

The second part of the chapter discusses some views on pastoralism together with political reactions. The first part looks at the distribution of pastoral people, the nature of arid and semi-arid environments, the operation of pastoral strategies, concepts of drought and desertification and relationships with sedentary cultivators. As Swift (1982) points out, projects aimed at improving the productivity and welfare of pastoral peoples have become a major development activity, but they have had mixed results and there is little agreement on how to proceed. There is still an urgent need to understand present processes and how such societies do and might change.

DISTRIBUTION AND DEFINITIONS

The number of pastoralists in Africa south of the Sahara is not very large, perhaps of the order of 10 million, or some 3 per cent of the total population. The most numerous and widespread group are the Fulani (some 6 million) who stretch from Senegambia and Guinea through to the Cameroons. Other important concentrations of pastoralists occur in Somalia (some 2 million) in Botswana and in Kenya, where the Maasai, who number about 250 000 occupy the Great Rift Valley and northern Tanzania (Burnham, 1980; Jacobs, 1975; Konczacki, 1978). There are other important groups of pastoralists, especially nomads such as the Moors and Twareg of West Africa who, although numerically small, occupy vast areas. Indeed it is important to realize that although pastoral populations are small, they are frequently the only people making use of very large tracts of land in tropical Africa where permanent pasture and non-agricultural land (desert, mountains and seasonal pastures) covers 34 per cent even of the area south of the Sahara. These areas of permanent pasture and non-agricultural land comprise the semi-arid zone with 250–500 mm of rainfall per annum and 7.5–10 months of dry season. All of these arid and semi-arid areas experience low rainfall which is also extremely seasonal and variable. Although semi-arid environments provide an ecological niche of particular importance for pastoralists, nonetheless large numbers of herders, especially the Fulani either make seasonal incursions into the moister subhumid savannas during the dry season, or are located in the grasslands as transhumant or semi-nomadic pastoralists.

The varying practices of pastoralists in the different sub-zones of the savanna and deserts demands some kind of statement about what we mean by 'pastoralist'. As in many other cases, the hard and fast lines adopted by classificatory systems can be less than rewarding, but it is possible to focus on certain aspects which help to handle the issue of pastoralism. There are three kinds of response to conditions of aridity and rainfall deficiency: first there is gathering and hunting; second a pastoral strategy, where animals become the processors of the available vegetation, allowing higher levels of human population and animal mobility; third there is the replacement of the existing vegetation by crops which reduces mobility and increases population but radically increases the risk of disaster if the crop should fail. It is important to realize that all these three options may be practised (a) by different populations in savanna areas; (b) by the same population as part of a mixed strategy; or (c) sequentially by a single populaton in the face of radical environmental change. To the three options we can add two more: the option of abandoning the dry grassland niche and the use of irrigation. Whatever the future may bring all of these uses have been widely deployed in tropical Africa.

The frequent distinction is made between pastoralists for whom stock is the sole source of subsistence (either directly or indirectly through the sales of meat and milk) and those pastoralists who keep stock but do not aim to achieve complete dependence (Burnham, 1980). These objectives can be associated with different degrees of movement over different distances and time periods. Nomadic pastoralists, for example, are predominantly dependent on their herds and they have no home or determinant centre (Monod, 1975). In addition, there are some pastoralists who do have permanent locations even if they occupy them only in the wet season when pasture is available and they can cultivate quick growing millet. Finally, there are pastoralists who have permanent villages continually inhabited by women, children and some men, while their herds are moved seasonally from one pasture to another. These three categories have sometimes been described as pure nomadism, semi-nomadism and transhumance, although these are not especially useful sociological categories.

It has been suggested that it is neither easy nor particularly useful to try to draw a sharp line between farmers and pastoralists, since many farmers own animals and many pastoralists cultivate land. Even the long-distance nomads, such as the Moors of the western Sahara, own palm trees in the oases to which they return for the annual date harvest (*guetna*) and formerly they had slaves (now dependent clients) cultivating millet in the oases and along the riverine tracts of the Senegal. The boundaries between peasant farming and pastoralism are complex and often more apparent rather than real. The boundaries overlap and nomads and peasants move either way into each other's domains in ways which reflect socio-political conditions rather than just physical parameters. There is, therefore, an indeterminate zone of overlap between areas where purely biological factors come into play. On the one hand there are indeed areas where it is too dry for sorghum or millet and on the other too humid for camels. The areas of extreme dryness are most accessible to men through the medium of animals, principally camels, which sustain an absence of water and limited vegetation, while providing man with food. Such a boundary is particularly apparent between the Sahel and the Sahara in West Africa.

Swift (1980) believes that it is more appropriate to look at the range of possibilities for herding and farming in different circumstances of 'settledness' and mobility. Also, there are groups which overlap simple boundaries, such as pastoral-nomad, semi-nomad and transhumant pastoralist. These groups oscillate across these categorical boundaries and the degree to which they are settled changes over time. Here mobility, farming and herding reflect adaptation to changing circumstances. A pastoral economy must be viewed as an on-going process where some families are more or less successful, while others leave and turn to other livelihoods. At the same time, among the Fulani of the Niger, for example, there are some who, having tried alternative employment, return to pastoralism.

A number of observers have noted that pastoralists of all kinds do periodically leave herding and take up non-pastoral and non-agricultural activities. Long distance trading and commerce has historically been a traditional facet of nomadic pastoralism but with the decline of traditional trade they have had to seek other sources of income, often in waged employment, which allows them access to goods only obtainable in this area. For example, the transhumant pastoralists of Botswana become temporary migrants to the Republic of South Africa to take employment in the mines and urban areas. In northern Nigeria circular migration has developed among some of the Twareg from Niger, especially among the lower caste of ex-slaves (Bouzou), who instead of watching and guarding herds have become night watchmen guarding building sites and houses in the rapidly expanding northern towns such as Sokoto. It would seem that this type of employment is organized within family groups, or among friends as one man takes the job for a few months and then is replaced by another, a method which maintains the wage earning basis of a group but using a series of workers employed in the one job. These kind of non-pastoral enterprises reflects the stress on pastoral societies in the face of hazards such as drought, as well as their changing external economic relationships. Frequently it is the convergence of drought and changing economic circumstances, which precipitates either a permanent break with herding, or a compromise of temporary employment.

ARID AND SEMI-ARID ENVIRONMENTS IN THE CONTEXT OF PASTORALISM

Pastoralists are familiar with periodic droughts which are recurrent and unpredictable. Major droughts occurred in many parts of Africa during the sixteenth, seventeeth, eighteenth and nineteenth centuries, in 1913–14 and in the late 1920s and 1940s. The Sahel drought of 1968-74 was the first to attract worldwide attention. Droughts, as Mortimore (1988) suggests, must be defined in the context of landuse systems and are as distinguishable from desertification as famine is from social impoverishment by the larger time-scale. While meteorological drought is an event understandable in terms of cause and effect, such a paradigm is inadequate for desertification. Desertification is a more difficult concept whose essence Mortimore (1988) believes to be ecological degradation where the diminution or destruction of the biological potential of the land leads to an extension of desert-like conditions of soil and vegetation into areas outside the climate desert, with the intensification of such conditions over time. Furthermore, desertification is a process not an event, nor is it an exoganous natural hazard. It is a process linking human societies and their natural environments and expressing historical changes in both. And human behaviour goes far beyond the response envisaged in covert environmental determinism (Hewit, 1983).

While arguments about drought and desertification obviously concern the areas used by pastoralists, it has been suggested that ecological degradation can at least in part be laid at the door of animal herders in general. Overgrazing by large herds is not only as academic issue, but has determined both colonial and post-colonial policies towards pastoralists and the balance between pastoralism and the natural environment is a recurring theme.

The environment of the pastoralist comprises an interdependent chain linking man, animals, plants, rain and soil. The animal–vegetation link is especially important, even more so than water, because water alone is of no use and in some cases vegetation will suffice to support animal life. For example, camels need vegetation more than water. Each animal species – camels, sheep, goats and cows have their own type of grazing or rather *grazings*. Some grazing is periodic or seasonal and comes after showers of rain, while other types of grazing are perennial. But even perennial grasses wither and die after prolonged aridity and it is necessary to think rather of seasonal cycles and cycles of years, a distinction which is reflected in the long-range camel nomadism of the Sahara and the shorter seasonal cycles of cattle movement in the Sahel. The importance of vegetation is often under-estimated by development agencies, who think that the provision of water – usually boreholes – will aid cattle peoples. But this may lead to a deterioration of the little vegetation available as animals become concentrated around water points.

As we have already observed, beyond certain levels of aridity pastoral nomadism is the only means of landuse and probably overstocking of deserts is not a severe problem. Pastoral nomadism in deserts and desert fringes involves continuous movement such that animals are grazed selectively and a balance is maintained. Also, in bad years there is a selective cut-back of the herds. Cattle rearing and herding by semi-nomads and transhumant herders in the savannas can lead to much greater problems. However, the optimum number of animals per hectare of grazing is a relationship which eludes precise definition, while the relationship between pastoralist and animals, that is, the number needed to support the group, is also difficult to estimate. For example among the Maasai of Kenya it has been estimated that 6.5 adults need about 15 000 calories per day comprising three quarters milk and one quarter meat. This diet would require seven cows in milk daily which means an actual herd of some 14–25 cows, to which one must add bulls, male calves and heifers, giving an equivalent herd size of 35–40 head.

The multiplication of cattle so often condemned as hoarding to enhance prestige may have a more functional justification in the light of the margins required for adequate provision of meat and milk. But it is of some significance that overstocking may be as much a matter of men as of animals; the number of animals is merely a consequence of the number of men. In other words the human and animal demographic cycles have slipped out of phase; the acceleration of the human population drags along with it the animal population. The imbalance between herds and grazing may also be exacerbated in some cases by an overdependence on milk. If milk becomes the dominant animal product then a much higher proportion of cows is needed, which leads to larger herds than in a milk/meat mix. On the other hand, a milk strategy (two-thirds of the herd as females) supports a larger human population than a meat strategy and allows rapid recovery after losses in a drought. For example, the pastoral Fulani of West Africa who occupy a relatively well-populated pastoral zone, traditionally rely on milk for subsistence combined with trading milk for grains and starchy foods. The dependence on milk means larger herds which increases the risk in semi-arid areas, but it may mean quicker recovery after losses.

Overgrazing is a recurrent theme in the discussion of pastoralism largely because it is held to contribute towards desertification. It is something which has preoccupied colonial and post-colonial administrators and development agencies and has coloured government policies and attitudes towards animal herders in general. The case for overgrazing rests on the concept of carrying capacity which in turn depends on the production above ground of edible herbaceous matter. Because of the absence of reliable data on livestock numbers and their territories, overgrazing is usually estimated indirectly from evidence of ecological degradation. This is something of a circular argument where the possibility of alternative causes and rangeland management may be ignored (Sandford, 1983). Recent research cited by Mortimore (1988) reports that in two projects in Mali and Niger in the Sahel under conditions of less than 500 mm rainfall, there is little evidence of rangeland degradation due to overgrazing.

In East Africa although there is little evidence that animal and human populations are too high and cause environmental degradation, this 'mainstream' view has influenced policies since the 1930s, which centres on destocking and grazing control. Range development projects classify land units and assign a carrying capacity which is not to be exceeded or in some cases raised. But as studies in Kenya by Homewood, Rodgers and Arnhem (1987) have shown, there is no simple linear scale of productivity. In the drought of 1983-5 the areas of 'highest potential' suffered the greatest losses. It is apparent that for pastoralists, pastures do not have absolute but relative rankings, which change. Thus in a drought, pastures normally infested by tsetse fly become drought refuges because with increased aridity disease transmission declines.

When estimates of average carrying capacity are produced they necessarily ignore fluctuations which occur from year to year as a result of rainfall variability. For those who use the pastures, land stocked at its *average* capacity means accepting losses of potential production in many years. To stock land at a *reduced* rate to avoid unknown losses once in every so many years would waste forage on a massive scale even assuming others could use it (Mortimore, 1988).

From an economic standpoint the costs of a conservative stocking policy in terms of forgone production are high but also rise with the variability of the rainfall (Sandford, 1983). Opportunistic strategies – increasing herd sizes and risking loss – make better economic sense. If such strategies are adopted then the scope for loss is lessened by transhumance on an annual cycle and by flexibility in the selection of pastures from year to year. Open rights to pastures and the freedom to cross borders are thus essential. Mobility over time and space is a basic strategy where erratic rainfall produces a highly variable plant cover. But the size of herds is a complex issue and has to be viewed as an insurance against risks associated with livestock rearing in semi-arid zones. Some ecologists have suggested that there is also the possibility that there is a natural cycle of 'boom and slump'; catastrophe and recovery, of the kind common in the natural world, as overstocking leads to environmental deterioration which in its turn promotes a reduction in animal and human populations until recovery allows a new upsurge.

Certainly cyclic crises are not unfamiliar to pastoralists and herd size is part of their awareness of these hazards. In East Africa during the droughts of the early 1960s the cattle of the Maasai of Kajiado were reduced from an estimated 737 000 to some 203 000. Faced with this kind of disaster and the knowledge that it is likely to recur, pastoralists need to keep herds at a level commensurate with this kind of occurrence, so that when it does happen, a minimum animal population remains from which new herds can be started, as well as being able to increase meat production to maintain subsistence during the crisis. This is to put the matter in general terms and of course not all pastoralists successfully survive the crises. Herds may be dispersed by loans and leasing which helps those who are temporarily short of animals or spreads the risk for those with larger herds. Also species diversification reduces risk by using camels, goats, sheep and cattle in different ecological niches, each grazing specific ranges of fodder. Thus the pastoralist is an active manipulator of his stock and while in the biological sense pastoralism is an adaptation to eco-climatic factors, this is too simplistic a view. A variety of strategies are required to deal not only with environmental hazard, but also external economic and political pressures.

PASTORAL STRATEGIES AND ORGANIZATION

The threat of drought, famine and disease may comprise an accidental series of events, but recurrent threats demand techniques or strategies if people are to survive. Pastoralists have a wide range of techniques and knowledge to enable their continued reproduction as pastoral groups. Mo-

bility, herd splitting, a knowledge of niches, division of labour and sym-
biotic relations with non-pastoral peoples are symptomatic in whole or part
of the lifestyle of all pastoralists. Also external supports through raiding,
transport and trading have traditionally been part of the pastoral practice
and behaviour.

Various attempts have been made to specify a range of pastoral strategies
available to pastoralists. The present behaviour of pastoralists can be seen
as a function of three sets of variables: physical environment, human
population and livestock population. The physical environment is manipu-
lated by skills rather than by tools. Grass burning and well construction for
example are direct attempts to manipulate rather than transform physical
conditions. But of greater significance are the cognitive maps and environmental knowledge preserved in the minds of elders. It is on their memories
of environmental states and of former response to crises that reliance is
placed. Swift's account of the Twareg of the Adrar in northern Mali shows
a similar interpretation, when he speaks of the pastoralist not as a labourer
but an environmental manager whose perceptions of the natural environment reflects this management role (Swift, 1980). The Twareg apparently
have good understanding of geographical space, are excellent topographers
with intricate naming systems for landscapes which appear featureless to an
outsider. Even so, their orientation is not primarily within geographic
space. Their system of reference points is tied to social and political
relationships.

Human populations, as we have already noted, are part of the problem of
overstocking and ideally pastoralists attempt to adjust the size of the
population to the feeding capacity of thier livestock. For example, the
distribution of population can be adjusted to the changing patterns of
available resources through a highly segmented form of social organization
in small family groups set within a larger sustaining ideology geared to
mobility and autonomy. Delayed or early marriage, birth-spacing and
temporary out-migration are other methods of population control.

But the manipulation of the livestock population itself lies at the heart of
pastoralism. Thus pastoralists practise multi-species herding, spatial deployment of flocks to follow the best grazing, successional lactation of
animals, for a constant supply of milk, stock reduction by slaughter and
sale at appropriate times and the organization of animals into convenient-
sized groups which can be managed by the labour available. Rainfall in
semi-arid areas is of course notoriously unreliable both in space and time
within any one year, as well as between years.

Swift's study of the Twareg gives some fascinating insights into the
management of herds by nomadic pastoralists and the manner in which
they use their environment in these circumstances (Swift, 1979). The
particular focus of Swift's studies have been the Kel Adrar, a Twareg
confederacy of some 20 000 nomads located in the Adrar n'Iforas of

north-eastern Mali. This area lies within the Sahelian zone of West Africa where rainfall depends on the northward advance of the Inter Tropical Discontinuity (ITD), that is, the boundary between the two pressure systems which generates the south-west monsoon from the coast and the north-east harmattan winds from the desert. The northward advance of the ITD varies from year to year. Toupet calculated that in Mauritania the 100 mm isohyet differed sufficiently for the years 1941-2 and 1951-2 as to affect 340 000 square kilometres, or 31.5 per cent of the country. In Sahelian countries, one year may bring heavy rains, the next nothing at all. In the areas Swift studied, a rainfall at Kidal has varied since 1926 from between 119.2 mm and 193.7 mm, which means one bad year in four and probably a disastrous rainfall evey 15 years. Also wet and dry years tend to come in clusters, for example droughts in the Sahel occurred in 1910-16, in the late 1940's and in 1969-73.

Given these provisos there are two types of grazing in the Sahel, first the extensive pasture of the annual grasses which depends on the quantity and distribution of rainfall and second the perennial grasses and vegetation concentrated around dry season wells and wadis. The former pastures are used from July to March, and the latter from March to June. Pasture, water, labour and herds form the essential ingredients of pastoralism and it is the herds which comprise the productive machinery transforming vegetation which is of no direct value to man into milk, meat and other by-products. The Kel Adrar studied by Swift keep camels, cattle, sheep, goats and donkeys, the latter to carry baggage and water. Each species of animal has different food, water and labour requirements and different reproductive characteristics and it is the manipulation of all these factors which lies at the heart of successful herd management.

Different ecological niches are exploited according to food requirements. For example, cattle and sheep are grazers and require grassland; camels both graze and browse, eating grasses and shrubs and trees; goats are mainly browsers and feed on shrubs and trees. The different species also have different dry season water needs; cattle and sheep drink often, every two or three days and have to be kept near the wells, whereas camels drink every five to six days and travel further afield. Goats drink very little but have to be watered each day and generally drink from water skins and stay around the dry season camps. The requirements of different animals demand corresponding labour inputs for herding, watering and milking. Sheep are the most labour intensive and must have full-time shepherding, whereas cattle and camels often wander unattended and need labour only for watering and milking. Like sheep, goats require constant attention but they are easy to manage and consequently are looked after by children or the elderly.

Another feature of the mixed stock of animals is that they have different economic and ecological characteristics. Camels and goats are hardy and will survive drought well, but they have a low market value. On the other hand, cattle and sheep have high pasture and labour requirements, and sell well but they are relatively fragile and in the bad years are the first to succumb to drought. Therefore in the good years the Kel Adrar find it pays to build up their herds of cattle and sheep and profit from limited sales, while the hardier camels and goats provide a fall back or subsistence base in the bad years. Part of herd management lies in the appreciation and control of the different breeding cycles of animals and the aim is to try to get a reasonably continuous supply of milk throughout the year. Although the Kel Adrar eat millet and milk they have to rely on the latter almost entirely for some part of the year. Cows and camels have a gestation period of 10 and 12 months respectively and conceive after the onset of the rains when pasture is good. Consequently their young are born in the following rainy season when pasture is at its best. On the other hand sheep are prevented from breeding until December or January, so, with a six-month gestation cycle, their lambs are also born in the rainy season. Goats are managed so that their kids are born after camels, sometime during October to January. Both goats and sheep are prevented from breeding a second time each year unless the pastures are exceptionally good. This programme of staggered breeding allows the optimum use of rainy season pasture and tries to ensure that there is some milk available throughout the year.

In addition to herding, the Kel Adrar engage in trading, particularly when pastoral activity is concentrated around the dry season wells. Utilizing their position between the Niger valley to the south and the oasis of Algeria to the north, they operate in both areas to acquire trade goods and supplies of millet and sorghum. These grains are obtained in the north either by purchase or exchange of animals which may be trekked 600 miles to the northern oases. Tea, sugar and other trade goods are also bought in the north and then sold in southern markets along the Niger for food-staples. Salt from Taodenni is bought for internal consumption by the Twareg as well as forming another element in the southern trade.

An inevitable problem for the pastoralist is the storage of surpluses against periods of shortage. Camel milk cannot be used to make cheese and meat will not store; the outcome is that surpluses are stored on the hoof and herds increase beyond the immediate needs of subsistence. The Kel Adrar are no exception to this pastoralist trait and surplus animals are kept so that in bad times they can be slaughtered or sold off for grain. Surplus animals may also be rented out for milking or loaned to kin and friends as a means of establishing networks of obligation and reciprocity, as well as spreading the risk of a large herd over a range of geographical locations and environments. Large herds even in poor conditions have a huge latent capacity for milk when a good year comes along. On the other hand small herds cannot be expanded rapidly to catch a good season, especially the breeding stock of females. As Swift points out, pastoralism is unlike agriculture where yields are proportional to the area planted and may be changed from year to year according to expectation and needs. Most pastoralists are attempting to achieve a balance between a maximum herd and the pressure on grazing resources in the good years so that they can use these accumulated resources and the social relationships they create, to carry them through the bad years.

Pastoral populations operate strategies of resource exploitation through a variety of organizational structures. There are four levels of organization: population, sub-population, local group and production unit (Dyson-Hudson, 1980). Populations (tribes) exhibit political autonomous structures, whereas the sub-population (sections) occupy named territories. At the next level local groups may comprise 15 to 20 camps, but the basic unit is the production unit or camp, which comprises several polygynous families. It would appear that of the four levels, two are of critical importance. The rights of resource use are, in principle, rights which belong to the whole population, that is the tribe, but in fact it is at the sub-population level with its named territories where the priority of use is allocated. What the tribal leaders do is to allocate a place in the queue for the use of resources assigned to other sub-populations when one's own area is under stress. Within the sub-population it is the independent moving production unit (camps) comprising humans and livestock, that is the operational basis of production, reproduction and consumption. This unit searches and finds the resources it needs and negotiates amicable arrangements with other similar competing units. But in the same way that the population level facilitates adequate response by the sub-population, the local group facilitate the activities of the production units. The local group or camp is a voluntaristic temporary grouping, which pre-structures collective exploitation and gives emergency help or distributes information.

Sub-populations vary in size from 2000 to 20 000; while production units may vary from 20 to 25 or 50 to 55 persons depending on the interplay of operator success, human and animal fertility, and micro-ecological conditions over time. Human and animal populations are linked to allow a strategy of resource sharing at individual and aggregate levels without removing individual responses and flexibility. This limits social liability under conditions of scarcity so guaranteeing a chance for all to compete. It should be noted that unlike West Africa where there is a complex intermixture of pastoral and agricultural peoples, in East and Central Africa there are ethnically formed blocks of territory where pastoralists interact with each other and with agriculturalists only along their frontiers.

CONTACT BETWEEN PASTORALISTS AND SEDENTARY FARMERS

In West Africa a social and economic map has long shown a complex interaction of pastoral and agricultural peoples and the exclusive dependence on milk and milk products which is an ideal among the Fulani no longer exists and may have been rare even in the past. As Burnham (1980) has observed institutionalized inter-ethnic relationships of various kinds have long played a central role in Fulani society and the nutritional practices of the Fulani mirror this fact. For those Fulani attempting to survive on herd resources alone in areas of low population density both of pastoral and agricultural peoples strategies of co-operation are imperative. In colonial and more recent times the Fulani have gradually spread into the drier regions of the Sahel which were formerly the domain of the Twareg and are areas of low population density. Likewise the Fulani have moved into the Adamawa plateau of Nigeria and the Cameroons. In the drier Sahelian regions of Niger, Upper Volta and Mali the spread of the Fulani together with their large herds aimed at milk production have made these areas particularly vulnerable in terms of the carrying capacity in drought years, as the recent droughts have shown. The movement of the Fulani and their cattle into areas hitherto occupied by the camel herding Twareg, is in part a response to the growing population densities in the Sudanic areas to the south, and the reductions in fallowing and the shift towards more permanent cultivation. The reduction of fallows restricts the possibilities for grazing for the Fulani and consequently they have moved into the areas occupied by the Twareg who are politically less stable and less able to resist the incursions of these cattle rearers.

It is usual to divide the Fulani into at least three groups: pastoral nomads, semi-sedentary pastoralists and settled urban Fulani. These broad distinctions based on ecology, economy and culture can be observed in Senegal, Guinea and The Gambia (where the Fulani are collectively known as Fula or Pular), as well as northern Nigeria and Niger. In Nigeria the settled urban Fulani are recognized as a sub-group and are known as *Torrobe* (Fula) or *Torankawa* (Hausa) who derive from an important aristocratic clan of Muslim scholars and reformists, who migrated eastward from the Futo Toro in Senegal. It was from this group that Shehu Usuman Dan Fodio emerged as the leader of the jihad which led to the formation of the Sokoto Caliphate by his son Bello in 1806, which became the largest and most populous state in tropical Africa prior to the partition of Africa in the late nineteenth century.

Within Nigeria and Niger the nomadic Fulani rear cattle, sheep, goats and some camels which involves them in an orbital cycle of periodic movements from north to south, or from upland to lowland in the dry season and back again during the wet. Grazing resources are limited on the one hand by the long dry season which preclude extended stays in the northern savannas and on the other by the tsetse fly the vector of sleeping sickness, which limits the use of the southern savannas in the wet season. It is during the dry season that cattle can penetrate into the tsetse zones of the south and animals are grazed along riverine tracts of the Sokoto-Rima rivers. Where cattle are kept within villages or towns, they are moved daily onto the river margins in the dry season, while in the wet season herds are moved into bush areas away from zones of intensive cultivation.

The seasonal movements of the pastoral Fulani are clearly influenced by the distribution of pasture, water and the tsetse fly, but of some significance is their relationship with non-pastoral peoples. The practice of selling milk from the herds to buy grains and vegetables bring the Fulani into densely settled zones, which, during the early dry season, gives them access to crop residues left after the harvesting of millet and guinea corn. Grazing over the farmlands provides food for the animals and manure for the agriculturalist; in some cases the farmer may provide a certain amount of fodder in return for manuring. But where dry season crops are grown on the *fadamas* and during the wet season on the uplands, herds must be kept away from standing crops and inevitably tension and litigation are part of the farmer–herder relationship. Cattle herders who are wholly dependent on their animals try to achieve an optimal age and sex composition in their herds, which approximates to 80 per cent females. The size of a herd necessary to support an average family depends on grazing and market conditions. With a good milk market, a herd of 20 animals will suffice, but in sparsely-populated areas where income is derived from the sale of surplus heifers as well as bulls, a herd of at least 60 is needed.

Another subdivision of the Fulani comprises those who combine animal rearing with agriculture. In this semi-sedentary form of pastoralism animals are dominant and it should not be confused with mixed farming. Farms are small, usually without cashcrops and with a preference for early millet, which interferes least with herding and can be grown on the poorer less-heavily populated margins of settled areas. The herds of semi-nomads are frequently smaller in size than the pastoral Fulani as farming reduces their dependence on milk and the herds move over shorter distances, averages of 117 km being recorded in the Gwandu area of north-western Nigeria (Hopen, 1958). Herding movements are similar to those of the pastoralist proper and assume an orbital form, with southward movements in the dry season and northward movements in the wet. Similarly the river margins and wetlands are used extensively during the dry season. The dual economy of these semi-nomads frequently involves the splitting and re-moval of part of the production unit for some time during the year and this type of pastoralism in effect becomes transhumance. The household head usually remains on the farm in the home village with a few milk cows while sons take the herds away during the dry season living in temporary bush camps (*ruga*). The return home is made in sufficient time to help clear farms before the rains begin.

In the north-western part of Kano state in Nigeria, the semi-nomadic Fulani live in settlements between the agricultural villages of the Kanuri people, and when the surface pools of water have dried up in December they move their herds some 50 km to the flood plain of the Hadejia river

(Mortimore, 1978). Here water grazing and milk markets are available until the onset of the rains when they return home in time to plant millet. A few herds remain at home all through the year (in demarcated grazings) but watering them from wells and feeding them on crop residues is quite a laborious business. In the Sokoto close-settled zone rather different patterns of transhumance occur. The towns and villages contain many cattle as this is predominantly an area of settled Fulani associated with the jihad, and these animals are moved out of the cultivated area in the wet season to the empty bush areas to the south and east, and brought back in the dry season when they graze on the extensive *fadamas*.

The Sokoto pattern is much nearer to what Mortimore (1978) has described as 'settled stock breeding'. The difference in this form of semi-nomadism is one of degree, where farming may gradually assume a less important role as the same grazings are visited each year.

It has been suggested that semi-sedentary nomadism is a transitional stage between nomadism and sedentary settlement and farming is begun after a reduction in herd size following serious droughts and a loss of economic viability on the herds. Even if this is true in some parts there is the possibility that the process is reversible. In the Sokoto and Gwandu areas of north-western Nigeria there are other important historical reasons for this change. The success of the Fulani jihad in the early nineteenth century attracted pastoralists both Fulani and Twareg, who lived close by the walled settlements (*ribats*) of the Caliphate because of the unsettled conditions. After consolidation of the Caliphate by the conquest of rival states and factions, land and slaves were given to the supporters of the jihad, which created a network of farming villages worked by slaves and provided the basis for an emergent semi-sedentary society. The abolition and decline of slavery in the colonial area was a crucial occurrence for the Fulani with large herds and lands, although many slaves simply stayed on and became assimilated into their owners' households.

PASTORALISM AND THE CHANGING POLITICAL ECONOMY: NOMADS AND THE STATE

Adaptation and change are central elements of pastoral societies and reflect a response to environmental uncertainty. But pastoralists have become increasingly subject to forces beyond their control embodied in the demand of the modern state and its administrative apparatus. Both colonial and post-colonial governments have considered pastoralists, especially nomads, as marginal elements in the national economy and groups who are difficult to embrace within precise bureaucratic frameworks. Untidy, uncontrolled movements over national borders make pastoral peoples natural anarchists in the context of a modern state. State involvement has often been allied to

increased population pressure in settled areas and the expansion of cultivation which has in turn pushed pastoralists into less favourable environments to the detriment of herding practices. Also, administrations staffed
by people from sedentary backgrounds, often with roots in farming communities themselves, harbour many misconceptions about the nature of
pastoralism and prejudices concerning pastoralists.

Administrative intervention is properly the concern of the second part of
this book but the response of pastoralists to this activity might prompt two
questions which need answering here; are there inherent features of pastoralism which make it difficult for pastoralists to change and develop and are
there inherent features of bureaucracies which make bureaucratic intervention so disastrous? Commercial involvement has been common in the
strategies of all pastoral peoples, whether they are the Maasai in East
Africa, the Lozi and Tswana in the south or the Fulani and Twareg in the
west. All use animal sales to obtain grains and trade goods in markets
outside their homelands. Yet in all these systems sales are peripheral. They
do not dominate the pastoral production system. Trade is necessarily
quantitatively and qualitatively inconsistent, reflecting periodic needs or
crises within pastoral societies. Nonetheless, both nomadic and semi-
nomadic groups have shown a response to the growing demand for meat in
the urban centres and in the forested zones of the coastal littoral where the
keeping of cattle is inhibited by the tsetse fly. This is particularly true for
the Fulani. In Sokoto state in north-western Nigeria in each good year
before the droughts, over 200 000 trade-cattle passed through the area.
This is in addition to the 100 000 slaughtered annually within the state.

This growing trade in cattle reflects changing tastes and needs within
pastoral societies which can only be satisfied through external markets and
the cash economy. One feature of this extension of the market principle
into pastoralist societies is the creation of social and economic differences.
Upper castes tend to be favoured, which creates imbalances within societies
which have delicate social as well as ecological equilibria. In Botswana, for
example, this has been extended by involvement in the migrant labour
market. Miners' remittances create wealth for the purchase of more cattle
and the generation of surplus which is directed to other forms of improvement. School fees are paid more easily, more young men and women take
their place in the urban hierarchy. Richer families become even richer and
the older systems of equalization begin to break down. Both colonial and
independent governments have tried to accelerate the involvement of
pastoralists to market opportunities where they do exist and in other areas
have tried to induce them by administrative means. The development of
road networks has assisted cattle traders and butchers in the control and the
marketing of cattle. For example, in Kampala the association of butchers
effectively dominated the buying of animals in Karamoja, controlling both
supply and pricing of meat. Thus pastoralists face pressures from many

directions: governments, external markets and sedentary farmers – and they have either adapted to or resisted these forces of change.

SOME EFFECTS OF EXTERNAL FORCES AND INTERVENTION

The Maasai pastoralists of East Africa are concentrated in the Great Rift Valley of Kenya and spread into northern Tanzania. Pastoral densities in this area work out at approximately 190 livestock units and 10 persons per square mile for Kenya, which when set against modern estimates of ideal grazing management of 8-20 livestock units, it can be seen that much of Maasai land is overstocked (Jacobs, 1975). Until the 1960s the Maasai were little interested in alternative modes of subsistence, in fact one of their differentiating features was dietary prohibitions; milk, meat and blood form their foodstaples with milk comprising as much as 80 per cent. Sheep and goats were kept primarily for meat and trading, while donkeys were used as pack-animals for transporting water in the dry season. Large herds, extensive grazing, a lack of centralized political authority and the absence of long-distance trade routes characterized the Maasai way of life.

To a large extent the present situation of the Maasai is the result of European settlement in the twentieth century and the encroachment of African cultivators and semi-pastoralists on their traditional grazing grounds. In 1904 and 1911 there occurred the Maasai 'moves' when the Maasai were contained in government-controlled southern reserves. As Jacobs points out, the deceptions used in this operation and the failure to honour promises have soured Maasai attitudes to all subsequent development plans. Under the control schemes of the early twentieth century, veterinary regulations meant the Maasai could not pass through European areas to the north from where they traditionally acquired stock to up-grade their herds. Consequently herd quality suffered. Furthermore, Maasai were prevented from buying at public auctions as it was held that they kept the prices high, so that ranching became unprofitable for Europeans. The outcome has been that the Maasai have been faced with reduced pasture and reduced herd quality, while experiencing at the same time increasing population pressure: the result has been an abandonment of traditional methods of management to the detriment of the physical environment.

The herding systems now operated by the Maasai can be divided into three types. First, some Maasai continue with traditional practices which promote a balance between their subsistence needs and the local environment. This herding system is focused on an alternation between permanent water supplies that provide high potential dry season grazings in the uplands and low potential scattered wet season grazings in the lowlands. In the wet season the Maasai engage in a systematic reconnaissance and movement among wet season grazings, which are managed in such a way as to leave enough standing hay back in the dry season reserves to which they eventually return. For example in order to extend stays in the wet season grazings donkeys are used to carry water to the herds so that they can remain as long as possible in order to build up the dry season reserves which are more restricted. This type of herding is found in the more isolated areas of Maasai land where external pressures are least experienced. A second category of herding is where herders have lost their high potential dry season reserves to European settlements, game parks, or agricultural development schemes. This loss of dry season grazing has seriously disrupted the herding strategy of the Maasai and although wells have been provided in the low potential wet season areas, this does not effectively allow the extension of pasture into these areas of low and erratic rainfall. The Maasai have become disenchanted and apathetic.. Some take wives from alien areas of sedentary cultivation, while others have tried trading and occasional wage labour. The third category of herding is the one practised by most Maasai and comprises those whose herding system falls between the two extremes. They continue to operate their traditional system of integrating high potential dry season and low potential wet season pastures, but it is set against a steady decline of the overall situation, as the dry season reserves are scheduled for alternative uses for company ranching, or game reserves. The Maasai also combine old and new management practices; they now use cattle dips and innoculation programmes to improve their remaining herds, as well as changing their dietary habits.

The effect of external political and economic change has been just as disadvantageous for West African pastoralists as for those of East Africa. If we look at the Twareg of northern Mali whom we discussed earlier, we can see how political problems exacerbated the effects of the droughts of 1968-74. In the early part of the twentieth century the French conquest of the Upper Niger Basin meant that the Twareg's domination of their sedentary agricultural neighbours was broken, as well as ending raiding between pastoral groups. As security increased, wet season grazing camps became more widespread and the French dug new wells for dry season watering. The French authorities dealt with the leaders of Twareg confederacies (*amenokals*), mistakenly believing they had widespread control over their subjects. When necessary force was used to crush resistance and in Swift's words 'the French aimed at organising the Twareg into a tight amenable administrative framework, to promote the development of a market economy, and in order to achieve these two aims to encourage sedentarisation' (Swift, 1980).

With independence in 1958 the new Malian government was socialist and had its power base in the black sedentary agricultural regions and the urban centres. They were opposed to the feudal society represented by the Twareg confederacies. The new government shared many of the former colonial attitudes to nomadic pastoralists whom they conceived to be irrational in their attachment to herds and livestock hoarding. The new currency of independent Mali effectively reduced Twareg trade with the traditional northern market in Algeria, as money earned in these markets was not convertible. Customs duties on goods were introduced at the border, identify cards demanded, and in effect the political boundary of the post-colonial period had become a diplomatic reality, whereas under the French regime it had been merely an administrative convenience. A further blow to the Twareg was the doubling of taxes on animals in 1962.

It must be conceded that for a poor country such as Mali the idea of nomadic livestock as an untapped source of food was an attractive proposition. Livestock disease and the lack of water were seen as the only things holding back development; in other words there were simple technological solutions. Sedentarization along Soviet lines was entertained although not much happened on the ground after the coup of 1968. Nonetheless sedentarization dominated government thinking and vaccination programmes were continued, new wells dug, boarding schools established for nomad children and government co-operative stores were set up to sell food grains, tea, sugar and other nomad goods at fixed prices. Thus over the years Twareg patterns of society and herding and trading practices underwent a change which they sustained without much material disadvantage, but the situation changed dramatically with the onset of the droughts in 1968.

The effects of the drought cannot be dissociated from the series of political and economic changes in the West African Sahel which occurred at the beginning of the twentieth century (Raynaut, 1977). The traditional social structure of the Kel Adrar for example reflected the different types of animals and the precise niches they occupied. Noble castes herded camels; vassals sheep and goats; but after the French conquest and after independence camel ownership became more general, therefore there was an increased use of long-distance pastures and caravanning was extended. Conditions of stability facilitated an increase of human and animal populations, while well digging encouraged more intensive and widespread use of pastures. The good rainfall years of the 1920s and 1930s and again in the 1950s and early 1960s encouraged herd growth, yet the natural check of disease and social limitations imposed by raiding had been removed. In addition the Twareg had become more and more dependent on markets and food controlled by the state, whose food policies had proved less than satisfactory and increasingly relied upon international markets and foreign aid. It is true that the Kel Adrar did well for several years out of animal sales and government co-operatives offering fixed price goods, but they were moving towards a position which was becoming more and more vulnerable and dependent on government agencies and supplies which were subject to sudden changes of direction and fortune. The collapse was triggered by the successive droughts of 1968 onwards and by 1972 many of the Kel Adrar had left their homelands for Algeria or the southern areas of the Illwemedden.

A point made by numerous writers on the Sahelian crisis is that the drought did not precipitate the Sahelian crisis, rather it triggered it off. The events leading up to the loss of human and animal life and the widespread distress began back in the early 1900s. Pastoralists have experienced severe droughts before and survived, albeit with reduced herds by resorting to the adaptive strategies we have referred to earlier. As in the case of the East African pastoralists, administrators have nurtured misconceptions about the nature of pastoral activity and attempts at developing or transforming nomadic societies have often been notable for the problems they have created rather than solved.

SUMMARY

It could be argued that despite intervention and attempts to transform pastoral societies, they are inevitably destined for decline in the face of modernizing tendencies and the growth of sedentary populations. Administrative control has merely accelerated the process. But the fact remains that there are large areas of tropical Africa which are not economically viable other than through some form of pastoral activity. Are these areas to be abandoned, or have they some future? A variety of technological solutions have been discussed such as climatic modification, de-salination of water for irrigation, the use of underground water, tree plantations, all of which range from the impractical to the hopelessly expensive for most countries.

In the immediate future some form of revived pastoralism seems the best solution for the more arid and semi-arid grasslands of Africa and improvements must be based on reviving the basis of subsistence compatible with the physical and social environments of pastoral people. In the Sahelian zone it would mean the improvement of camels and goats rather than a preoccupation with improving beef cattle and a restoration of complementary exchanges between nomads and sedentary farmers. In East Africa the complementarity of high potential dry season pasture and low potential wet season pasture will have to be grasped, which may mean game reserves and extensive ranches will have to be sacrificed in the interest of pastoralists, if the problems of maintaining pastoralists in less viable areas are to be avoided. Unfortunately, the outlook for pastoral economies is not particularly bright given the locus of political power in most countries and the dominance of sedentary and urban-based interest groups.

In many ways pastoralists exemplify in sharper and greater detail the problems experienced by all rural Africans and the changes which have occurred during the colonial and post-colonial periods. Like agriculture, the nature of pastoralism has been widely discussed, largely by outsiders, and there have been a multiplicity of plans and programmes of change devised for the future of these people. In our next two chapters we try to address the question of agrarian change and transition, first in a historical context and then in terms of the plans and policies of intervention implemented by modern African states and aid-development agencies. In this way we shall try to put the dimensions of rural life which we have discussed so far in the larger structural contexts of international and African political economy, while not forgetting that local peoples are not passive agents in the process of change, but react in various ways including by outright resistance.

7

Traders, Settlers and Cultural Brokers: the Context of Colonial Intervention

In any political and economic space, even with a well-developed independent legal system, exploitation is a natural product of the relationship between the powerful and the disadvantaged, the rulers and the ruled. Colonial history is not simply a question of European exploitation. Many African societies, without the benefits of a literate culture, had developed sophisticated mechanisms of social and economic control and were familiar with the nuances of well-defined power relations. At the same time Europeans brought not only notions of conquest and prejudices of racial and cultural superiority but a wide range of more benign paternalistic perceptions.

In this chapter we draw particular attention to both the co-operations and the collisions of will between Europeans and Africans and their very different perceptions of value. We shall suggest that the path towards independence was proscribed not so much by changing political circumstances following World War II, but by clash, compromise and subversion expressed over a much longer period than the direct interventionist phase of colonial rule.

The grid of these values may be represented as divided along an axis which leads from greed at one extreme to selfless idealism at the other. Traders and invaders, Africans and Europeans, the god-fearing and the godless, shared with each other their very different experiences of both these extremes and took lines of action which represented their different perceptions of each other's motives and worth. Within such a perspective it is possible to view the role of chiefs, missionaries and colonial government officers as cultural brokers in these relationships. Moreover, the dimensions introduced by all these agents, both European and African, were fed into the theories, policies and attitudes of the spatial, social and economic reality of contemporary African rural life which is in no small respect a product of the tensions generated out of these interactions, which found their early focus in the slave trade.

The manner in which an indigenous trade in slaves was transformed into the trans-Atlantic slave trade was a function in part of the increasing opportunities provided by European slave trading ships, but it was more significantly the product of changing social and political relationships in tropical Africa as population densities and competition gradually increased.

In the period when this traffic was developing, Africa was a continent of many polities, varying from small independent and relatively peaceful forest tribes to large hegemonic empires both in the forest and in the grassland areas. In the forest zone, the wealth of the natural environment and relatively stable populations sometimes allowed the development of a sophisticated ecology of the kind identified in the utopian subsistence ideal of our model (see chapter 1). The social and economic relationships were defined by lineage kinship systems which revered old age and placed women in the role of fertile labourers blessed with the means of repro- duction of the labour. In such areas periodic shortages of labour were often overcome by selling or pawning women and children or by raiding other communities for slave captives who were added to the lineage system. In many other areas moreover, the instabilities of weather and climate meant that tribal groups were essentially mobile and their attitude to space was territorially unspecific. In this way, competition and raiding were preferred to intensification. The increasingly competitive behaviour of groups who had moved over territories as a strategy for allowing regeneration of exhausted pasture or cropland, became a characteristic feature of African history. As we have argued earlier in this book, this emphasis on forage stemmed from an attitude to land as an unlimited resource over which range established rights of usage. This was at its most severe in the conflict between pastoral and agricultural peoples which often led to the feudal subjugation of the latter by the former. It was an activity which was given a special dimension by the Islamic jihad where slave captives were a natural by-product. Such movements, over considerable distances, eventually created ever more opportunities for conflict, made more impressive by the introduction of firearms.

As European explorers were keenly aware, many African kingdoms were based on tribute. Large areas of the interior were subject to feudal and semi-feudal polities, oligarchies and fiefdoms in which weaker tribes paid the price for protection or peace with their womenkind or other labour obligations. This extended domestic slavery which was endemic through- out the continent into a cross-continental trade as the power of imported firearms changed the pattern of relationships, exaggerating the potential for large-scale terrorism. Eventually, European and Arab traders merely sup- plied the guns to more effectively carry on and develop a mode of life euphemistically referred to as negative reciprocity (chapter 5) or more prosaically, raiding and warring of which slaves were the natural and increasingly numerous product. Within the household economy, slaves could be incorporated as extra labourers who did not threaten existing social and lineage relationships but were in all other respects part of this system. But involvement in long-distance trade with powerful outsiders increasingly shifted the function of the slave from use to commodity value. In other words, the black tide which flowed across Africa and, by the seventeenth century, across the Atlantic to America was in the first instance a product and then a perversion of African attitudes to land and labour.

It is not surprising, therefore, that during this long pre-colonial phase, where only the highest unit values were of interest to traders, slaves became a valuable commodity as well as gold, ivory and kola. Systems of negative reciprocity with an indigenous traffic in slaves extending across the whole of middle Africa left few openings for well-developed systems of long-distance exchange for agricultural produce. Such trade as there was depended on the secure alliances with coastal and some interior rulers and these alliances were eventually the basis of the slave trade. Few agricultural items entered external trade via the coast and possibly because of the disruptive effect of the activities of slave traders, endogenous trade in anything but slaves and the other valuable commodities which they were forced to carry, played little part in life over large areas of underpopulated African space. It was not until the effective end of the slave trade, towards the end of the nineteenth century, that perceptions changed. They did so in response to two pressures. The first was a drive towards enlightenment which began with journeys of discovery activating the European sensibilities to the continuing horrors of the slave trade. This led rapidly to a major conscience-driven impetus to convert and to 'civilize'. The second, and more important, pressure was the rising demand for new agricultural produce and raw materials by the new urban industrialized populations of Europe. The two new components in the emergent matrix of interactive forces were the trading company and the missionary.

Both traders and missionaries were engaged in the exploration of terri-tories for expansion of interest into the essentially rural spaces. On another axis, the entrepreneurs of the earlier trading period, especially but not exclusively in West Africa, were soon turning their attention to the growing towns of the colonial states. If the opportunities for African advancement were restricted during the period, there were plenty of lessons to be learnt. It was at first an atomistic activity, closely related to the local marketing system and it is no accident that in many non-Muslim areas it was domi-nated and organized by women. The market women of West Africa were among the first entirely indigenous manifestations of powerful commercial forces at work below the surface of colonial rule, bypassing and in some cases subverting the mechanisms established by European commercial interests to generate and control the movement of agricultural surpluses. In the early stages of commercial agricultural expansion to meet the growing European demand for products of the coast, it was the African states of the coastal zone and their market traders who frequently organized and controlled the commerce. Those Africans who had profited from the slave trade developed plantations, chartered ships and crews to transport the crops to England. The development of the Gold Coast trade in cocoa is a classic case of African enterprise.

In East and Central Africa indigenous peoples were not slow to take advantage of the opportunities afforded by trade and by mining enterprises in the early days of contact. Powerful interest groups in the stronger African polities of Central Africa who had controlled the flow of slaves and the trade in ivory, but also extracted surplus foodstuffs from subject peoples had experience to deploy. So it is not surprising that as Palmer (1977) has shown, in the early days of expansion into the southern middle-veldt of Rhodesia, it was Europeans who lived at a subsistence level while their African neighbours made rapid progress towards peasantization by supplying the emergent mining towns with foodstaples.

Certainly colonial agencies and Europeans were responsible for restricting the opportunities for commercial involvement by rural Africans, but at least in the early years these were restrictions which given the right opportunities African rural entrepreneurs were well able to subvert. Eventually, however, as colonial powers took control these restrictions were tightened or elaborated and African entrepreneurial behaviour began to change in character.

EUROPEAN COMMERCIAL INVOLVEMENT

If African attitudes to land and labour had been changed first by the competition for land and then by the development of the slave trade from a regional to an international scale, they were further altered by European trader perceptions of the role Africans could play in commercial development. Throughout this period of increasing colonial involvement there was a struggle between African attempts to engage in a wider range of functions and the efforts of Europeans to restrict and manipulate this involvement to their own advantage. It was a struggle in which, as we shall argue later in this chapter, the missionaries and, to a different degree, some colonial officers and district officials and advisors played the role of cultural brokers.

European commercial involvement in rural Africa may be caricatured as a mixture of taxation, coercive control, plantation and expropriation. The approach varied in relation to the density of population, the qualities of the environment and the existing political structures and attitudes of the colonial power. Taxes were used as the main mechanism to concentrate the minds of the new peasant producer so that new production targets could be met. Any surplus labour would then be obliged to find paid employment off-farm. Poll taxes, hut taxes, yard taxes, water and land taxes, cattle taxes and colonial tariffs were some of the many methods of taxation used in the early days of colonial influence. The most unpopular were those involving capitation of some kind. They provoked riots and local wars, for example, those in Sierra Leone in 1896, and in the Gold Coast in 1895, and they were widely avoided. They may also have been an instrument in provoking labour migration with all its ramifications (chapters 2 and 3).

For those crops and products which could not readily be produced on plantations, collecting on a regular basis from forest and bush demanded coercive control of labour and marketing organization which provided further mechanisms to extract surplus and labour from small-scale producers. In the colonies of the Portugese, the French, the Germans and the Belgians, coercion was more common than direct taxation. The most notorious of these forced labour requirements was the product of concessionary company activities most particularly in the Belgian Congo, where immensely profitable collections of rubber and ivory were the product of a system of forced labour which decimated the population by more than 50 per cent in 20 years following the establishment of colonial rule in 1884. Similar methods of extraction characterized large tracts of equatorial Africa held by French companies. Such crude simplicity was, however, a feature of the early phase of colonial enterprise. Soon the plantation replaced the forced labour gang as the more characteristic form of controlled extraction of production for export.

Although in some areas concessionary trading companies also relied on coercion to force labour on their plantations, the development of plantations in Africa is more typically characterized by the search for social and political environments in which companies could rely on compliant labour. The great trading companies aimed to maximize returns through large-scale enterprises and established plantations and worker camps. They tended (and tend) to mine either the soil for agricultural produce, or the substrata for minerals. For them it was important that rural Africans be transformed as quickly as possible into a docile proletarianized low-paid workforce. Africans did not always respond well to this. Lever Brothers, for example, found that African producers were not very willing to sell to them when they established an oil mill in Sierra Leone in 1904 and they were forced to withdraw from this territory two years later.

If it was advantageous to control directly the supply side, the costs of setting up plantations were high, with a lengthy period for maturation of the crop before a return could be made on investment. To offset these problems, companies demanded the freedom to operate at very low costs. In contrast to Lever's experience in Sierra Leone, Firestone Rubber Company was able to negotiate with the freed slave aristocracy in Monrovia for a vast tract of interior Liberia at nominal cost, and their rubber plantation became the largest single unit in the world (80 000 acres). A similar pattern was followed in other territories by other large companies. Lever Brothers were quick to learn the lesson of their early mistakes and were soon well-established in the Congo, in the Gold Coast and Nigeria. Brooke Bond ensconced themselves in Kenya in the 1920s and then extended their interests to Uganda, Tanzania and Malawi. They were quickly followed by other British tea companies. Soon plantations for the production of all the characteristic tropical products flourished throughout the intertropical zone, producing, as we have seen (see chapters 2 and 3), a division of labour which is still a feature of many African rural economies as preferred labour, usually but not exclusively male, leaves the provision of subsistence in the hands of women, children and the elderly. This response is particularly marked in areas where mining concessionary companies also draw on labour and in the case of multi-nationals like Anglo-American in Central Africa, manifest themselves across both sectors of the economy.

THE SETTLERS

The next ingredient in this matrix of external influences which affected the direction and pace of rural change in the periods of African history leading up to independence and which continue to give differential shape to attitudes and responses, is provided by the colonizers who came to stay. These colonizers comprise not only the more obviously powerful invasion of land alienators who came to live and farm in the climatically congenial areas of veldt and highland Central and East Africa, but also the Indians in East and Central Africa and the Lebanese in parts of West Africa.

The Indians came first as indented labour to build the railways of East Africa. Soon, however, they occupied a niche as entrepreneurs, using their well-articulated family networks and caste-related skills to serve and eventually to dominate the burgeoning retail trade. As the demand for European products extended further and further away from main lines of communication, the Indian trading store became a focus for social as well as retail activity and other social and administrative services. Schools, clinics, bars, police posts and agricultural services grew alongside them. Whereas such enterprise deprived Africans of the opportunity for engaging in retail activity except as pedlars, it could be argued that Indian family and trading networks were the essential catalyst for an early extension of a necessary function, the rural trading store which acted as retail focus over large areas of Africa where population densities were too low to sustain a network of market-places of the kind described in chapter 5. Indeed this development provided the spatial framework for rural service planning in many such areas in the post-independence period (Siddle, 1980). Although the Lebanese traders occupied a similar niche in West Africa, their influence was much more localized. In terms of their political and social as well as their economic impact, the settlers who came to farm rather than to trade in Africa were clearly more important.

The European view of African rural space was that any suitably healthy land which was ostensibly unoccupied by strong indigenous polities was open for settlement. In some areas at least Africans were not unfamiliar with this concept of use. Where they differed with Europeans lay in the concept of land ownership. As we have argued above (chapter 4), until quite recently the most common African view of land involved concepts of use and occupancy by groups rather than private ownership in perpetuity by individuals. For Europeans the occupation of land meant 'long lease' permanent alienation for permanent settlement. In Kenya large areas of the highland zone occupied by a famine-decimated, demoralized Kikuyu population, was simply alienated and long-leased to land investors from England. Wealthy titled land speculators frequently mortgaged their English estates to acquire vast tracts of grassland. Before World War I Lord Delamere 'owned' 100 000 of upland Kenya, and similar swathes of veldt fell into the hands of the landed aristocracy in Cecil Rhodes Africa to the south. For such families it was a return to the times when monarchs handed out privileges. Throughout the settler zone of East and Central Africa the sequence was very similar. Missionary explorers and game hunter–traders identified suitable areas for settlement. Trek routes were established, trading companies acquired rights of exploitation and leased land to first-comers at very low prices. African chiefs often went along with early European proposals for mineral exploitation in return for what appeared to them to be suitable trading terms. Their opposition to increasing evidence of something more than a transient European presence was quashed, usually by force or the show of force.

Having eliminated the rights of native populations to free access to their hunting and grazing lands, their movement was further restricted by the designation of reserve areas, a hypocritical benevolence already familiar from North American and South African settlement experience. Railway lines were constructed to confirm the line of settlement and to provide access from the coast. Land acquired on long lease was made freely transferable. Advertisements for settlers appeared in the English papers and after World War I in particular, the flow of English settlers grew to something approaching a small flood. By 1930 there were more than 7000 settlers in East and Central Africa each occupying land averaging over 2500 acres in Kenya and Uganda and 5000 acres in the Rhodesias. Distance from prospective markets seemed amply compensated for by the ready access to capital through loans and subsidies, the low price of land and the inevitably cheap labour. The expansion of markets for luxury crops in post-war pre-depression Europe and the growing local market for cereals created the prospect of an early bonanza for settler farmers with readiest access to railways and bullock cart routes.

Very soon however, African subsistence farmers began to respond to market forces as the opportunity to buy an increasing range of imported luxury items peddled from the burgeoning network of Asian rural stores was matched by rising prices for commodities which they could also produce on their small holdings in reserve lands adjacent to the European farming areas. By the mid-1920s, for example, Tonga farmers in Northern Rhodesia, where the European farming presence was always rather tenuous, had already accumulated sufficient capital from cattle trading to invest in ploughs and to expand their production of maize. Soon they were producing a considerable proportion, perhaps as high as 50 per cent, of the colony's cattle and a quarter of its maize. Local markets were soon glutted, particularly by maize, the new staple 'urban' cereal of upland Africa. The response was swift and inevitable. Regulations were already in train during the early peiod of settlement to extract labour, like the *thangata* labour-rent system in Nyasaland. Now there were more overt forms of restriction on production like the grain quotas in the Rhodesias and the imposition on the Ndebele of the regulation that their farmers could cultivate only 40 acres.

Soon, as the depression began to take hold in Europe, farming associations and marketing control boards were established in Kenya, the Federation of Rhodesia and Nyasaland and monopoly supply and price controls, reinforced by the strong lobby of land-owning interests in the United Kingdom, extended to all territories of the colonial East and Central Africa. Before the end of the 1930s, the size of the very active nascent peasantry was firmly regulated by quota and by market controls which ostensibly could not be so easily circumvented as they were in West Africa, where as we argued in chapter 5, a system of open rural markets allowed free enterprise to flourish.

Even in the Centre and East, despite these controls, a little-documented vigorous black market developed and this sharpened the perceptions of rural Africans as to the role perceived for them . In West Africa, their function was to provide cheap products for export, but in the Africa of the native reserves it soon became clear that the function of Africans was not to compete with the European estates but to provide them with cheap labour. As far as the European settlers were concerned, the main product of this system of support was the encouragement of the inefficient and the tolerance of the incompetent. Far too many settlers came with over-blown ambitions and few skills. Whereas all sound farming practice involves the balancing of risks and the calculation of the margins of possible profit against the chance of crop failure and soil depletion, farming in African environments is inevitably more than just risky, it is positively hazardous. It demands particular skills and particular qualities of mind. While there is little doubt that the best of the European farmers were (and are) very efficient producers, fully aware of conservation techniques and the careful management practices which allowed them to raise levels of production without depleting land resources, there was a long tail of less efficient farmers and there soon emerged a clear distinction between the highly motivated risk calculators and the gamblers. The effect of protective legislation was to keep the latter in business well beyond the time when they may have reasonably expected support.

For their African neighbours, the Land Apportionment Acts divided land into racial blocks, creating African Reserve areas adjacent to the white farming areas. By the 1930s these occupied many thousands of square miles throughout the region. In Rhodesia, for example, over a half of the national territory was alienated for European use. Grain Marketing and Maize Control Acts, Tobacco Boards and Commonwealth preferences for coffee and tea, subsidized white farmers and controlled the market surplus of the emergent African peasantry both in the Native Trust Areas and in the reserves. The establishment of reserves as overcrowded commercially underproductive reservoirs of migrant labour was the most effective of the mechanisms of control, ensuring a low-paid highly competitive and docile labour supply. For example, between 1930 and 1940 something close to 50 000 people had been moved from European farming areas into the Southern Rhodesian reserves.

A similar picture emerged in Northern Rhodesia with pressures particularly acute in the Tonga areas in the southern Province and the Ngoni reserves in the eastern area of European settlement around Fort Jameson. Both were areas in which European occupation remained patchy and the problem of 'squatters' was ever present. Both were areas in which, like Ndebele areas to the south, African peasant farming (signalled by the development of plough agriculture to replace shifting cultivation) was making inroads. In the period between 1916 and 1951 African-owned ploughs in this region of the Rhodesias increased from 9245 to 163 492. A similar pattern emerged in the Kikuyu Reserves in Kenya.

At the same time the government developed a wide range of support mechanisms for white farmers. Soil surveys and extension services expanded rapidly in line with the expansion of the white farming communities. The pattern was established early. In the period of settler expansion after World War I (1918–28), the Rhodesian expenditure of the Department of Agriculture on European farming rose from £33 468 to £75 636 and the average amount spent on each white farmer almost doubled. By the 1950s the 2400 white farmers in Southern Rhodesia absorbed £1 675 373, representing an average of £700 for each farmer in the territory. Small wonder that in Rhodesia and Kenya the research and extension services were among the best in the world. Surveyors and environmental scientists surveyed most new holdings and recommended appropriate management practices. Grants and loans were always available. In the Rhodesias this service culminated in the Conex farm survey reports of the 1950s. Using the elaborate land capability classification devised by Trapnell and Clothier (1953), these farm-by-farm surveys were among the most detailed analyses of potential for any commercial farming area in the world. The limits of successful conservation and intensification were clearly specified (Clothier, 1956) and became the basis for all subsequent planning activity in the commercial farming areas.

Despite all this attention and the increasingly aggressively unfair competition between European and African farmers for fluctuating markets, the increasing dependence on export crops and the fluctuations of the world economy through booms and slumps encouraged a gambling element. Indeed it is possible to suggest that the frontier atmosphere which encouraged many of the least proficient to look for quick profits in inappropriate agricultural activities was artificially projected well into the colonial period by the combination of economic uncertainty, quota support and cheap African farm labour. This was particularly true at the margins of the white settler economy in the railway belt of Northern Rhodesia (Siddle, 1981).

THE CASE OF NORTHERN RHODESIA (ZAMBIA)

For 60 years this narrow zone, comprising only 3 per cent of the national area, with its copper mines in the north, and its few hundred commercial European farmers raising beef and growing maize for the urban markets, was the effective territory of the colony of Northern Rhodesia responsible for over nine-tenths of the commercial activity in the colony.

This somewhat paradoxical dual role of the 'line-of-rail' as both frontier and core-area was a function partly of its position in relation to more firmly-based settler societies to the south and partly of its isolation from alternative routes to the ports, but it was also a function of the marked disparity between the settler economy and the indigenous system upon which it was superimposed.

Much of the territory of Northern Rhodesia (Zambia) comprises the dry and sandy woodland savannas of the Congo – Zambesi divide. This region, little more than a migration corridor before British rule, was occupied at very low densities by peoples at the simplest levels of social and economic organization. Shifting cultivation systems produced meagre returns and there was little surplus for exchange (Richards, 1961; Trapnell and Clothier, 1953; Allan, 1965), and this unstable ecological situation with its low population density prevented the organization of anything but the crudest marketing system (Bohannan and Dalton, 1962). Moreover the area was shielded by its mid-continental position from all but the most persistent long-distance traders. It was therefore not exposed to the interplay between internal and external cultures that was the catalyst in the process which led to the development of marketing organizations in more densely settled parts of West and East Africa. On the Central African plateau there were no towns, no markets, very few nucleated villages and therefore no *foci* for a system of central-places.

The impact of the harsh forces of settler-orientated colonial development on such weakly developed pre-colonial material cultures was predictably damaging. Early economic growth was inevitably diversive and exploitative. European miners, farmers and administrators quickly dominated all aspects of the growing cash economy except local trade and this vacuum was quickly filled by Asian immigrants who opened stores in non-European areas to cater for a growing demand for imported consumer goods. Africans occupied the lowest rung of this rapidly established three-tier society in which ethnic, economic and cultural differences ensured the virtually complete isolation of one group from another. Indeed there was little opportunity for anything beyond the most superficial contact between peoples at such widely different stages of cultural and economic development and most of the response to this situation reflected little credit on the conquerors and produced little in the way of positive reaction on the part of the conquered.

Historical circumstances further mitigated against positive developments. Central Africa was conquered and drawn within the economy of the developed world during a period of rampant commercialism on the one hand and declining colonial responsibility on the other. In these latter years of Empire, central governments no longer exerted moral authority and control over affairs at the limits of its vast territories, leaving many decisions to concessionary trading and exploration companies. As a result, the governments were often swept unwillingly into fresh responsibilities by the ruthless exploitive vigour of the officers of these trading companies who became adept at using the goodwill built up by missionaries during the 30 years of activity after the death of Livingstone and the good name of the British Queen – whose protection was offered without authority – as a means of acquiring mineral concessions and then land rights from local chiefs. The effects of this approach on the rapid development of mining and the urban economy are clearly evident.

Less obvious is the impact on rural environments. During this period, when pragmatism and opportunism had more influence on policy than foresight and morality, deep wounds were inflicted on fluid rural socioeconomic systems delicately adjusted to a highly unstable ecological environment through a cultivation cycle based on 'ash-patch' (*chitemene*) cultivation. These systems involved long fallows and were heavily reliant both on a male labour force and on low population densities for their survival (Allan, 1949, 1965). Under the circumstances of a rapidly expanding urban economy they were soon drained of their strength, both through widespread male labour migration and through local imbalances of population. The delicate rural economies were neither improved, complemented nor replaced under this regime: they were merely allowed to degenerate.

The economic function of the inhabitants of this rural backwater was to provide a labour pool for the narrow European mining and agricultural sectors of the economy. In the year of independence and depending on region, between 40 and 70 per cent of the male labour force in the 16 to 40 age group were absent from their rural homes at any one time working in the mines, farms and towns of the Rhodesias and South Africa (Kay, 1967). In that year it was estimated that 4500 farming families in the areas away from the railway line grossed a total output worth only $62 million, one fifth of which was converted into cash income. This in its turn was only slightly more than the $8.5 million remitted to the rural areas from the wage packets of those employed in the commercial sector.

Bearing in mind these gross sectoral and spatial imbalances, the total dependence of the economy on external factors and the clear commitment of the political party which won the independence election on a policy of radical reform, and bearing in mind also the political and economic disturbance which followed Southern Rhodesia's unilateral declaration of independence in 1965; then few countries could claim a more dramatic and potentially disturbing background to economic planning.

Three main factors were responsible for the imbalanced spatial economy which had developed in this part of Central Africa during the period of colonial rule: the very low level of indigenous economic development in the area before colonization, the traumatic rapidity of the transformation and the high degree of pragmatism governing policy decisions during a formative development period which coincided with the declining years of a great empire.

After the collapse of Rhodes's grand imperial design, few of the changes which took place in the spatial economy during the colonial period were the result of positive policy. The formative phase from the signing of the first mining concessions and the construction of the railway until World War II was one of exploitation governed only by pragmatism. Such pragmatism was an inevitable consequence of the nature of Northern Rhodesia as a primary frontier zone so far as both European and African cultures were concerned, a character which it was not to lose throughout this unsettled period. The small group of white farmers, miners, traders and missionaries who struggled to maintain a frequently marginal economy at the end of a mid-continental railway line were sustained by the knowledge that if things became too difficult they could always retreat south of the Zambesi. Unlike South Africa and Southern Rhodesia, Northern Rhodesia never became a zone of real settler expansion. Successive waves of immigrants never consolidated earlier positions. Along the 'line-of-rail', early bridgeheads were tentatively maintained rather than reinforced. Even many of the former settlers came to find short-term gain.

The pragmatism of this early period is evident in every new line and surface etched into the developing spatial structure. The railway line, diverted to cross the Zambesi at the Victoria Falls after linking Bulawayo and the Wankie coalfield, followed the easiest route to the mining *dorp* of Broken Hill (now Kabwe), establishing watering and bunkering points for the growth of minor townships. These in their turn became the centres of administrative districts and when Livingstone was abandoned as the capital in 1935 (for being too unhealthy and too far south) it was also natural that a loop near Chief Lusaka's village, in the central part of the rail line between Livingstone and the Copperbelt, should be chosen as the capital site.

A similar pragmatism governed the dimensions of the narrow zone of development on either side of the railway. In the early days of settlement it was convenient both to farm and to administer the lands within about 30 km of the railway line, a distance which represented a journey of one day by bullock-cart. This area became the zone in which land was alienated for farming expansion by European settlers. By a natural progression it was the need to secure this narrow foothold which led to the establishment of 'native reserves'. During the first decade of settlement in the railway belt there was no real land shortage and little competition with African subsistence farmers, but population movements as the economy developed altered this situation and it became necessary to compensate Africans dispossessed of land within alienated 'crownland' areas, and to establish African reserves.

Although formal recognition of these areas was delayed until 1947, competition for resources caused early friction in the densely settled areas of the Eastern Province close to Fort Jameson (now Chipaka) and a reserves commission was established in 1904. It was this early commission which tended to establish precedents for the much later 'line-of-rail' allocations.

In the railway belt, the inter-war period saw the creation of a number of reserves and here, as in the Eastern Province, the size of the unit was based on a population density allowing 2 ha of land per person. Corridors to the railheads were left open through the European farms to allow for eventual African commercial enterprise, but otherwise separation was complete.

Although some officials argued against the long-term wisdom of this segregationist policy, the reserves remained. In this situation, as in all others, the easiest solution at the time was adopted and in this way the administration lost its opportunity to encourage the diffusion of innovations by the juxtaposition of African and European farms. Except for those African farmers on the edge of a reserve who happened to have tolerant European neighbours, African advancement received little encouragement until the post-war period (Makings, 1967). Yet despite this generally restrictive attitude some progress was made, particularly in the Hyenja-Kgani reserves of the Eastern Province and in the Tonga reserves of the Southern Province (Kay, 1967). By 1936 African farmers, although individually selling one or two bags of maize a year, were collectively producing almost half the marketed maize in the territory. The precarious European economy, slowly recovering from the effects of the world depression, could not accept this competition. Quotas were established to limit African participation in the cash economy, a restriction which bore heavily on people in reserve areas already feeling the effects of population densities in excess of those which would permit the maintainance of soil fertility under traditional methods of agriculture (Allan, 1965).

In the towns of the Copperbelt, company rule remained the dominant force until well after independence, exerting a pervasive influence on many aspects of life. Copper mining began in earnest in 1922 with the invention of the flotation method of processing these sulphide ores. An initial investment of £1.5 million by the Roan Selection Trust was followed six years later by £3.5 million from the Anglo-American Corporation. These two major companies, linked by both management and investment, controlled the mining economy and were responsible for much of the urban development in the country. During the period of initial growth, the companies followed a policy similar to that pursued in South Africa. Company townships were constructed with houses of different quality according to status. African employees were employed as target workers on short-term contracts, housed in two-room dwellings and not allowed to bring with them their wives and families. The colonial government did not have funds to invest in planned urban development, and the mining companies were allowed to follow their own policy in this matter.

By the end of the 1930s a clear outline was emerging of the colonial frontier economy which was to become the major constraint on national development during the period following independence. Close to the railway a small group of 300 European farmers and 1000 miners struggled to maintain a slowly developing commercial economy. When it suited them to do so they employed African workers to help them in this task. Such workers were tolerated within the European zone for short-term contractual periods, but were not allowed to earn or produce enough to challenge their precarious position. But as African population densities increased in the reserves, target workers began to stay for longer than their target periods. Those without contracts began to settle hopefully in unauthorized townships outside the mining areas, bringing with them an increasing tide of relatives and dependants. Urban crime rates grew in proportion to the distress which this considerable urban migration began to cause.

With so many faces staring anxiously and hopefully over the fences of the well-organized mining compounds and over the boundaries of the under-utilized European farms in the core area, this zone began to resemble nothing so much as a *laager*. Much of the period between the end of World War II and the granting of independence may be represented as one of struggle between those Africans and Europeans enlightened enough to see that such a political economy, which artificially restricted the forces which change was generating, was not only short-term in character but positively damaging to the long-term needs of the territory and the conservative elements in all racial groups who wanted to preserve a *status quo* which ensured at least some prospect of financial gain.

During the period of maximum duality in the economy a small group of enlightened agricultural officers and academic anthropologists produced evidence to show the serious nature of the problems engendered by the pragmatism of colonial policy. If some attempt was made in the post-war period to recognize a responsibility for the ecology of territory in the 'off-line' areas of Northern Rhodesia as well as for the well-being of those who lived in an area previously regarded solely as a labour pool, it was largely due to the work done by Trapnell and Clothier (1953, 1957), Allan (1965) and Peters (1950) in the Department of Agriculture, and of social anthropologists in the Rhodes Livingstone Institute led by Gluckman (1948), Richards (1961), Colson and Gluckman (1951), Colson (1971) and Scudder (1962), who carefully documented and lucidly described the rural systems which were so rapidly being destroyed by population instability and indirect economic pressures. Their papers and reports provided the basis for a post-war planning strategy which in some respects at least was 30 years ahead of its time and for which, by consequence, neither the financial nor the human resources existed (Hadfield, 1960; Makings, 1967).

For Africans, two types of scheme were conceived: the African Farmers Improvement Scheme and the Peasant Farmers Scheme. The first aimed to encourage commercial individualism through grants and loans and expert advice. During the 10 years of operation 2863 farmers were helped in this way, and by achieving incomes of between £60 and £100 per annum, they were not only able to build brick houses and to buy bicycles and wireless sets, but also to achieve social superiority over their kin who still followed communal and interdependent traditional practices. Increasing mistrust of colonial administration and rapid changes in supervisory staff, as well as a paternalistic rigidity in the regulations regarding loan repayment, caused a good deal of dissatisfaction and the scheme did not survive until independence.

The Peasant Farmers Scheme, on the other hand, was the colonial precursor of many post-independence attempts to create development conditions through resettlement. Areas where population pressure was greatest, in the Eastern and Southern Province reserves, were selected for this much more demonstrative form of rural aid (Kay, 1967). After initial settlement by carefully selected families, crop areas were prescribed, rotations fixed and subsidies were given to cover initial improvements and capital expenditure. Although ostensibly more successful than the Improved Farming Scheme, the investment in this highly-privileged group was still meagre. During the period of its operation in the 1950s the scheme involved 2000 farmers and a total cash investment of £300 000, and the cash returns were not more than those in the alternative scheme. Bearing in mind the aim of the plan was to bring the maximum help to the largest number, it is interesting to note that during the period of the plan barely one-tenth of the rural population received any benefit from the small investment in improvement in the rural economy.

Whilst African farming development remained at a low level there were considerable advances in the European sector both along the 'line-of-rail' and in the Eastern Province. The concentration of farming in the railway belt and in the area around Fort Jameson (now Chipata) allowed an effective deployment of resources and expertise in a manner entirely consistent with the plan. A post-war boom in prices and a new wave of immigrant settlers from the more austere economic environment of post-war Britain resulted in a rapid expansion in European farming, especially of tobacco. In 1939 there were only 300 white farmers in the territory. Between 1949 and 1953 this number increased to 1200 and by this date very few farm plots in the alienated Crown lands along the railway had not been taken up (Hellen, 1968), while a new farming block near Mkushi had been opened. In response to this situation an extremely efficient regional planning and resource management programme was devised (Clothier, 1956). The 'line-of-rail' farming area from Livingstone in the south to Mkushi in the copperbelt in the north was divided into Intensive Conservation Areas (ICAs), which were then subdivided (1954–60) into regional planning units of between five and 30 farm holdings. For each area a survey by provincial agricultural offices provided information on a wide range of physical and economic factors. Planners used Trapnell's and Clothier's valuable pioneer surveys and contemporary aerial photography to draw up soil and vegetation maps, to devise management improvement programmes for each individual holding embodying the best principles of conservation and management and to specify the amount of financial aid to be made available for fencing, contouring, baulking, ridging, irrigation and waterpoint improvements.

Much of this work was carried out during the period of the Central African Federation (1953–63) as part of a broader policy, and it is difficult to establish the total amount of investment in this scheme, but bills of costing in the Ministry of Rural Development files indicate that a total investment of £1 500 000 may have been given over to this end. This was an amount equivalent to the total value of African farming for two years (Makings, 1967).

The period between 1952 and 1962 must be accounted one of 'high farming' in the European sector and there is little doubt that in different political circumstances the next decade would have seen marked improvements in the efficiency of management practices in this sector. But political events had already overtaken management and conservationist programmes of this sort even before they had been fully implemented and the decade of independence was inevitably one of uncertainty and declining ecological standards in commercial farming as quick profit became a more realistic aim than long-term improvement.

What was true in Northern Rhodesia, was also true throughout the settler states of Africa. There is little doubt that a buoyant African involvement in the cash economy would have been a product of this period of albeit spasmodic expansion in markets. Nor is there any doubt that an emergent African peasantry would have been better equipped to withstand the sharp vicissitudes of the economy in this period of urban expansion and boom and slump in world markets. Indeed, a peasant system of production with its characteristic resilience (opening to commercial opportunity when times and prices were good and retreating into subsistence when they were not) was a much more valid response to these economic circumstances.

In direct proportion to their political power, (strong in Kenya and the Rhodesias, weaker in Uganda, Tanganyika and Nyasaland) throughout the colonial territories of British East and Central Africa, African farmers felt what Palmer (1977) called 'the full blast of competition from heavily subsidised European farmers', while being periodically squeezed out of access to markets, heavily taxed and persistently underpaid. In the Portugese territories of Mozambique and Angola a policy of miscegenation blurred the picture of exploitation, but similar policies ensured privilege for Portugese estate owners and managers, many of whom lived like feudal lords. These policies ensured that the European settler presence in Africa was destined to be short and to end in conflict. In the event it was to be only one generation before the tide began to turn and the bright mission-trained sons of the dispossessed began to organize political responses to this oppression. It is no accident that the blood shed in this struggle for independence was and is in direct proportion to the scale of the settler presence on the land.

For a long period, then, the main trading contact between Africa and the rest of the world was for high stakes, with rich profits measured against a real cost in human misery and danger from which no participant, European as well as African, was exempt. The conquest of Africa was for the most part not a question of soldiers followed by priests or mullahs followed by traders. It was a much messier process of interactions driven on both sides by greed. It was only fairly late in this process that European missionaries imported a genuinely new and much more subversive morality to the continent. They were joined by district and agricultural officers who, together with missionaries, became the cultural brokers.

THE CULTURAL BROKERS: MISSIONARIES AND COLONIAL OFFICIALS

In many areas the Christian missionaries – idealistic, evangelical, and at first very innocent, preceded or accompanied the new traders and commercial explorers at least some of whom seemed at first to be driven by the same idealisms. Many District and Agricultural Officers, trained within a public school ethos, shared similar attitudes. Very soon, however, missionaries and government officers were working entirely different seams of African consciousness from traders and settlers. While Livingstone and the missionary societies promoted commerce and Christianity as the twin props of advancement towards enlightenment and colonial officers worried about stocking rates, carrying capacities, plant breeding and new crops, their commercial co-religionists were, as we have seen, less idealistic.

This paved the way to dichotomous and frequently confused African images of the intentions of these powerful outsiders. From the 1860s and throughout the colonial period, missions of every known creed and fervour from every part of Western Europe and North America established schools and churches in all parts of tropical Africa. The main effect of this was that a new generation of mission-trained Africans were brought up in the spirit of new European and American visions of justice, fair play, social democracy, salvation through hard work and honesty. They quickly learned not only a new independence of spirit, but also to despise those other Europeans and Africans around them whose motives were less pure.

Although many mission stations have been involved in small-scale rural development programmes and village relocation enterprises, the main effect of this drive to self-improvement was to take people away from their rural environments. Mission schools were all too pleased to see their better pupils succeeding in the offices of the colonial bureaucracy, as they began to find their places as members of the new urban African middle class. This process began surprisingly early. Communities of freed slaves in Freetown, Monrovia and Libreville spearheaded the invasion of new value structures. Often hated or despised as 'black men in white clothes', some kind of cultural quislings, nonetheless they provided role models for indigenous Africans who were soon separating themselves from their rural backgrounds, precursors of a generation of white-shirted, be-suited urbanized Africans who were already divided from their rural heritage well before independence.

It was from this group of the upwardly mobile intelligentsia that the new political formations began to take their leaders. Some were given the benefits of a university education, frequently on Christian charitable trust scholarships to England, Europe and the United States. It was from this group that the first African political leaders was drawn, particularly in English-speaking Africa. Their perceptions of African society and what they see as the conjunction of the best of European and African moralities and political philosophies, have given shape to the more distinctively innovative forms of intervention in the process of rural change since independence.

A much older and perhaps more pervasive missionary impact has been made by Islam. Muslim influences on tropical Africa are almost as old as the spread of the faith out of its core area and were certainly well-established in what in Europe is called the Middle Ages. Islam provided the lubrication which allowed for the spread of endogenous African trade across the desert as well as the firm base for the development of the empires of the Western Sudan in the long period when European influence was very marginal.

The gradual extension of Muslim influence out of the savannas and into the forest zones of tropical Africa is one of the most significant and least reported influences on the shape of rural societies throughout the region. Among the most important of these influences have been the division of labour and land rights. The Islamic faith alters the position of women and their role in the domestic economy. In many of the Muslim areas of West Africa and in East Africa, it is men rather than women who trade in the market-places, while Islamic law lays down definite rules of inheritance and land division. It might be argued that the essential fatalism of Islam persuaded its followers to accept the status quo. On the other hand one might suggest that the disciplines and regimes of the faith provide a structure within which strong and stable social and economic formations can flourish.

In contrast with the largely local scale of the missionary impact, colonial civil servants and agricultural officers influenced all levels of African rural life and were instrumental in changing attitudes. This had far reaching implications not only for rural change in the colonial period, but also in the period of independence planning. The role of agricultural officers, charity officials and planning consultants from aid agencies in moulding African attitudes to commercial agricultural production has received little emphasis. In large measure they bear responsibility for appraisal of the merits of large-scale (export) and small-scale (domestic) production which has played a crucial role in development planning. They have also encouraged prejudices against indigenous and 'small-scale peasant production'. Perhaps the most important single consequence has been to further undervalue and marginalize women and to disregard their crucial contribution to rural development as both producers and traders.

If benevolent paternalism was the best that Africans could hope for in this period of colonial intervention, it is possible to identify three levels of interaction between agricultural services and African producers. These levels are well-defined, both in terms of the ecological model in the first chapter and the theories of development which will be the subject of the ninth. With varying degrees of commitment associated with regional opportunities, levels of benevolent paternalism were represented by the formal distinction we have made between settler and non-settler economies. At the first level, colonial agricultural agents concentrated their attention on primary local exchange crops, on 'small-scale peasant production', attempting to integrate new crops into the village economy or to provide a new context for small-scale co-operative or individual farming. Secondly they encouraged activity at what we have called in chapter 1 the intermediate regional scale. They provided infrastructure, principally advisory services and marketing organizations. And finally, at the large-scale of the plantation and the development scheme, they aimed to provide for capital intensive, efficient, basically monocultural production at the level of the economy of the colony as a whole.

Viewed like the missionaries as cultural brokers, the main if frequently inadvert function of colonial officers was to introduce African rural people to possibilities which may or may not have emerged as a product of the normal dynamic of social and economic interaction. But they did so within the limits imposed by the interventionist attitudes and behaviour of the colonial period. This created a set of paradoxes which were to become part of the ethos of colonial rural development and to pass quite naturally into the thinking which governed initiatives in the post-independence period. Many of the questions colonial officers asked themselves are still being asked, albeit in different circumstances. How could one help to create circumstances in which African producers could become commercial farmers and at the same time (as it was perceived) threaten the essential subsistence-oriented rhythms and adjustments of farming life? Could Africans become peasant producers without endangering the fabric of social and economic relations or the delicate balances of the environment? Could incipient ecological and economic disaster actually be prevented by a programme of gradual commoditization? Should African rural areas be merely the providers of labour to the expanding commercial sectors of advanced settler agriculture? Could capital be substituted for very inefficient low-skilled labour in areas of low population density to create large-scale improvements in exportable commodities?

As we have argued above, and as we shall see later, the ways in which these questions were asked and the answers that were produced varied with the colonial experience. More explicitly it varied with the style and expression of a benevolence, sometimes warped, which lay at the heart of most policy formation. This benevolence was associated with the inevitable paternalism of a period when the sense of empire was coloured by the elitist attitudes of the public school and the *ecole polytechnique*. It was from these institutions that the colonial services recruited.

Despite the efforts of enlightened officials, the style of interventionism of East and Central Africa responded, as we have seen, to the demands of a settler culture and the growing problems associated with overpopulated Native Reserves. The focus here was on conservation and small-scale peasant farming either through carefully controlled schemes for the native purchase of land, changing the concept of land ownership 'at a stroke', or through producer and marketing co-operatives and villagization. The small-scale of investment in such activity reflected its low priority in political terms. Such schemes were almost invariably the equivalent of demonstration farms. Surrounded by a social and economic sea of indifference or resentment, the 'demonstration farmers' frequently suffered at best isolation and at worst jealousy and social ostracism. Few could be accounted successful. But they created the basis for a debate about the nature of self-sufficient autonomy (which would give the African the power to withdraw his labour from the European commercial and mining sectors), the virtues of small-scale peasant production and the damage inflicted on the environment by policies which encouraged alternatives. They also sowed the seed of an approach which found an echo, within the framework of different political philosophy, in the co-operative and villagization schemes of independent states (chapter 8).

In West Africa, colonial service local-scale interventionism took a form which was governed by a very different set of circumstances. Here small commodity production was already well-established and, as we argued in chapter 1, in some instances new crops were integrated with existing systems with minimal disruption; in other cases it was disruptive (see chapter 2). Agricultural departments concentrated on the establishment of botanical gardens and thus gained experience of the improvement of native strains of, for example, palms, bananas and cocoa, which could be grown as part of the regime of village agriculture. Improved varieties and seeds of many other crops were developed by native administrations and eventually by producers themselves throughout the zone. They were also anxious to introduce economic plants which would yield quick returns and feed quickly into the export trade. New American cotton strains were successfully introduced in northern Nigeria, the Gold Coast (Ghana) and in the French territories of the Western Sudan. Coffee became a cashcrop for peasant producers in Ivory Coast and the Cameroons and improved varieties of groundnuts spread throughout the sudanic zone, but particularly in Senegal, The Gambia and Northern Nigeria.

The role of the agricultural services sector at the intermediate scale was to square the circle of encouraging production without creating circumstances of over-supply. Everywhere, one possibly inadvertent mechanism was to ensure that agricultural support services were always understaffed and served very large areas. The other more overt instrument involved the control and protection of trade. The protection of trade concentrated on three objectives; the subsidization quota and zone protection of settler producers, the maintenance of district level self-sufficiency (by preventing imports and encouraging famine staples) and finally the regulation of trade to protect African producers from the worst effects of price variation and oversupply. Having given attention elsewhere in this chapter to the effects of settler protection, we concentrate here on the function of the marketing boards.

The main function of the marketing boards was to create monopolistic purchasing agencies to stabilize prices, so that whatever the fluctuations in the international market, African producers could rely on a guaranteed price. The main reason for the extension of this activity was the world recession and more particularly World War II. By consistently underpricing, this policy resulted in a very convenient form of indirect taxation for the administration and profit maximization on the part of the exporters. It also became an instrument for the control of inflation. In some West African countries and in Uganda, considerable quantities of the easily stored cashcrops were 'withheld' in the post-war period. In the two decades before independence between a fifth and a third of all the palm oil and cocoa in Nigeria, a half the cocoa in the Gold Coast and a third of all the cotton and coffee in Uganda was withdrawn. This represents a considerable brake on African potential earnings in a period of market expansion which could only be justified if the money had been in some measure ploughed back into rural infrastructural improvements. The extent to which this happened varied widely from one colony to another, but was never great.

In other words, the encouragement which agricultural services gave to African producers at the microscale of the individual farming family through advice and improved strains was to some extent nullified by the restrictive practices of the marketing boards. It was a classic case of giving with one hand to take with the other. Many of the adjustments and changes outlined in the chapters of this book might be seen in the light of these restrictive practices introduced (and often continued into the post-colonial period), as a means of raising taxes.

At the largest scale of intervention, motives were certainly much less ambiguous. The creation of economies of scale became an official preoccupation following the early exploration of possibilities for plantation agriculture by private enterprise, principally for palm oil, rubber, coffee and tea. Here the aim was to improve the flow and quality of production at what was an economic price, a preoccupation which again grew during the years of economic depression between the wars.

It is no accident, therefore, that the most impressive of the initiatives by agricultural departments in conjunction with colonial governments, were the large-scale schemes. These large-scale development schemes, designed in the age of economic rationality, aimed to lift export production by economies of scale, were the precursors of many others in the post-independence period. These schemes have been extensively reported and critically assessed and we have chosen to illustrate the thinking of those who were responsible for all the large-scale improvement schemes by taking only one example, the East African Groundnut Scheme.

At the end of World War II Britain was almost entirely dependent on imports for oils and fats. World shortages of these commodities were chasing up the prices. The Groundnut Scheme was designed to reduce the shortage and at the same time to produce nuts at a cost below the then current market price of £32 per ton. The scale of the enterprise was to be truly monumental. There were to be set up 107 blocks, comprising 30 000 acre fields (the size of Russian state farms). They were to occupy 5000 sparsely populated square miles of East and Central Africa with 80 blocks in Tanganyika, 10 in Kenya and 17 in Northern Rhodesia. In the event only the blocks in Tanganyika were developed. The scheme was to be implemented over five years, 1947–52, occupying at its maximum, over 1000 Europeans and nearly 60 000 Africans in both land-clearing and agricultural operations. The staggering scale of this operation was only conceivable in the atmosphere of command economy which followed the war, with the experience of vast capital investment enterprises and a skilled workforce geared up psychologically to a war effort. Indeed the parallel with a military operation was made quite explicit by comparisons with enterprises like the Mulberry artificial harbours which made the D-Day landings possible and by the appointment of a retired general as a managing director. The analogy was further reinforced by the use of converted Sherman tanks as tractors. In hindsight it is easy to see why the scheme was doomed to failure. No one seemed to think it necessary to consider the logistics of such a mammoth venture. Forward and long-term planning was practically non-existent. At almost every level in the operation there were fundamental mistakes. The land was inadequately surveyed using poor and inaccurate maps. Basic information on rainfall variability was lacking. Soil conditions were imperfectly understood. The army surplus converted 'tractors' proved wholly unsuitable for the job, broke down frequently and were inadequately serviced with spare parts. The infrastructure was grotesquely inadequate to cope with an operation on this scale. The port of Dar es Salaam suddenly had to cope with a fourfold increase in tonnage for which no preparation was made in the form of deep-water wharfs. The railway was unable to clear the cargoes. Alternative road transport absorbed the diesel fuel that should have gone to the tractors. Bottlenecks occurred at all points on the supply route. No provision was made for the rapid increase in the workforce who were inadequately housed, fed and watered, causing damaging labour discontent. Costs escalated while scale estimates were revised downwards. By 1950 the cultivated acreage projection had been reduced from one and a half million acres to just over half a million, while the projected cost had more than doubled. The project was struck by drought and insect infestation. Production of groundnuts barely covered the re-seeding requirement, let alone produce a commodity. In consequence, groundnuts were quickly superseded by cattle ranches and tenant farming schemes in which groundnut production was positively discouraged. Perhaps the most remarkable feature of this *débâcle* was that expansion of the highly-effective peasant production of groundnuts in northern Nigeria was at this time being actively discouraged by the marketing board policies outlined earlier in this chapter.

CONCLUSION

At the level of the individual and household, there is little doubt about the benign intentions of much of the work carried out by missionaries, planning agents and, more particularly, the agricultural departments of colonial Africa in the six decades of their effective operation. Government servants who worked in the colonial service as scientific and agricultural officers often made an important contribution to European understanding of African systems of land tenure, ecology and economy. The quiet work of plant breeding stations has been seen as not always closely enough related to the needs of African farmers (Richards, 1985), but the successful introduction of high-yielding varieties of good staples as well as cashcrops often owes much to painstaking work on strain improvement over many decades. Similarly, and often working in conjunction with anthropologists like those who were employed, for example, in the Rhodes-Livingstone Institute in Lusaka, and with the more dedicated and far-seeing of the district officers, scientific officers did much to alert the administration to the dangers of overpopulation in African reserves and to the disastrous effects of soil erosion and overcultivation which were the indirect product of labour migration (Trapnell and Clothier, 1953; Peters, 1950; Allan, 1965). Similar claims might be made for the rice, cocoa and cotton research officers in West Africa. If their attempts to introduce European concepts of soil conservation were sometimes misplaced or inappropriate to the economic circumstances of the people they were serving, it was often because attitudes were not always in tune with either imperfectly understood African rationality or the misguided policies of a remote central administration.

In the contrast between the East African Groundnut Scheme and the Nigerian marketing board strategy, there can be no better illustration of the clash of attitudes which represented colonial development policy, nor is it surprising to find these differences of attitude represented in the theories of development which came to underpin the development strategies of the decades of what might be termed 'neo-colonial independence'. The conflict of interests in departments of agriculture who were serving both the demands of colonial governments and commercial interests and the needs of native producers (who were inevitably competing 'less efficiently') could never be properly resolved, but it created spatially differentiated strands of intervention. It also created further sets of possibilities and questions to alter the perceptions of rural Africans concerning the relationships between land labour, subsistence and commercial production, gender and social divisions of labour, wage or in-kind payments, 'on-farm' and 'off-farm' activities and the integration of migration behaviour with the demands of the land. The varying ways in which Africans adapted to these changes and fed them into the development strategies of the independence period, will be explored in the next chapter.

8

Interventionism and the Independent State: Plans, Schemes and Radical Transformations

The rural development strategies of newly-independent African states were (and still are) usually a mix of three not necessarily mutually exclusive objectives: first, the raising of exchange crops, to provide for a growing urban population, to facilitate imports and subsequently to service the escalating foreign-exchange debts; second, the reorganization of land, settlement and production (ostensibly to serve immediate political objectives of greater equity); and third, the raising of rural incomes to improve the quality of life and to reduce the movement to towns. New states were faced by immediate problems not encountered during the colonial period. Whereas colonial powers could prevaricate, very few states in Africa have been able to avoid the pressures of imperatives stemming from these three objectives, though the mix has clearly varied with the colonial experience, the political complexion of the government and the opportunities offered by the environment.

The outcome of most development schemes have been different from their stated objectives and both liberal and Marxist writers agree that intervention by the state to promote agrarian change has been generally abysmal. Neither state-led accumulation, nor resource redistribution have succeeded because the state has been too weak and poorly integrated to oversee such developments. Yet there is evidence that state intervention has led to significant socio-economic differentiation in rural areas and opened up opportunities for indigenous capitalists. One of the interesting aspects of contemporary Africa is the capacity of an indigenous bourgeoisie to divert and influence state policy towards their gaining access to land and capital and the limitation of foreign investment (Lubeck, 1987). This is particularly relevant in countries such as Ivory Coast, Kenya and Nigeria. In the later colonial period chiefs, educated elites and merchants were excluded from opportunities for investment in shipping, banking and industry, and as there were no *latifundia*, the emergent political–administrative class used the state as a medium of accumulation. As export crops were the basis of state revenues, so this class supported the push to increase exports and later government plantation and mechanization schemes. The state has come to represent an alliance of political, bureaucratic and managerial interests which rarely includes the peasantry.

It is important to remember that rural development was not the first priority of many states. Industrialization was a primary concern together with the pride associated with new nationhood which demanded the trappings of prestige projects to impress both the neighbours and the new influx of foreign officials and potential investors. There were high profile demonstrations of independence; new airports, new government offices, presidential and parliament buildings, new hydro-electric schemes and, in the spirit of the times (see chapter 9), new capital intensive industries. Even the poorest countries managed at least one of each from this shopping list. All required the importation of skills, machinery and raw materials. It is not surprising that new governments rapidly acquired debts which had to be serviced. Currencies, once detatched from the pegging support of the colonial power, deflated rapidly as their credibility waned. Aid, loans and grants served mainly to create leeway for governments under pressure. Also, the inability or unwillingness of farmers to provide food surpluses led to food imports to meet the demands and tastes of urban populations. The rising costs of imports and the need for cheap food in turn gave an impetus to rural development schemes, although the attempts to transform agriculture have not provided the required surpluses to feed the cities. But debt burdens accumulated and aid agencies and banks have gradually laid down firmer rules for repayment which bound borrowers ever more tightly into use restrictions. A product of two or more decades of aid and loans is the tightening grip of a new form of clientship which adds a new dimension to the concept of neo-colonialism. The strict controls of the IMF on the servicing of debts provides for further potential embarrassment. Although the reduction of food imports and lack of foreign exchange generally may advantage capitalist farmers, the loss of political manoeuvrability makes it difficult for states to accept even string-free aid except within very clear parameters of internal control.

To the imperatives outlined above we must add the pressing problem of the ecological deterioration of which clear warning was given in the colonial period (chapter 7) in all those parts of tropical Africa where unreliable rainfall and increases of population have been pushing against the margins of existence. It is a problem which has been exacerbated by civil wars and the refugee displacements which these frequently long and fierce conflicts have caused. It is here, too, that one can most clearly identify the interface between the 'new missionaries' of the international aid and charity community and local prejudices and conflicts. The pride of nationhood and vested interests makes it likely that governments are slow to identify their inability to cope with a problem until it becomes a crisis. Political differences between, for example, capitalist donors and marxist recipients has added a further element which, in the case of Ethiopia, created the kind of impasse that only a media event, the world of popular music and youthful idealism seemed able to break.

In the end it seems and has seemed very difficult for most African countries to keep pace with the demands of emergent classes and established interest groups on the one hand and for all the ostensible advantages proffered by the schemes of the agents of development on the other. The problem of squaring this circle and turning an erratic process of stimulus and response into a steady and stable improvement in material well-being for the rural population as a whole remains unsolved. As we have implied above, many states have taken the easier route of increasing foreign indebtedness and overvalued currencies rather than risking the alienation of both disaffected and corrupt elites (well versed in diverting funds to private foreign accounts) and the new urban masses working on the certainty that an unorganized peasantry carries no political clout.

It is a significant feature of the development policy of many new states that even if there has been some level of ideological commitment to smaller-scale diffusionist activities and enterprises, they have been forced by the burden of debt to adopt the larger-scale *dirigiste* approaches, where aid agents can clearly be seen to control both inputs and outputs. But it is also true that the larger the scale of the input the more likely it is that one will either create or exaggerate the differences of wealth and opportunity which many rural development planning policies specifically set out to alleviate or prevent. The 'basic needs' approach of the World Bank has only gone part way towards redressing this problem.

In the limited space available it is impossible to give any more than the flavour of these problems and paradoxes so as in the last chapter we have chosen to use case studies to examine how governments have responded to the opportunities and constraints of independence, looking first at an example of the 'the scheme' approach through large-scale irrigation projects and integrated rural development in Nigeria, then at the ways in which ideological commitment to social restructuring has had to be trimmed to the harsher economic and political realities, especially in the settler states of Central Africa.

IRRIGATION SCHEMES AND INTEGRATED RURAL DEVELOPMENT IN NORTHERN NIGERIA

The development of sophisticated water control systems in the Chad, Kano and Sokoto-Rima river basins comprise the largest development schemes currently being undertaken in tropical Africa and partly stem from the political necessity of re-distributing some of the benefits of the oil boom of the 1970s towards the economically poorer, less advanced northern region. But they are aimed also at reducing imports of rice and wheat which feeds the urban sector, although food importing in the 1980s became an important source of accumulation for the Nigerian ruling classes. The Nigerian Third National Development Plan (1975–80) was explicit about irrigated farming in the north being part of a general policy for rural areas which seeks to raise rural incomes and narrow the differentials between rural and urban dwellers, to produce raw materials for industry and food for the urban sector and to earn foreign exchange by exporting agricultural products. At a more local level the introduction of irrigated farming is seen as a means of curtailing the annual dry season exodus of rural dwellers, as well as the more permanent drift into the towns. But as Wallace (1979) observed, a basic assumption of this plan designed by the World Bank is that increased rural productivity will automatically result in widespread improvement in rural incomes and welfare. The link between increased productivity and rural welfare remains ill-defined and unexplored. Another assumption of the plan is that present low productivity is the result of illiterate peasants who lack modern technology and information on how to improve their farming.

The implementation of large irrigation schemes inevitably means that some people will be dispossessed of their land as the building of dams floods considerable acreages. The building of the Tiga dam in the Kano river basin led to the resettlement of some 13 000 people, while the Bakolori dam on the Sokoto river displaced some 18 000 inhabitants. Resettlement villages often have poor water supply and poor land. In heavily populated areas such as the Kano and Sokoto regions land is scarce, and even if peasants have enough money to purchase land, good farms are frequently not available. The result may be that many resettled villagers leave and move on, or if they stay become agricultural labourers to offset the limited viability of the poor land they have been allocated. At the moment evidence of village desertion is limited, but after the building of the Kainji Dam there was a discernible depopulation of resettlement villages (Oyedype, 1973).

For those on the schemes the new technology of irrigated farming has proved difficult and for some farmers virtually impossible. Wallace (1979) has given some attention to the labour problems encountered by farmers on the Kano river project and suggests that planners misunderstood the nature and organization of farm labour. It was assumed that the basic production unit was built around joint-families of the paternal and fraternal kind we discussed in chapter 2. Under this kind of domestic organization, the head acquires unpaid labour from juniors, but as we observed such structures have undergone considerable erosion, not least in areas of high population density on the periphery of large towns such as Kano and Sokoto. Hausa farmers in the Kano valley rely very much on non-family labour, such as young migrant workers and local village labour.

The planners also failed to take into account the fact that the wet and dry season farm labour forces are not the same. Dry season labour migration is a long-established practice in Hausaland and many farmers found that dry season irrigated farming posed serious problems. Young men were not interested in farming during the dry season on irrigated land because the returns for their labour were not sufficiently attractive, compared with jobs available in the expanding urban sector. This is partly a reflection of low prices and inadequate marketing arrangements offered by government and private traders. Planners paid little attention to how farmers might dispose of their produce and, for example, almost up to the point of starting irrigated farming at Bakolori, little consideration had been given to marketing. Farmers in Kano complained of having produced tomatoes from their irrigated land as part of the cropping schedule insisted upon by the river valley authority, only to have them rot by the roadside as they attempted to sell them. Alternatively they were bought-up at rock-bottom prices by merchants with lorries coming out from Kano. The result of low prices is that men migrate, particularly from smaller, poorer households in the dry season, often with the approval of their families, who then resort to alternative and less efficient sources of labour provided by young children and women to try to keep irrigated farms in production. If the land is not wholly farmed then it is rented out, either to more prosperous local farmers, or to urban traders and salaried government workers who then hire either local or migrant labour. Thus farmers with limited or seasonally depleted labour resources rent out land and may themselves become part of the growing local labour market, as they find it difficult to continue farming in the dry season. Wallace (1979) found that in Waziri ward of Chiromawa town, 25 per cent of household heads and 30 per cent of their dependent sons had worked as wage labourers on the Kano river valley project. Irrigated farming requires a range of inputs such as fertilizers, water, seeds and crop sprays, which are expensive for smaller farmers and while two-year credits were offered by the authority, no credits were available for hiring in labour.

Renting of land was one outcome of irrigated farming in Kano, but to what extent land was being sold was not readily discernible. At Bakolori on the Sokoto-Rima scheme there were some indications of land sales even before plots were used (Wallace, 1980). On the Bakolori scheme farmers were allocated irrigated farms equivalent to their previous holdings of upland and floodland, minus 10 per cent for the absorption of land by the river valley authority for canals, roads and offices. Although this method of allocating new blocks of irrigated farmland is equitable, it also presents some farmers with a farm which is difficult to handle. For example, the cultivation of seven acres of wet season upland and one acre of dry season floodland is quite a different proposition, from eight acres (minus 10 per cent) of irrigated land which has to be cultivated intensively throughout the year. The shortage of labour for irrigated farming may lead to land resales and renting, as farmers cannot cope, but it may be that some farmers are using less land on the new system to produce the same incomes and levels of subsistence as they had from the old system and they have settled for this and rented surplus irrigated land, which together with off-farm work secures an adequate living. This, of course, does not fulfil the stated objective of the planners, who wish to raise rural productivity, farm incomes and state revenues. What does seem to have happened in common with mechanized rice farming in Ghana is that an impetus has been given to capitalist farming with the growth of an increased agricultural wage-labour force. The benefits, far from being widespread, have become limited to the bigger rural farmers and urban entrepreneurs.

In many ways the effects of post-independence development schemes have not been all that dissimilar to the introduction of cashcrops by the colonial regimes, except that they are not just exacting surpluses from the peasantry, but also expropriating the land to set up schemes. What has happened in Nigeria (and elsewhere) is the creation of opportunities for capitalist farming which is subsidized by the state. The element of risk capital is almost nil since farmers have access at low prices or rents to land which has been improved to the tune of £3000 per acre. Moreover, there are the benefits of cheap inputs and credits. On the other hand it may be that the state is producing amounts of wheat, rice and vegetables which might reduce imports, or at least have a political pay-off in that certain classes or interest groups are well-served by the schemes. Meanwhile many middle and poorer farmers sit tight and adopt their own strategies for coping with new events, or households become increasingly 'proletarianized' as members enter the urban and agricultural labour markets.

In addition to the river basin development projects in northern Nigeria parallel initiatives have taken place through integrated rural development schemes. The first of these projects was started in the mid-1970s in Funtua, Gusau and Gombe but in the 1980s the whole of the north was covered by such schemes renamed as agricultural development agencies. Their objective is to bring packages of inputs such as ox-ploughs, pesticides, much needed seeds and fertilizers to farmers over wide areas, together with improved roads and water supplies. Such schemes became a major instrument of development policy in the 1970s throughout Africa and had their origins in the equity and basic needs issues of the 1970s. Disenchantment with large-scale projects, the discovery of the informal sector, the populist advocacy of the importance of the peasantry, nationalistic sentiments and the Green Revolution all contributed to the adoption of policies of integrated development. By the 1970s the World Bank supported this approach and began to address the problem of reaching 'the poorest of the poor' who were disproportionately located in rural areas.

The progress and success of integrated rural development in northern Nigeria has a not dissimilar history to the larger schemes. Changes in production and production relations have created problems of adjustment for villagers. Some have preferred to opt out of new methods or have partially adopted new inputs (Iliya, 1988). But once again it has been the alliance of traditional rulers, bureaucrats, politicians and merchants who have been able to use the projects to improve and consolidate their access to inputs and credit, thus accumulating land and labour and increased surpluses for local and regional markets.

It would appear that schemes designed to provide farmers with better inputs, as well as large-scale irrigation schemes built to give farmers a perennial water supply have not succeeded in realizing the aims set down by governments and planners. The improvement of basic needs for a large proportion of the rural population and a widespread increase of productivity and farm incomes, have often been less conspicuous than the advantages which have accrued to the already better-off farmer, or urban-based merchant and town-dwellers. According to one line of thought, the shift of industry into developing countries with their cheap labour markets is dependent on cheap food supplies, otherwise urban industrial wage rates will rise. A depressed peasantry and poorly-fed city invites revolution, and there is therefore an imperative to defuse the time bomb of poverty and food crises with a 'basic needs' programme (Gakov, 1987). Such strategies of basic needs and equity run counter to the interests of dominant classes, but if northern Nigeria is any guide, they are well equipped to manipulate integrated development schemes. So the deepening of capitalist relations in the countryside which ensues may well ultimately provoke antagonisms from the dispossessed and those with reduced access to resources. It may be that the ensuing struggle among classes and interests is the real hope for restructuring society on more radical lines.

But what of these more radical programmes of change? So far we have looked at state intervention which tries to improve infrastructures and introduce innovations to peasant farmers by the injection of state capital and large-scale schemes administered by state or para-statal agencies. However, there have been other methods of agrarian change employed in Africa aimed at the transformation of rural society as part of national programmes of socialist or humanist reconstruction. Although both Soviet and Chinese and latterly Cuban models have been closely studied, there has usually been an attempt to come to terms with Africa's past and indigenous values to lend a distinctive colour to and indeed allow us to speak of, African socialism.

SOCIALISM AND HUMANISM IN AFRICA

Many states which became independent in a phase of development when foreign markets were buoyant enjoyed a market for their high value specialist products, and enjoyed a honeymoon period when it was possible to experiment with interventions at all scales, serving the needs of both expediency and idealism. Frequently they are both allowed scope to operate within a pragmatic political environment which sees no inconsistency in a massive capital intensive agribusiness plantation of a major multi-national with a proletarianized workforce, spatially juxtaposed with a small-scale community development project, aiming to encourage self-help and low-level peasant production, supported by foreign aid and serviced by the expatriate technicians of a communist state.

In Ghana, when cocoa was fetching a high price on the world market in the early 1960s, the Nkrumah government introduced ambitious plans to develop industry and agriculture along socialist lines. These plans included state farms, tractor mechanization and marketing agencies, intended to increase productivity through extensive mechanized farming, in particular for the production of foodstuffs such as rice and maize. Ambitious schemes involving large-scale irrigation and dam projects accompanied socialist co-operative endeavour by 'young pioneers', while at the intermediate level the market women of Accra and Tamale organized their own vigorous trading network served by the new roads and rail networks. The perform-ance of the state farms was dismal, partly because of difficulties of adminis-tering and controlling such innovations and ultimately private capitalist farmers benefited from cheap machinery as the farms were run down (Van Hear, 1982).

Other revolutionary programmes have been attempted in Ethiopia, which highlight the problems of radical transformation and how they can be beset by external factors which can lead to the terrible conditions and food-shortages endured by many Ethiopians from the 1970s to date. The 1974 socialist revolution in Ethiopia was partly sparked off by food short-ages and corrupt mismanagement of aid during the 1973 drought in which at least 200 000 died. In 1975 all land was nationalized, holdings limited to 10 ha, elected peasant associations were created charged with organizing co-operatives and communal farms and the collection of taxes. By 1978 there were 30 000 peasant associations comprising seven million farmers, while in 1982 state farms had been inaugurated and 850 producer co-operatives set up.

But the whole of this radical programme has to be set within the disruption caused by the revolution and the persistent fighting in different parts of the country. In 1977 there was the war against Somalia over the occupation of the Ogaden province, which was won only through large-scale help from the USSR. However, a more formidable problem has been the independence movement within the northern province, which was formerly the Italian colony of Eritrea. This area has seen prolonged fighting causing economic disruption which has been made worse by drought. The Eritrean freedom campaign has been split into two factions, while the Ethiopian government itself has been split by ideological disputes about the nature of the revolution. Terror campaigns have been part of this factionalism and in 1982 the Provisional Military Advisory Council headed by Colonel Mengistu launched an all-out attack on Eritrea, which included programmes of 'development and politicization'. On an other front, fighting has broken out in the Tigre province just south of Eritrea, organized by the Tigre Peoples' Liberation Front, which now controls much of this northern territory.

The persistence of insurrection has meant the need for a large standing army which deprives the economy of its most able-bodied workers, while at least half-a-million people have been displaced as they have fled the countryside to escape the direct consequences of the conflict. Many have abandoned the countryside and locusts have thrived on unoccupied farmland, especially in Ogaden. The distribution of what food surpluses are locally produced, together with food-aid from outside sources are seriously hampered by the disruption of the transport network. Just to complete this dismal picture we have to note that while prices for the country's main export crop, coffee, held firm in the mid-1970s, they slumped in 1982, at the same time as droughts were affecting 10 out of 15 provinces. In 1983 some five million people were at risk because of food shortages and although food-aid from abroad may help to reduce the problem, it can hardly cure it. It can be argued that some progress has been made by the transformation of agriculture and that the redistribution of land may, in the long run, be of benefit. But given the chronic political instability in Ethiopia, the continued warfare, the cost of maintaining a large army and periods of erratic rainfall, then it is hardly surprising that rural hunger and depression are so apparent.

UJAMAA AND VILLAGIZATION IN TANZANIA

A rather different, but equally fundamental attempt to change rural life was spearheaded by Julius Nyerere in Tanzania, whose programmes of *ujamaa* (villagization) owed much to his interest in the formation of peasant communes in Mao's China and the belief that socialist transformation could come from peasant societies and not necessarily have to proceed via 'machinification' and urbanization, as suggested by more orthodox Marxism (Nyerere, 1974). The Tanzanian experiment has attracted much attention, not least because of its adherence to incorporating African traditional values. Like other socialist programmes it firmly believed in promoting equity and self-sufficiency and cutting the ties of dependency with the external world, especially the Western bloc and the world trading system. In this respect there was a link with the rise of dependency theory and neo-Marxism, while the policy of communal village agriculture in Tanzania also falls within the realm of populist strategies.

The Arusha Declaration of 1967 set forth the belief that Tanzanians should return to collective and communal values if their material conditions were to be rapidly and equitably improved. These values were to be found in the communal labour groups, *ujamaa*, which could be developed into a set of principles for living and working together and provide a socialist framework for the transformation of Tanzania. The goals of the *ujamaa* policy were self-governing communities, a better use of rural labour, the ability to take advantage of economies of scale, to improve production, to disseminate new values, to avoid exploitation, to facilitate national planning, to increase the standard of living and to facilitate national defence. Apart from wishing to curtail individualistic tendencies encouraged by the colonial regime and the power of small capitalist farmers, there was a concern not to make the same mistakes as large-scale development schemes, which were generally over-capitalized. Economies of scale were to be achieved through a larger labour force, using existing technology in the first instance, with the introduction of mechanization at a later stage (Hyden, 1980).

At first voluntaryism was accorded a high priority in the formation of the *ujamaa*, and there were some notable successes, but they were usually in lightly populated and poorly developed areas which had hitherto a limited exposure to the market economy. As the majority of rural Tanzanians lived in dispersed settlements rather than villages, *ujamaa* needed a re-grouping of population to create effective communal labour forces working on communal farms. The creation of nucleated villages was an integral part of *ujamaa* policy, and villagization was seen as the means of introducing centralized services such as dispensaries, schools and extension services. Those in charge of planning believed that to fulfill their functions, villages would have to be sited along roads, therefore the relocation of peasants would be not only into larger communities, but they would be sited in specific places.

By 1970 it was apparent that *ujamaa* was proceeding slowly and a more positive attitude was required towards villagization if it was to become the key to the rapid development of *ujamaa*. In 1973 droughts underlined the natural constraints under which agriculturalist work and compulsory villagization was decided upon by Tanzanian African National Union (TANU) with the declared objective of relocating the rural population by 1976. This comprised the largest resettlement in African history, and by 1974 2.5 million of a total 13 million rural dwellers were settled in villages, although this did not mean that communal farming was widespread. The new villages were not popular, as they required longer journeys to fields and labour time was being lost. Also in some cases water supplies were not secure and farmers were moved into areas where soils were less than satisfactory. The farming ecology of close-nucleated settlements was different from former locations and the concentration of cattle around villages and centralized water points can be destructive of the soil complex, while distance from farms meant a less effective watch on crop predators such as baboons. Roads became the focus of villages in order to provide viable services and infrastructures, but in some heavily populated areas such as the Highlands and the medium density areas of Sukumaland, villagization was scarcely needed, as service centres at selected points would have reached the majority of dwellers (Cliffe, 1973).

Communal farming and villagization have met considerable resistance which has arisen from hasty planning, the conflict of interests between peasants and bureaucrats and not least a misunderstanding of the fundamentals of peasant production, especially in northern areas where it was well-established and successful. It is true that communal labour was widespread in Africa and still exists today, but it does not extend to the ownership or sharing of the product, except in special cases. As we saw in chapter 2 the most important forms of communal labour are exchange work-groups operated on a reciprocal basis by a small number of farmers who pool their labour and who are quite clear about the 'rules of the game'. Although forms of communal work are part of rural tradition, the organization of labour and the distribution of the product is rooted in domestic groups built on principles of age, sex and kinship. It is true that in many instances rights to the use of land is vested in the village community, which determines its allocation, but once allocated, the organization of farming and patterns of cropping are directed from *within* domestic groups. Rural communities often contain a good deal of tension between the interests of individual households and the interests of the community at large; they are forces which divide as well as bind the community. Exchange labour and festive work-groups may represent communal values, or the helping of one by another, but they are not primarily designed to produce surpluses; rather they exist to ensure an acceptable level of subsistence.

The semi-autonomy of domestic groups and their individualistic traits provided a ready basis for the emergence of small-commodity producers during the colonial period and in some parts of Tanzania such as the Highlands and Sukumaland, the market economy made substantial inroads. Planners seemed to have taken little account of regional variations in the penetration of the 'pre-capitalist' economy by market relations, other than to see *ujamaa* programmes proceed. Yet there was sufficient awareness of peasant attitudes to allow *ujamaa* villagers the right to cultivate their own private plots, but as elsewhere private plots have become something of a stumbling-block to full-time peasant commitment to community and national interests.

The hours worked on communal farms show tremendous fluctuations, although there are few small-scale in-depth studies of the workings of *ujamaa*, especially on a comparative basis. Sumra (1979) provides some insights into the workings of communal farms in a survey of several villages in Handeni district of Tanzania. More workers turned out for communal farming when food was short and numbers varied according to the type of job, whereas under traditional systems of labour exchange, jobs were done as required by the host. The timing of work on communal farms was less than satisfactory, as clearing tended to take place after it was completed on private plots and once the rains were underway weeding and vermin control were poorly done for the same reason. Communal farms devoted to commercial crops such as cotton also suffered, because insufficient workers were available for intensive and continuous jobs such as spraying and picking. Labour bottlenecks have become a constraint on production levels, just as they have in other farming systems. but the conflict has arisen not between foodstaples and commercial crops, but between private and communal plots. Sumra (1979) suggested that perhaps communal farms should have been devoted to certain tree crops, or animals and poultry, where labour demands were complementary. Alternatively labour on communal farms should be compulsory, or confined to committed members of the village.

In the West Lake Region, less than half the potential working days in season were spent on communal farms and even then the working day was reduced to around four or five hours. During any one day only one-third or one-half of the potential labour force actually came to work on the farm. Many villagers felt that communal farms were rather a waste of time, and that yields were poor, a feeling which grew out of their lack of firm commitment on the one hand and on the other, poor management. The organization of labour on communal farms is not easy and requires considerable managerial effort and expertise. The recording of the quantity and the quality of work and the correct reward is difficult and in many instances attendance becomes the only criterion.

The food requirements of households often lack a direct equivalence to the input they can muster. A small group of active adults with a large number of young or old dependants is in a stage of imbalance, although formerly the adult workers could resort to adjusting working hours, call on their kin or use labour exchange groups. It must be stressed again, labour exchange was a means of pooling labour inputs, and apart from food and drink did not affect the product. Also labour exchange works best where small numbers are involved, say a half-dozen, whereas the planners of *ujamaa* villages set much higher ceilings and it was this that exacerbated the organizational problems (Barker, 1979). Smaller communal groups of about 30 seemed to work much better, because there was cohesiveness and mutual trust, which makes record keeping irrelevant. When planners demanded lower limits for villages of 250 families, or about 1000 inhabitants, their objectives were being determined not by the requirements of efficient farm labour, but of the thresholds for the provision of certain services.

Communal farms and farming in many villages have become little more than symbolic gestures and the necessary strategy for the acquisition of services and farming inputs provided by the state. Communal farming raised many doubts in the minds of peasants as to the objectives and benefits, primarily if they worked harder, who would benefit – the government, bureaucrats, urban dwellers or foreigners? The latter qualification became more apparent as there was a shift towards export crops in the mid-1970s in order to increase state revenues to pay off increasing debts and provide infrastructure. Also, village members were never clear on their rights to accumulated wealth and collective property. Under traditional relations of production there were general, if not unquestioned, rights to land and property and if divorced wives or brothers left a household, rights and responsibilities were understood.

HUMANISM, SOCIALISM AND THE SETTLER ECONOMIES: ZAMBIA AND ZIMBABWE

Enriched in its early years of independence by high copper prices and the heavy demands of the world market, Zambia was able to indulge in a wide range of enterprises extending across all three scales and every political philosophy from African socialism, populism, capital intensive mechanization schemes, large-scale state farms, agribusiness enterprises led by multi-national firms, dam and irrigation schemes, land redistribution, median scale infrastructural improvements, worker co-operatives, to media-led farming improvement schemes and price manipulation.

At the end of the colonial era, Northern Rhodesia still retained the *laager* economy which had been established 30 years earlier (see chapter 7). Nothing deliberate had been done to alter a situation which Federal policies had merely made worse. The only really liberal legislation had been the lifting of restrictions governing residential status to allow long-term immigration to mining towns and the repeal of laws governing quotas for commercial maize production. Both these reforms were no more than remedial measures which were made necessary by mining nationalization and a rapidly expanding urban population.

The new government, led by Kaunda's United National Independence Party (UNIP), was clearly committed by its radical political stance during the struggle for independence both to reforming a very imbalanced economic structure and to tough policies towards the South. Its dilemma was one of reconciling the demands of the electorate and the harsh realities of political power without economic independence. During a colonial regime people are conditioned to believe that paternalism is part of the natural order of authority and power. An underprivileged, but newly-enfranchised population therefore readily believes that it will inherit the riches of the developed sector, not through its own labours, but through the beneficence of government. Extravagant promises at the hustings encouraged this population to assume that there could be a rapid transformation of their economic condition. The logic was apparently unassailable. White government gave white men power, wealth and comfort. White power had been replace by black power. Black power would now provide wealth and comfort for black men.

This not unfamiliar background to early development planning created an impossible situation for a government already philosophically committed to a radical foreign policy as well as a liberal domestic one. The verbal barrage which Zambia has continually maintained against the governments of Southern Africa, upon whose ports it has relied to maintain its industry and to supply its urban consumer market, has left the country open to a charge of hypocrisy, a charge of which the government is only too painfully aware. In this respect, the sanctions policy which followed Rhodesia's illegal declaration of independence (1965) exposed all the weaknesses of the Zambian position but it also provided the government with the necessary evidence to support its radical stand.

The Kaunda government has not been without opposition, particularly in the southern and western provinces. It was from these areas that the flow of labour migration to South Africa and Rhodesia was most pronounced and the curtailment of this flow by legislation in 1966 provoked a good deal of resentment. Those who saw their main means of livelihood cut away also saw government support going to the northerners who formed the major part of the privileged workforce of the Zambian Copperbelt, and who provided the voting strength for the ruling party. But, as the flow of supplies from the south were drastically reduced and problems took on national rather than regional proportions, political dissent was muted. In fact, it has been threats from the outside that have produced the internal solidarities necessary for a policy of radical reform and which have contributed in no small measure to the political tides which carried the government towards a one-party state and unchanged into the present decade.

In these difficult circumstances it is not surprising that the First National Development Plan (1966–71) was not effective in reducing disparities between the line-of-rail growth region and the rural areas. Despite a liberal nationalization of mining and industry in 1969, considerable improvements in education and in urban employment opportunities and substantial investment in a rural development programme, the economy itself has remained firmly dualistic, with an obvious concentration of planning resources on improving conditions within the space occupied by the colonial *laager* now transformed, politically, into a 'national growth pole'. Most aspects of spatial planning in the first eight years of independence reflect this concentration of energy in the nodal region along the railway.

The 1966–71 plan had three main aims: to diversify the industrial economy, to improve and extend the infrastructure and to reduce the inherited disparities between urban and rural areas through a regional planning strategy. If one disregards for the moment the spatial aspect of planning, there can be little doubt concerning the considerable achievements of that first period of independence, despite the constraints on development imposed by Rhodesia's Unilateral Declaration of Independence (UDI) and the subsequent imposition of economic sanctions. During the period of the plan the gross domestic product (GDP) increased by 80 per cent at a rate of 10.6 per cent per annum, bringing the *per capita* average to K. 303 in 1970 compared with K. 226 in 1964. This high growth rate resulted in great measure from favourable terms of trade through high copper prices, but it allowed the government to embark on a considerable public investment programme, increasing the annual budget expenditure from an average of K. 92 million in the four-year period before independence to over K. 300 million at the high point of expansion in 1967.

An early priority for Zambia following Rhodesia'a UDI was an attempt to reduce the balance of payments and foreign dependency by 'one-shot' schemes. A large sugar estate was established at Nkambala in the country's main commercial farming district of Mazabuka, aiming to reduce Zambia's increasing reliance on imported sugar in the face of a demand which had been rising by 20 per cent per annum since 1963. Trials in 1965 indicated that the Kafue alluviums were suitable for cane sugar using irrigation methods and the first plot of 2023 ha was established in 1968. A further 7163 ha were set aside for development. A refinery was completed in 1970 with a capacity of 60 000 tons of sugar per annum. In that year 214 000 tons of cane gave a yield of 45 000 tons of sugar; about two-thirds of Zambia's needs. The estate, run on strictly commercial lines, at present provides employment for 2700 workers and three settlements have been created to house immigrant workers from all parts of the country. Apart from sugar production, the estate developed other subsidiary activities. Molasses was converted into cattle food and a dairy herd was established. There were plans, too, for a distillery and experimental horticultural plots (citrus fruits, vegetables, bananas) indicated the potential for extending the irrigation channels to provide for urban markets in yet another way. There seems little doubt that Nkambala could act as the catalyst in the initiation of many small-scale intensive agricultural projects in this accessible region close to both Kafue New Town and Lusaka.

The spectacular improvements in communications and the diversification of fuel supplies, the increased control over mineral exploitation and revenue and the increase in range of industrial enterprises and social services were the most successful aspects of economic change during the period of the First Plan. Yet the 1970 Mufulira mine disaster which temporarily cut Zambia's copper production by 25 per cent and the fall in copper prices during 1969-71, demonstrated all too clearly the influence which this industry still exerts on the economy, as the government was forced to curtail its development programmes.

As the plan progressed, there was increasing recognition of the fact that real development must be based on a regional planning design and a new economic and social philosophy (Kaunda and Morris, 1966; Kaunda, 1980). This was in part a response to the fact that the regional planning strategy was the least successful part of the plan. Despite the improved investment in rural development activities, growth in this sector was disappointing. Agricultural production did little to reduce the increasing tide of agricultural imports as new wage structures and an increasing range of consumption created new demands. Imports of foodstuffs doubled in value between 1964 and 1969, whereas the share of agriculture, forestry and fishing in the GDP declined from 11.5 per cent to 6.8 per cent during this period.

Part of the reason for this decline has been the instability of the European farming industry. Of the 1200 farmers in 1964, less than half now remain and many of these now concentrate on short-term profit maximization, shifting from tobacco to maize as the basis of their farming system. Thus in 1968, 62 per cent of the land under cultivation by commercial farmers was under maize and only 9 per cent was under tobacco, whereas in 1964, 47 per cent had been under maize and 14 per cent under tobacco. The lack of success in agriculture is not merely caused by disturbances in the European sector. Planners failed to appreciate the fact that rural development cannot be achieved merely by capital investment, as in the industrial and commercial sectors. Too many settlement and production schemes were initiated without careful forethought, and with the idea of reaping quick political and economic returns. Too much conflicting advice was sought and acted upon, and there were considerable discrepancies in advantage between one area and another.

Despite the claims of the plan to be regional in character, there has been a continued concentration of activity in the line-of-rail and its neighbourhood. Davies (1971) has shown that the *per capita* shares in planning investment for each region demonstrate the strong pull exerted by the nodal region. A study of rural development schemes in relation to their potential service areas reveals a similar, though not so pronounced, concentration of rural development activity in areas well served by communications and close to the nodal region (Siddle, 1970).

All these trends revealed the strong pressure on a new government to concentrate its limited resources and to follow established economic lore regarding the nature of economic development. It also reflected an approach to development which relied on paternalistic provision of localized amenities and assistance through schemes, grants and loans rather than the generation of a spirit of re-education towards self-reliance. It is interesting to note in this context that by far the most successful rural development schemes were those which relied on local support for their existence (Siddle, 1971).

The African socialist philosophy of Zambian humanism (Kaunda and Morris, 1966), presented by the president as a guideline for development, denied the validity of development processes which foster personal advancement and wealth accumulation. Kaunda's proposals, which favoured communal action, group decision-making and profit sharing, need time to diffuse through a society committed for 60 years to the alternative approach. Zambia prepared itself, through the Second National Development Plan (1972-6), for a major shift of emphasis along these lines.

By far the most important new aspect of the second plan was to increase emphasis on regional and rural development. Top priority was given to provincial programmes and to an intensive development of the rural areas which have a 'high natural and human potential for agriculture development'. The second part of the plan was given over to the detailed breakdown of regional planning proposals. The basic philosophy of the new plan was clearly stated as one in which regional planning would rely on the resources inherent in a properly organized population. This organization was to be achieved through a 'participatory democracy' of village and ward development committees, which would both channel ideas for local improvement and carry out the organization of those local projects which were clearly specified and costed in the plan Second National Development Plan (SNDP). 'More than any other single factor in the SNDP, development of grass roots through these committees and the Intensive Development Zones was to mark one of the most fundamental differences between this Plan and the FNDP' First National Development Plan (Republic of Zambia, 1971: 36).

The Intensive Development Zones (IDZ) reflect a 'major new policy strategy to concentrate public services and investment for integrated development of rural areas', which bore remarkable similarity to the strategy outlined but never implemented in the post-war plan 25 years earlier. The notion was to concentrate development 'in areas with the greatest inherent potential' in the provinces so that these should not become 'islands of development' but provide 'an impetus to national and provincial economic and social development'. This is to be achieved by providing an integrated package of interlocking services (technical advice, production inputs like fertilizer and credit and marketing) complemented by adequate provision of social services.

The criteria for selection of an IDZ were that enough ecological capacity existed for concentration of energies; that a basic community structure already existed; that population density was high enough to justify investment; that aptitudes and incentives for improvement were already existing within the population; while the existence of tarred roads, railways, processing plants and other actual or expective propulsive factors was 'preferable'. The plan also stated, more realistically, that these criteria could not be expected to apply to every zone under consideration. Indeed if they had been then few zones would be 'selected', even within the railway belt, let alone outside it. Management of the zone was to be undertaken by a 'team leader' who would act as a co-ordinator of local, provincial and national organs of administration. Special training was envisaged to provide sufficient agricultural extension, marketing and credit staff as well as other health and education officers.

The objective of this most significant aspect of rural development policy was the increase of *per capita* rural incomes by four or five per cent per annum. A tentative K. 17 million was allocated to this end. In addition to this specific programme, a policy of provincial investment was to be followed, using the new freedom of decision-making in provincial affairs which followed the decentralizing of local government in 1969. Ministerial and provincial investments were to be balanced in such a way as to be reflected in 'spatial as well as sectoral investment allocation'. A total of K. 80 million was to be given over to this programme of provincial development and there is a marked difference between the spatial distribution of this amount and that designated in the FNDP. This time there is a clear and shrewd attempt to balance political interests between the influential tribes of the north-east and the socially, politically and economically disadvantaged groups in the west and south. Most of the provincial programmes concentrated on the provision of services and facilities in all districts, aiming to improve primary schools, feeder roads, rest houses, water supplies and to add their own network of agricultural schemes.

There is little doubt that during the early phase of development, sustained by high copper prices, rural populations benefited from improvements in infrastructure. Wider provision of health centres and schools brought 85 per cent of the population within 12 km of a free clinic and 8 km of a free primary school by 1974. At the same time investment in the agricultural sector away from the railway belt had been transformed, with *per capita* spending doubling in the first decade of independence. One of the significant side benefits of this policy of subsidizing maize production had been the pegging of maize-meal prices in the copperbelt and in the towns where support for the government is essential to stability. In fact an apparently benign rural development policy was increasingly driven by the demands of an urban population for cheap food. Faced by political problems engendered by the independence struggle to the south and the

possibilities of urban discontent the government has felt obliged to continue to 'buy off' the urban population by maintaining these subsidies on
basic staple commodities, particularly maize. Crop collecting depots were
established throughout the country and pricing policies which had discouraged market production in remote areas were reformed. By 1975 uniform
prices were offered at all maize depots with the government bearing the
costs of transportation, and subsidies on fertilizers were increased (Wood,
1983). At the same time generous inducements were offered to farmers to
join producer co-operatives, tractor hire units were established throughout
the country and settlement schemes were still used as a mechanism for
assisting peasants to become commercial farmers. Many schemes, dominated by the old paternalist ethos referred to above made few real attempts
to engage the peasants in a politically aware way in their own self-
improvement. It was inevitable, therefore, that many such schemes were
inefficient, corrupt and poorly led. Large-scale para-statal ranches and rural
reconstruction centres suffered the same fate. In fact, many of the impressive policies ran away into the sands of poor motivation and inertia.

However politically inevitable these policies were, the Zambian economy
was operating in a fool's paradise. Eventually the balance between the
demands for rural social justice and maintained or enhanced urban living
standards could not continue to be sustained by reliance on one major high
value export commodity. The precarious balance of this strategy was
exposed by the rise in fuel costs following the oil crisis of 1974 which
pushed the support of maize prices to half the economic cost of production.
Agricultural subsidies, negligible at independence rose to 26 per cent of the
government revenue by 1980.

Even more significantly, the oil crisis of 1974 had a similarly dramatic
effect on copper prices as economies faltered and governments sought
substitutes for this expensive mineral. By the early 1980s copper was only a
quarter of its 1970 price and at its lowest real value since the years of
pre-war depression. From its position as the main, almost sole provider of
export revenue, the copper industry now teeters on the brink of total
collapse. Since 1975 it has made a negligible contribution to the Zambian
economy, even needing subsidies to maintain operation at all.

The crisis has at last produced some diversification with a move away
from large-scale para-statal organizations, heavily dependent on government funds, to small-scale village and craft-based industries, and there has
been a freeing of the informal sector from restrictive licensing legislation
left over from colonial days. The reduction in agricultural subsidies has
clearly affected areas away from the main focus of development near the
railway belt. The growing and marketing of maize is once more concentrated in the hands of a few hundred European commercial farmers and
probably 50 000 peasant producers (Wood, 1983). The reliance on subsidized maize production in areas much more suited to cassava and millet has

at last been replaced by the marketing of what was in an earlier period purely subsistence crops. Almost a quarter of government spending in 1980 went on keeping the price of maize and cooking oil artificially low in a period of rising prices – a policy which is in effect subsidizing urban wage-earners – and the increasing burden of foreign loans has become intolerable. The IMF's rescheduling of these debts has carried with it a stiff financial penalty. Food subsidies are under strong pressures with rising prices and real shortages of supply. A new rurally-educated primary school generation have voted with their feet and joined the rural–urban exodus. By 1990 Wood estimates that half the rapidly expanding population of the country will be in towns, swelling the ranks of the young, unemployed and disaffected who already live in the shanties. Malnutrition is once more evident among the urban poor and the opportunities for wage employment have become more limited. Any attempt to change the priorities towards the support of the rural areas, along the lines suggested by Lipton (1977), will potentially carry with it severe political penalties.

In Zambia, as in Ghana, the high egalitarian idealism of the leadership was dissipated by errors of judgement and political ambivalence and the economy collapsed because it was based on a single export commodity. So much seems to depend on a politically committed organizational infrastructure at what is often referred to as 'the grassroots level', to create and maintain a wide base of marketable products and a relatively low profile in terms of the scale of state intervention. Although some capital intensive schemes have been singularly successful in tropical Africa, as Dumont (1969) continued to point out, many have followed in the path of the Groundnut Scheme (see p. 146), leaving in their wake a wasteland of regenerative vegetation and the abandoned carcasses of unserviceable machinery.

In Zimbabwe, the newest independent state, there are clear indications that the lessons learned elsewhere in tropical Africa have been absorbed into political and economic policies. But the new leadership is fortunate in having inherited a country which had profited from the sanctions imposed by the international community on the illegal Rhodesian regime under Ian Smith, which had broadened and deepened its base towards a measure of self-sufficiency in all sectors of the economy. It emerged from the struggle for independence as economically healthy as any country in tropical Africa (Stoneman, 1981). Ecological assessment (see chapter 7) has also given Zimbabwe one of the clearest perspectives on limitations and opportunities of any country in the tropical world (Palmer, 1977).

The most serious immediate post-independence problem has been the redistribution of land and the satisfaction of the needs of those who struggled for a fairer share of good quality soils in rainfall-reliable zones close to roads and railheads. At the same time there was a perceived need, despite the avowedly Marxist stance of the new leaders, to leave sufficient room for the specialist skills of European farmers who wished to remain as Zimbabweans and to continue to make their vital contribution to the economy. The ZANU (PF) government prioritized the land problem in its manifesto, promising the swift collectivization of peasant agriculture and the establishment of state farms, while at the same time retaining an efficient European farming sector on which the modern economy depended. As with many other socialist transformations, redistribution of land to the landless was to precede collectivization and state farming projects. The problem has been the inequitable distribution of land in relation to land quality.

Land is classified into five agro-ecological zones (see figure 4.2). More than half the large-scale commercial farms occupy land in the best regions. Three-quarters of the communal African land is still in regions IV and V, regarded as marginal or unsuitable for agriculture. But the best lands in natural regions I and II occupy less than 20 per cent of the country. At the same time population pressure in the communal areas means that they carry more than 200 000 more households than their carrying capacity. The problem is very severe in the south where as many as 10 per cent of households are landless while a quarter of the white-owned land was underutilized or abandoned. At the same time the 6300 commercial farms produce three-and-a-half times the gross output, four times the value by hectare, as the three-quarters of a million communal holdings. Up to 80 per cent of the agricultural output is produced on European farms. Three-quarters of the production from African communal farms is consumed actually on the farm. A third of the African workforce is employed on European farms and estates. These are the harsh facts faced by a reforming government. The administration has chosen to concentrate on the most sensitive issues – the resettlement of the underutilized European farmlands through an intensive resettlement programme.

Initiated soon after independence in 1980, with support from the British government, the aim was to settle 18 000 families on a million acres of former commercial farmland. The land was not confiscated but repurchased at rates which were commensurate with land prices in 1976. The scheme is now well advanced with infrastructure in place (access roads, dip-tanks, bore-holes, clinics, schools) and the settlers comprise the landless, those with too little land to sustain themselves and their families and refugees. Squatters on the farms were treated with great circumspection and some became settlers on the schemes. Resettlement follows one of three models taking account of the agro-ecological zones, all aiming to provide the families with a basic minimum income of Z$400.00. The first model involves intensive village settlements with five hectares per family and an ecologically adjusted number of approved livestock units appropriate to the available grazing area and the region. No land is further than 3 km from the village dwelling. Twelve schemes of this kind had already settled 25 000 people at the rate of 10 families per day by the end of 1982.

The second model is based on the principle of co-operative farming and communal living. Only livestock will be owned individually – all land, property and implements are to be owned communally. The programme is designed for young ideologically inspired ex-freedom fighters and refugees and directed towards intensive enterprises. This is in many ways the preferred model for the socialist transformation of Zimbabwe. The third model is similar to the first but with a central core estate to provide essential services, demonstrations and advice. The core farm is a unit for large-scale commercial production served by settlers who contribute labour. A fourth approach called the Accelerated Resettlement Programme was designed as an emergency relief programme to deal with the immediate problems of serious over-population and squatting. It involves purchasing any Euro-pean farm that comes on the market wherever it is and resettling it without the benefit of services or support. Planning is minimal and settlement has been taking place on a piecemeal basis.

The remarkable speed with which resettlement programmes have been implemented reflect as much as anything political necessity encapsulated by the facts and figures of spatial and economic deprivation, which was the driving force of the independence struggle. In only 18 months following independence, Zimbabwe achieved almost as much as Kenya over 15 years of the small-holder resettlement initiatives and land purchase, though the environmental restrictions allow for a lower level of intensity of occupation in Zimbabwe. The end product of this process would be the occupation of about two-thirds of all the commercial farming area outside the prime quality agricultural land of the first and second natural regions.

Although it is too early to make a full assessment of the success of this bold set of initiatives, the demands on budgetary resources are clearly enormous and the dependence on foreign aid is bound to increase. It seems unlikely on past experience of similar enterprises in Kenya, Zambia and elsewhere, that many of the objectives for minimum incomes will be met in a time-scale sufficiently attractive to keep the people on the land. Moreover the concentration on the immediate political objective of resettlement of the most needy means that the main problem of the old reserve areas, where the majority of the rural population still live and the pressure of population continues to increase. The 're-education' of the rural majority still remains an issue. As we have indicated earlier in this chapter, rural people are not going to accept change unless they are fully involved in the process of desicion-making. It remains to be seen whether or not the Zimbabwean 'one-party state' has learnt this lesson of the independence struggle.

PEASANT RESISTANCE AND STATE PERSISTENCE

Attempts to transform agriculture have met with some spectacular rever-
sals, as time and time again peasants seem less than willing to meet the
demands of the state and their agencies. Neither agrarian state capitalism
nor socialist reconstruction have proved infallible bases for rural change,
while the populist philosophy of 'small is beautiful' has not yet proved to be
a panacea either.

It is not surprising that peasants stuck so closely both to their private
plots and to their communal lands, because they were able to retain control
of their labour and its product, in a manner to which they were accustomed, as small commodity producers. Also they were fully conversant
with the capabilities of particular pieces of ground which their families may
have farmed for generations. This was particularly true of smaller and
poorer domestic groups, who had most to lose from investing their limited
labour time in a communal enterprise from which the returns were far from
certain, or appropriate. Better-off households had spare labour and could
afford the risk, and so this was another reason for the fluctuating levels of
labour found within communal enterprises. Such attitudes are entrenched
in concepts of anteriority and posteriority and the production and reproduction of domestic groups, controlled by individuals, not elected village
bodies. It is in this context that peasant resistance to villagization and other
schemes must be seen.

There is no shortage of explanations of why peasants are difficult to
integrate into national economies as 'efficient' producers; the more common
ones are lack of education and illiteracy coupled with capricious environments and poor administration. As we have seen, interest in peasant
resistance has grown among academic researchers, but there has been less
interest among politicians and bureaucrats. Problems of environment, poor
personnel and administrative infrastructures do play a part in the failure of
development projects, but it is necessary to go beyond these more obvious
shortcomings and inquire about who is resisting whom, what form resistance takes and whose interests programmes of agricultural transformation
actually serve (Cohen and Hutton, 1978).

Peasant resistance takes a variety of forms. We have seen that under
collective systems, private plots are given preference, with the common
good often coming a poor second. In other instances, peasants vote with
their feet and either leave development schemes or continue to engage in
non-farm employment as migrant workers, if the returns appear to be
better for the domestic group as a whole. Finally, peasants on occasions
resort to violence and rioting, especially when many have to be removed to
make way for large dams required for irrigation schemes. Yet very rarely is
resistance co-ordinated, cohesive and long-lasting, rather it resolves into a
stubborn lack of interest.

Peasant farmers do not perceive the advantage of complying with schemes which incorporate them into national objectives and markets from which experience tells them they have little to gain. Also, the penetration of agricultural production by state capital can lead to increased economic differentation and like many 'green revolutions' works in the favour of the already better-off farmers or urban entrepreneurs, rather than for the bulk of the peasantry for whose interests the schemes are supposedly designed. It is also necessary to consider the continuing access of peasants to farm land through traditional systems of landuse, land rights, or inheritance, together with labour-intensive farming systems and the production relationships which characterize them. Many schemes misunderstand the nature of the production process and the relations of production, so much so, that resistance and poor performance are almost inevitable. For example, in northern Nigeria large-scale modern irrigation schemes, which in essence are designed for operation by capitalist or state wage labour under strict managerial controls, have been constructed to accommodate thousands of farming households who initially have been allowed to retain some control over their labour and land, although the latter has been reorganized and consolidated to facilitate irrigation. The inherent contradictions in this situation, together with the ability of some households to succeed, often at the expense of others, has created class distinctions and changed social and political relations. It is for these reasons that arguments about relations of production, economic differentiation, systems of land-holding and property relations between peasants and small commodity producers and migrant labour are not just academic issues, but have a direct relevance to the attempts to restructure rural communities.

Why then do African states persist in their attempts to transform the agricultural sector, pursuing policies which have a history of failure, or limited success? In the view of Hart (1982), what appears parlous by standards of economic efficiency or public welfare is very rational in the context of the institutional and material requirements of emergent states. In the wake of independence, modern African states were naturally keen to correct the shortcomings of colonial rule and political and ideological goals were foremost in the minds of the cadres of graduates who formulated and administered policies. But their expectations frequently exceeded the revenues available. As we have seen in the previous chapter, colonial administrations had not been overly ambitious in the development of physical or administrative infrastructures, other than to facilitate the growth of exports, and the development of transport networks had been secured cheaply by using varying amounts of direct or indirect forced labour. Nor were government institutions, except in Kenya and the Rhodesias, developed to serve advanced capitalist production. Now all states have a pressing need for liquid resources to continue and expand their functions, which means raising revenues from as wide a base as possible.

Both colonial and independent governments were faced with limited options for raising sufficient revenue. The taxation of peasant farmers and petty producers yields small returns, given the difficulties of administration, while direct taxes are impractical. Import and export duties are frequently avoided by smugglers and border traders and the expatriate companies, are often given long 'tax-free holidays' to encourage investment in the first place. Under these conditions emergent states have had recourse to milking the funds of the co-operatives, seeking foreign aid and suppliers' credits, or of floating their own currencies and financing public debt by the printing of money. When these circumstances are set within the context of the terms of trade, increased food imports and rising world oil prices, the urge to intervene and transform the most basic sector of the economy, agriculture, is overwhelming. The aim of grand rural development schemes is not efficiency, but gross controllable output, which at least yields some surplus and income for the state to offset balance of payments deficits, even if overall agricultural performance is worse than peasant production (Hart, 1982).

On the other hand, rural development schemes also serve the interests of the indigenous bourgeoisie – an alliance of politicians, bureaucrats, merchants, traditional rulers and capitalist farmers. Such schemes are the means whereby members of this 'alliance' accumulate land and capital, consolidating their positions and extending their influence. A number of writers have suggested that the crucial and tantalizing issue is whether this situation will really lead to a progressive deepening of capitalist relations as production investment occurs or whether it will encourage merely parasitic accumulation (see Lubeck, 1987).

SUMMARY

The state as initiator and manager of economic change is well-established in tropical Africa. Because the colonial powers were dealing with unfamiliar situations and they wanted to meet certain metropolitan interests, they were led into attempts to adapt or change rural structures. These attempts in many ways were in advance of state intervention and planning in the metropoles, although by the depression years of the 1930s the intellectual and political climate had changed in Europe and America. After World War II policies developed in Britain and America were transferred to African colonies, where the objectives were to stimulate industrial growth and raise levels of saving investment.

As faith in these strategies declined, the emphasis was shifted towards rural-led development schemes, while newly-independent African countries became aware of the alternatives offered by socialism and radical programmes of national reconstruction. Therefore the penetration of agriculture by the state has taken a variety of forms and has been based on different theories and ideological premises. Both state capitalism and state socialism have faced similar problems, in as much as they have to deal with a multitude of domestic groups shaped by age, sex and kin, which have been drawn into small commodity production, and who are not willing or able to embrace national plans and objectives. Hyden (1980) has referred to an 'uncaptured peasantry' who have too many 'exit options', compared with the majority of those living in modern capitalist and socialist states who have little choice in offering their labour to entrepreneurs or state managers.

It will have been evident from the argument in the last two chapters that without the opposition of a strong merchant landowning class, states, either socialist or capitalist, have been free to initiate as many new policies as they wish. But with minimum control over the rural economy, they have less power to make these policies adhere in such a way as to lead to benefits for rural populations. It can be argued that peasants were, and are, captured by the state through commodity marketing boards and the need to produce to meet tax payments and other expenditures but the impact is uneven. The attraction of schemes is that the state or its agents has control over the means of production. But it is often at a cost to those who live in scheme areas. For example, in northern Nigeria, those who have lost land to irrigation schemes or who are unable to continue farming within them have few options other than joining the landless, the land poor or the unemployed. For all these reasons, the drift towards urban migration and the situation identified at the bottom of the taxonomic model in our first chapter (figure 1.1) seems depressingly inevitable, even in areas where population densities are high. The ecological impact of such a drift in environments which are fragile is incalculable. Yet despite the resilience of African farming systems in many areas, their inability to rapidly increase surplus production to feed urban populations remains. In our final chapter we explore the contribution of European and American scholarship to interpreting all these processes and proposing strategies for rural development.

9

Development and Underdevelopment: Theories, Explanations and Strategies

INTRODUCTION

The explanations and interpretations of the commoditization of African agriculture over the past 150 years are often contradictory and have a certain geographical and historic specificity. There are those who see the colonial experience and European intervention as the means whereby rural Africans were drawn into a larger international trading economy, which brought positive advantages. There are those who see European merchant and industrial capital protected by colonial rule as a means of incorporating Africans into the world capitalist economy, thereby pushing them into a subordinate and marginalized position of underdevelopment from which the only escape is radical political and social restructuring. The first of these perspectives is associated with what is known as the *vent for surplus* theory, which sees economic change, especially the cashcrop revolution, as being part of the response from indigenous farmers to new market opportunities. The second is associated with radical or Marxian interpretations of the transformation and, indeed, for some, the evisceration of African economies.

VENT FOR SURPLUS

The *vent for surplus* model of international trade has been principally associated with Myint (1971), although its origins may be seen as far back as Adam Smith and the development of *laissez-faire* capitalism. This model attempts to explain the processes of export crop development in Third World countries as the interplay of the indigenous domestic economy and the forces introduced by foreign trade. The theory's concern with domestic economy is a recognition of the significant contribution to world trade made by small-scale producers in those areas which are outside the mining plantation and agribusiness sector. Myint believed that prior to the inclusion of tropical Africa in international trade, there was substantial underemployment of land and labour in the area and international trade eventually provided the opening or 'vent' for this surplus in the form of export crops.

The theory can be expressed as a standard partial equilibrium model, where cost differences of goods arise between areas of high demand and low (or non-existent) supply, and those of low demand and high supply. This gives rise to a price differential allowing trade to take place, always providing the costs of transport do not exceed the differential. A major role of international trade is the provision of an effective demand for export commodities and it is this demand which activates unused or surplus resources. Improvements in transport may make such trade possible, or improvements in transport may be stimulated by the onset of trade. Furthermore, producers are encouraged to enter the export market by the increased opportunity to spend earnings on imported foreign-manufactured goods which become more readily available, thus creating the incentive for increased effort.

Myint's elaboration of *vent for surplus* has had a wide appeal for many authors wishing to explain the mechanics of the expansion of export crops in Africa, especially as it emphasizes the response of small-scale producers who are the source of significant proportions of the world's cocoa, cotton, coffee and groundnuts (see Szeresewski, 1965; Helleiner, 1966; Hopkins, 1973; Hogendorn, 1977). The appeal of *vent for surplus* has diminished since the 1970s and has been attacked by both radical and neo-classical writers. However, it still has some resonance with current IMF and World Bank initiatives. The IMF conditions for development financing stress lower levels of public spending, balancing the books and open-door trading regimes. The implication is less state intervention in agriculture, the free play of market forces and a return to an agriculture which is export-led through the production of crops for which there is an effective international demand. To this end, aid financing assists in particular projects such as rural feeder roads which facilitate the evacuation of crops and reduces locally high costs of transport. These prescriptions are contained in what is popularly known as the Berg Report (World Bank, 1981).

The *vent for surplus* theory rests on three major assumptions about the areas of cashcrop production. First, that the increase in the volume of exports has occurred without a corresponding increase in population. Second, the expansion of new export crops was achieved without a corresponding reduction in time spent on the production of goods and services in the domestic economy. Third, export crops were expanded without the introduction of new agricultural technology. From these assumptions it follows that export expansion was managed by the increased use of the remaining factors of production, land and labour, which had hitherto been underemployed. In this situation the economics of labour-use have to be related to areas with differing population densities. Underemployment may occur in over-populated parts of the world because insufficient land is available, or in areas of low population density and surplus land because there is a lack of effective demand for its potential output. It is little use in producing goods for which there is no market, and in the African case, where population densities are generally low, it is argued that it required the stimulus of external demand. New crops became substituted for leisure as Africans chose to improve their incomes by earning cash to buy imported goods. According to the *vent for surplus* theory, the risks of becoming involved in export crop production are negligible because farmers are using or 'venting' both surplus land and surplus labour, so that there is not a shift of resources from domestic food production. However, Myint did allow that as export cropping developed farmers might begin to specialize and to rely increasingly on other farmers for food supplies.

The *vent for surplus* theory puts much emphasis on population and land ratios and, in the African case, labour not land is clearly identified as the major internal constraint on production. But it is precisely on the issue of population and labour supply that Myint's thesis has notable shortcomings. The cultivation of export crops may have taken place in areas of relatively low population density (although it is always difficult to arrive at limits and thresholds for such parameters,) but the mobility of labour was of the essence. The Senegambian groundnut trade is a good example of how from its very inception in the 1830s there was heavy reliance upon seasonal migrant labourers who came from the interior (Swindell, 1979). Crops such as groundnuts and cotton are grown and harvested during the wet season and their cultivation cycle parallels that of foodstaples. Much of African agriculture is subject to a seasonal regime in which rainfall or the lack of it are the crucial variables. In the absence of irrigation, farming is limited to the wet season and even within this limited cultivation cycle there are short-term peak demands for labour, especially for weeding and harvesting. As we observe in chapter 2, it is not simply the stock of labour, as Myint implies, but the flow of labour which is also of crucial importance. In order to fill this gap farmers have increasingly sought to recruit casual employees. The use of migrant labour, drawn from large catchment areas has been critical in the development and continued production of many export crops, such as groundnuts, cocoa and cotton. Because of the seasonality of African farming, short-term labour peaks are common and if they cannot be resolved they become a severe constraint (see chapter 2).

For this reason Tosh, (1980) has suggested that in the savanna areas, where these crops are grown, the problem of resource allocation is much more severe than for the forest areas where tree crops such as cocoa, coffee, rubber and palm can be integrated more easily with foodstaples (see figure 1.1, chapter 1), especially as they are harvested in the dry season. In fact, even here, much depends on the mixture and types of food and non-food crops. However, competition can be just as problematic within forest agriculture. The changes in the allocation of labour, the division of labour and work patterns (chapter 2) in one sense represent a technical 'revolution', albeit one not involving machinery. In other words we would argue that the factors relating to the organization and supply of labour are misconstrued by the *vent for surplus* theory, even for those areas where it seems to provide a generally satisfactory causal framework. Other misconceptions arise over the role of entrepreneurial ability and capital accumulation in the process of agricultural development.

Expatriate capital may or may not have been necessary depending on circumstance, but as the Ghanian cocoa industry and the groundnut industries of northern Nigeria show, systems of group co-operation developed from past economic experience and capital accumulated from previous economic activities were of considerable importance (Hopkins, 1973).

Many authors broadly sympathetic to the *vent for surplus* theory have nonetheless drawn attention to its limitations, but there is also a body of opinion which rejects its explanations of how African farmers were incorporated into world trade, because they believe its limitations are more fundamental. Opponents of *vent for surplus* have argued that the development of export crops was not 'costless' and that a severe distortion of African economies occurred, autonomous development was hindered and economic dependency increased. (Freund and Shenton, 1977). The spread of export crop production is here seen as part of a structural reorientation of African economies set within the context of the world capitalist system first dominated by Western European colonialism and subsequently by the neo-colonial behaviour of the US. *Vent for surplus* inadequately explains the mechanics of export growth in the nineteenth century, neither does it account for the failure of African countries to achieve sustained economic growth in the twentieth century. It is for these reasons that opponents of *vent for surplus* and classical international trade theory have sought to emphasize political economy and Marxian principles in an attempt to understand the relationship between capitalism and underdevelopment in Africa. Here we shall identify and discuss first the neo-Marxist paradigms of *dependency theory* and second the structuralist theses of the *articulation of modes of production*. The former emphasizes relations of exchange, while the latter is set within classical Marxist theories of production relations and the labour process.

DEPENDENCY THEORY

The most comprehensive statement of links between developed and under-developed countries comes from analyses of Latin American economies, notably those of Gunder Frank (1971), although his work has several precursors such as Baran (1957). But as Kitching (1982) points out, whatever the origins of dependency theory, and whatever kind of scenarios its adherents draw, the central concern is one of pessimism about capitalist development. They are concerned with the blocking of the transition to capitalist relations of production in Third World countries, which results in either a distortion of pre-capitalist economies, or their evisceration. The key to this 'blocking' lies in the dependent nature of peripheral capitalism, which is linked to, and controlled by, the domination of international capital by the United States and west European countries. In effect, they see Third World economies as playing a subordinate, or marginalized role in world capitalism. (Goodman and Redcliffe, 1981).

Dependency theorists are particularly concerned with the non-dynamic and non-progressive nature of Third World economies, which they see as being located on the periphery of capitalist systems of production and exchange. Furthermore, because many parts of the Third World are ex-colonies, foreign domination and dependency have been associated with imperialism, and underdevelopment is seen as having a necessary part in the development of capitalism in Europe. Yet dependency theorists break with the classical interpretations of Marx, Lenin and Luxemburg, in the belief that capitalism is arrested and will not develop further in peripheral areas. Marx believed that capitalism would be destructive and exploitative in the short run, but the destruction of pre-capitalist formations was a necessary part of the historical progression to capitalism and eventually socialism. Dependency theorists reject equally the progressivist thesis of classical Marxism and the possibility of 'take-off into self-sustaining growth' advocated by modernization theory and *vent for surplus* ideas.

Under this radical scheme there are two important questions associated with imperialism and the colonial experience of Third World countries: first, to what extent is present poverty due to the policies of the colonial powers and second, how far did industrialization in Britain and other European countries depend on the creation and maintenance of surpluses from their colonies?

Kitching (1982) gives a good resumé of the chief tenets of dependency theory, as developed for Latin America, which are identified as follows. First, the contention that the ruling classes in Latin America, unlike the bourgeoisie of Western Europe, have little interest in industrializing the economy because they enjoy their wealth and status by performing a managerial role for international capital and multi-national companies. As the state depends on the support of the ruling classes, it protects their interests by minimizing the constraints on multi-national capital. The reinforcement and reproduction of the ruling classes depends on their ties with international capital and on the state ensuring the interests of both parties. Second, the ruling classes are usually landowners, but as their real interests lie elsewhere they normally view agriculture as being stagnant, technically backward and unable to provide surpluses on a sufficient scale to allow for capital accumulation and industrial investment. For the most part, the organization of agriculture is feudalistic and, where it exists alongside plantation and commercialized agriculture, remains untransformed. It is also contended that much of Latin America's industry is capital intensive and unable to provide much employment, as well as being geared towards the production of consumer goods bought by the privileged such as urban dwellers. This underwrites the disparities between rich and poor, urban and rural and formal and informal sector workers. These ideas are of less relevance in tropical Africa, because of the low level of industrial development, though the germs of such processes might be discerned in those areas where urbanization is progressing most rapidly.

An important issue for dependency theorists is the transfer of surpluses from Third World countries by international capital. The principal mechanism whereby this transfer takes place is through persistently negative terms of trade which obtain in international markets to the detriment of local producers, especially of export crops. Other means of transfer are the repatriation of profits, management fees and the over-invoicing of imported goods. Also, amortization and interest payments on loans contracted in international capital markets move surpluses out of underdeveloped countries. All these mechanisms reduce the available surplus for investment to a level below what it might be. This creates a theoretical distinction between the 'actual' surplus and the 'potential' surplus (Baran, 1957). Moreover, in underdeveloped countries there are important spatial inequalities between regions and between urban and rural areas, which produces inequalities in incomes and 'price-twists'. The theme of spatial inequality has been developed by Lipton (1977) who believed that an important cause of poverty lay in the urban–rural dichotomy and a prevailing bias in favour of urban dwellers and consumers. Though this argument fails to take full account of the mobility of labour and the significance of urban–rural remittances, there are areas of Africa (as in the case of Zambia outlined in the previous chapter) where the urban–rural divide has grown deeper despite both these counteractive forces.

Dependency theory has also been applied to Africa, notably by Rodney (1972) and Amin (1976). It is suggested that in Africa, European capitalism penetrated the continent from the time of the slave trade onwards and external exchange relations have distorted indigenous economies by encouraging those sectors such as agricultural exports, which best served the interest of foreign demand. As a result surplus value has been transferred to the metropoles from the periphery, a process which was reinforced by colonialism and has continued afterwards by the co-operation between national bourgeoisie and multi-national corporations. International trade has become a 'zero-sum game' the gains of one player (the metropoles) are the losses of the other (the periphery). Thus international trade has done nothing to help industrialization, rather it has caused local economies to atrophy and locks them into a dependent role *vis à vis* the advanced capitalist industrialized countries of the North.

A common theme of all dependency writing is the rapid penetration of pre-capitalist relations of production and their incorporation into the world capitalist economy, which condemns them to a subordinate position in the international system. But it should also be noted that unlike orthodox Marxian theory, dependency writers such as Frank (1971) and Wallerstein (1974), believe that the capitalist transformation of peripheral areas is now complete, while Amin (1976) sees peripheral capitalism as a historically specific thing in itself and a necessary part of the establishment of capitalist systems in the developed world (Goodman and Redcliffe 1981). In this more pessimistic view, peripheral countries are not experiencing just a temporary blocking in their transition to economic development, they are rather permanently condemned to structural underdevelopment through their subordinate role in the world capitalist system.

Dependency theory in general, and its application to Africa in particular, has come under strong fire from both Marxists and non-Marxists alike. Kitching (1982) points out that if one attempts to assess the damage done to a colony's economic development, or the extent to which industrialization of an imperialist power was due to exploitation of its colonies, you face a formidable problem of logic and method. In order to develop the dependency position one has to know what would have happened if circumstances had been other than they were. What would have been the form and speed of, say, Africa's development if it had not been conquered by European powers? How would its agriculture have developed without the export of commodities such as cocoa and groundnuts? Once this realm of alternatives is entered, all kinds of possibilities emerge which are contingent upon the assumptions one makes. One cannot have a re-run of history to test out different scenarios. One solution is to try to indicate the actual constraints which were due to colonial or foreign control. There are clear indications that most applied quotas and taxes and the failure of colonial governments to protect indigenous industry and land rights were of crucial significance in many colonies, not only those of white settlement. It was these kinds of arguments which were advanced by nationalists demanding independence, but when independence was achieved new sets of impediments had to be identified and as Kitching argues, it was under these conditions that theories of dependency and neo-colonialism emerged.

Dependency is a model based on comparative statistics which involves problems of orders of magnitude, categories and cut-off points. Can we compare advanced capitalist countries now with underdeveloped ones, without recognizing that the former have not always been developed? Yet equally can we compare nineteenth-century Britain and present-day under-developed countries? Also, many modern industrial states of today once had considerable degrees of dependency. For example Norway, Sweden and Finland supplied agricultural produce to advanced European countries, while in 1980 American capital owned 50 per cent of Canadian industry. Dependency theory is often weak on the periodization of change and the processes of change and does not recognize sufficiently that capitalist Europe has a long history of discontinuities and contradictions in its development.

But it is the emphasis dependency writers place on the relations of exchange rather than production, which have led many Marxists to attack the dependency paradigm as representing a break with orthodox ideas of imperialism. Whereas Frank believes that it was capitalism which pen-etrated Latin America from the sixteenth century onwards, Amin (1976) sees both dependency and capitalism as beginning with the slave trade and ending with the establishment of colonial rule. Such a stance is clearly at odds with the progressivist notion of pre-capitalist societies in the Third World being slowly transformed through the emergence of an indigenous bourgeoisie. But within the neo-Marxist dependency school there exists rival claims; new dependency theorists such as Cardoso (1979) have argued that it is inevitable that international trade brings wealth in its wake, and some underdeveloped countries have experienced dependent, or limited development through limited industrialization sponsored by multi-national corporations. It is thus incorrect to see uneven development as no develop-ment.

But the core of the disagreement between more orthodox Marxists and dependency theorists lies in their respective interpretations of capitalism. Dependency writers lay great emphasis on the relations of exhange and this particular issue forms an important element in Brenner's critique of Frank and Wallerstein. Brenner (1977) agrees that capitalism is a system in which production for profit via exchange is dominant, but this does not mean that the opposite holds true. Production for the market does not necessarily in itself signal the existence of capitalism. Production for exchange is quite compatible with a system where it is either impossible or unnecessary to reinvest in expanded or improved production in order to profit. However, production for profit via exchange will have the systematic effect of ac-cumulation and the development of productive resources only when certain specific relations of production obtain, namely a situation where free wage labour occurs and where labour power is a commodity. It is when labour power is effectively separated from the means of production and when labour is 'free' of direct dominations such as serfdom or slavery, that both capital and labour can be combined at the highest possible levels of technology. Such a combination must not only be feasible, but desirable. Therefore, the origins of capitalist economic development *vis à vis* pre-capitalist modes of production lies in the origins of property, labour extraction, systems of free wage labour, which is part of a historical process whereby labour power and the means of production become capitalist.

One of the problems of dependency is that it is so concerned with the dominance of the centre, it fails to take adequate account of the continuing dynamism of the periphery. Hopkins (1975) suggests that dependency theory is not so much an explanation, but a signpost and that what really is required is a theory of interdependence which will leave scope for a variety of outcomes. However, to attack dependency theory is not to deny that there exists a set adverse circumstances under which Third World countries operate within the international trading system, or that it is biased in favour of the advanced industrial nations of the West. The rising price of oil and petroleum products into the 1970s, the collapse of many commodity prices, spiralling interest rates and the problems of financing debt in the 1980s bear witness to the problems of Third World countries. Indeed one of the shortcomings of the Berg Report (World Bank, 1981) was that its data base did not capture the worst crisis in the global economy since the Great Depression. The collapse in the terms of trade for African countries since 1978 has been dramatic, for example, deterioration of the order of 27 per cent for Ethiopia, 36 per cent for Ghana and 30 per cent for Ivory Coast.

Concern with the external effects of the world trading economy without a full espousal of dependency theory has led some to make a distinction between 'dependency theorists' and 'dependency worriers'. The latter urge a concern which embraces the introduction of reforms to minimize the effects of dependency, such as tougher policies towards multi-national corporations, heavy industrialization, diversification of export structures and a new international economic order brought about by negotiations between the 'north' and the 'south'. But for dependency theorists on the other hand, this is not a tenable position; it is impossible for real Third World development to occur within the capitalist world systems. For them revolution and socialism are the only alternatives to continued stagnation and poverty.

ARTICULATION OF MODES OF PRODUCTION

Like dependency theory, articulation of modes of production is a rejection of *vent for surplus* and modernization theory. It attempts to address the question of why the transition to capitalist relations has not occurred in Third World countries. Unlike dependency theory it is concerned with production relationships rather than those characterized by exchange. During the 1960s African studies were much concerned with the politics of chieftaincy and the development of elites, but gradually there has been a shift towards consideration of the rural sector and the organization of domestic production. This has been undertaken by both neo-classical and Marxist writers, the former for more pragmatic reasons, the latter for theoretical ones. The literature of the 1960s has a valuable body of household budget surveys and farming systems surveys, which has increased our knowledge of the rural sector, especially agriculture. Another important landmark was the reinterpretation of economic anthropology by the French Marxist anthropologists of the 1960s, (see Kahn and Llobera, 1981) who sought to focus attention on the analysis of pre-capitalist societies in Africa and their modes of production and reproduction.

The concept of modes of production has led to a whole literature attempting to characterize the modes, or mode, of production which best fits African pre-capitalist societies. Thus we have the lineage mode of production, the slave mode of production, the exchange mode of production, while the more familiar Asiatic and peasant modes are also contenders for the role. A 'mode of production' is generally taken to comprise two elements; the forces of production (land, labour, tools, raw materials) and the social relations of production (that is, the patterns of co-operation) involving patterns of worker co-operation in production and of the people involved in the exploitation of these forces, together with sharing of the product. The problem is that while Marx outlined a process of successive modes of production which led up to the capitalist mode, he was less explicitly concerned with the details of these transitional phases than in the working of capitalism itself. It was this that formed the core of his major work. Indeed, Marx never really considered the possibility of a combination of modes, nor the possible effects of the penetration of non-capitalist modes by different forms of capitalism and the likely effects these would have on indigenous modes of production and reproduction. Following this line of argument we arrive at the conclusion that underdeveloped countries comprise social formations which are in the process of change from non-capitalist modes, but are characterized by the *articulation* (linkage) of both non-capitalist and capitalist modes. Non-capitalist and capitalist modes of production can be seen to exist in parallel but are articulated in mutually reinforcing modes. This conjunction has arrested transition from one mode to the other. It is contended that this re-working of Marxist principles produces a richer and more subtle analysis of the Third World situations than Marx's early writings, which predict the destruction of peasantries under the progressive forces of capitalism by means of imperialism.

The articulation approach has been used in the interpretation of African agrarian structures and is particularly associated with Meillassoux (1964,

1972), Terray (1972) and Rey (1971, 1973). Rey (1973) argues that the transition to capitalism is delayed because the reproduction of each mode of production (pre-capitalist and capitalist) is dependent on the reproduction of the other. The productive and reproductive needs of metropolitan merchant capital may be met by pre-capitalist societies and such interaction through exchange strengthens rather than, as Frank would have it, dissolves the pre-capitalist mode. In such circumstances capitalist relations of production have to be installed by force and that is what colonialism was trying to do. Much of Rey's theory is worked out in his analysis of the transformation of a lineage 'mode of production' in Congo-Brazzaville, where he believes that by the 1930s a proto-capitalist mode was established. So ultimately, even in agriculture, pre-capitalist modes disappear.

The notion that the preservation of pre-capitalist society can be of direct interest to metropolitan capital has been put forward by Meillassoux (1972)and Wolpe (1980). The argument runs on the lines that under certain conditions articulation is structured so that the maintenance of non-capitalist modes acts as a reservoir of cheap labour for the capitalist sectors of the economy. For example, with migrant labour, part of the long-term cost of reproduction is born by the non-capitalist sectors, that is the domestic economy to which migrants return, while the wage paid by employers is correspondingly lower. Meillassoux regards the long-term reproduction costs of workers employed in the capitalist sector as surplus labour extracted from the domestic economy and forms a 'rent'. Therefore, the maintenance of the domestic sector and household production of export crops can be advantageous for capitalists and allows primitive accumulation to be a continuing process in the modern sector. Marx's notion of primitive accumulation outlines the establishment of capitalism through the transformation of relations of production on the land, the disappearance of the peasantry and emergence of a property-less class of wage labourers. Articulation theory proposes that this process is taking place without a unilinear transition from non-capitalist to capitalist modes of production.

QUALIFICATIONS AND CRITIQUES OF RADICAL THEORIES OF
UNDERDEVELOPMENT

Articulation theory replaces a linear scheme of change by a multiple one and argues that capitalism maintains non-capitalist modes as a necessary part of its own reproduction, especially by the provision of cheap labour. This contention is unacceptable to many observers as it seems to represent a voluntarist conception of capitalism, which downplays class struggle and conflict. It is also true that proponents of modes of production analysis have been uneasy about how to relate the economic base to class structure, political institutions and religion (superstructure). Likewise, there is some uncertainty about appropriate units of analysis – individual units, regional units etc. There is also disagreement about how to conceptualize modes of production and processes of reproduction, especially when non-capitalist and capitalist modes are linked. If, as articulation theory suggests, there is a co-existence, with capitalism as the dominant mode, then contrary to formal appearances, are non-capitalist modes really separate or are they in essence capitalist? Perhaps they are non-capitalist laws, because capitalism has eroded or destroyed the conditions for the reproduction of other modes. If this is so then it renders articulation redundant. As Goodman and Redcliffe (1979) have observed, the crucial question is, does capitalism need an articulation of modes? It is not necessary, they argue, to secure external markets, raw materials or labour to provide a permanent and universally necessary condition for the expanded reproduction of capitalism. Rather it can be explained by the contingencies of historical circumstance. The conditions mistakenly regarded as universally necessary relate not to capital as a whole, but to individual capitals, or branches of capital at particular times. Articulations with capitalism and individual capitals will be determined by the internal conditions these modes exhibit. In other words, the specificities displayed in these encounters by both 'capitalism' and 'non-capitalism' explains the particular structures and processes of social transformation found in peripheral social formations. Thus historical contingency avoids necessity and the monolithic species of capitalism and it is not a general universal necessity for capitalism either to destroy or to maintain non-capitalist modes of production for its expanded reproduction. The task is to discover and analyse the historical conditions which lead to either destruction or maintenance in particular cases. But it can be argued that articulation, shorn of its more theoretical trappings, can be a heuristically valuable concept for explaining a number of complex interactions in Africa (Lubeck, 1986).

Since the mid-1970s there have been a number of radical analyses of underdevelopment which have looked for a less deterministic Marxism (for an overview see Corbridge, 1986). For example, dependency writers such as Cardoso believe there is diversity as well as unity in capitalist-associated development and that the logic and demands of the world economy are in a state of continuous reconstruction. Decolonization, the post-war rise of the US, the power of the Soviet bloc and the influence of multi-national capital provide a constantly shifting scenario of world capitalism and socialism. Writing of northern Nigeria in the early twentieth century, Shenton (1986) points to the complex conflict of different kinds of capital: (merchant, industrial, local, international) interacting with the interest of the local Muslim aristocracy and the British administrators. Similarly, British policy on land tenure initially slowed the development of a land market to facilitate merchant capital and the interests of indigenous rulers (Watts and Shenton, 1984). These arguments reflect Kay's thesis that capitalism created underdevelopment not because it exploited the underdeveloped world, but because it did not exploit it enough (Kay, 1975). There are also ethnic groupings and classes which may either resist or comply with external forces. There are different indigenous ideologies which attempted to cope with the imperial and post-colonial challenge and there is now an acceptance that given the external forces of international capitalism, there is room for some autonomy of Third World states and the development of an indigenous capitalism. We must add to this matrix resistance from peasants and small commodity producers, the conflict between men and women in identifying new roles for themselves and the different interests of young and old. Asymmetries of power and wealth in specific historic and regional circumstances are part of the process of change.

In East and Southern Africa the disengagement from colonialism has been particularly violent and long drawn out and the various freedom struggles and their aftermath are crucial to the kind of agrarian transformation these countries are witnessing. Yet as Ranger (1986) points out, comparisons may be superficially attractive, but less than useful. While it is fashionable to compare Zimbabwe with Kenya on the one hand and Mozambique on the other, in terms of the direction that country may take (the reinforcement of a black bourgeoisie or the grass-roots mobilization of the peasantry) it is absurd to select either model for Zimbabwe. Ranger is not against comparisons, but he is hostile to the free-floating type which is unanchored in historical reality. What is needed in Zimbabwe, he argues, is an understanding of the traditions of and changes to the peasantry itself, and the role of the whites in the development of the country.

Corbridge (1986) also urges the need to make allowances for different resource endowments and climatic variations; such conditions of existence cannot be ignored or assumed. Likewise, although different levels of population and rates of growth have their origins in changing relations of production, they still may have a feedback into the economy and society which is also part of the conditions of existence. There is nothing *inherent* in the concept of capitalism he argues which decrees there must be high population densities in the peripheries to secure a cheap labour force or for that matter which preclude industrialization.

A number of writers, notably Kitching (1980), have argued for the dismantling of 'grand theories' into lower level concepts which have thereby a greater generality and specificity. For example, Kitching disclaims the usefulness of mode of production analyses, articulation of modes and class theory in African situations and favours lower order concepts such as mode of appropriation of surplus labour, mode of appropriation of nature, division of labour and circulation (of commodities and money), which are more applicable to any historical situation where commodity production occurs. In tropical Africa, production relations are varied and flexible and categories such as 'pre-capitalist', 'peasant' and 'proletarian' need handling with some care. Perhaps it is better to talk about 'capitalizing' and 'proletarianizing', terms which stress the process of change. As Sender and Smith (1986) point out, Marx stressed the extremely long period required in all areas of Europe for the decisive establishment of capitalist social relations. And (after Lenin) capitalism at a low level of development does not require the complete separation of workers from the land.

But as we noted in the introduction, while largely non-indigenous scholars theorize about the nature of underdevelopment, African rural populations face both real and potential economic and ecological crises which demand immediate action. Either as a matter of political necessity or on humanitarian grounds African governments, in conjunction with external agencies, must formulate policies and strategies to alleviate rural deprivation. And whether such interventions fail or succeed, and whether they are accepted or rejected, they nonetheless contribute to the process of rural change.

In chapter 8 we identified the differences in perspective which were the catalyst for change in rural Africa in the period before and during colonial rule. We wrote of the tensions between exploitation and greed on the one hand and benign if paternalistic strategies for improvement on the other, we also explored some of the differences between African and European perceptions of value. In the post-colonial period various forms of intervention and control, and purposive, structural and technical innovation have continued to be part of the policy of independent states and a body of theory has grown up around these changes. But it must be emphasized that planning theory and practice, for all its benign intentions, has about it the same tensions between endogenous and exogenous perceptions of value that were a feature of the colonial period.

Although the apparent objectives of both the planners and African policy makers have been to improve the lot of all farmers, out of this mix of interventionist perceptions and inputs, state planning policies and peasant attitudes and behaviour, there has been a persistent tendency to exaggerate differences of wealth and opportunity. It is a process which most rural Africans understand only too well. In effect, many rural development and aid policies are still seen as essentially paternalistic and their moral concern frequently rooted in protecting and advancing national and international interests whether of socialism or capitalism. They represent something done to rural Africans by outsiders even if the outsiders include members of the African urban elite as well as foreigners. As we have seen most farmers and rural communities have had some colonial or post-colonial experience of the direct or indirect effects of mechanization schemes, irrigation projects, planned resettlement, marketing boards, integrated rural development projects and the effects of IMF prescriptions. It is therefore not surprising that in the past response to intervention from rural communities has varied from slow or partial acceptance through indifference to subversion, corruption and outright resistance, especially when whole ways of life seem threatened by major transformations, or where the opportunities for diverting public funds into private accumulation are too tempting. In this context, it is worth remembering that the ideal of accountability and disinterested public service were the product of at least a century of ethical transformation in West European countries and that African attitudes to the activities of those who held power were formed from an African experience of clientship and patronage which were often reinforced by colonial policies and behaviour.

PRESCRIPTIONS FOR CHANGE AND DEVELOPMENT

In the remainder of this chapter we shall concentrate first on the thinking that conditioned the sytle of external intervention, the background to state intervention and the growth of development theory. We shall then attempt to present an African perspective of this process by examining the ways in which, through their rural development plans, new states responded to these theoretical imperatives and alternatives and out of sheer political necessity sometimes substituted ones of their own. These priorities are expressed in the spatial allocation of aid and the unequal effects of schemes and other initiatives. Here we must distinguish between the different priorities of post-colonial settler states: between those which had a narrow colonial economy and those which inherited a broader base; those with and without the immediate problem of land reform; and those which have a semi-politicized peasantry following a freedom struggle and those which do not.

The origins and growth of development planning theory are to be found in the Great Depression of the 1930s which proved such an unnerving experience for Western Europe and North America. In the nineteenth century, economic liberalism and free trade were seen as prerequisites for the wealth of nations, a doctrine which was convenient to British industry and its domination of manufacturing and trade. But in the 1930s Western capitalism was in crisis and there was a shift towards protectionism and restrictionism. In addition to economic depression in America and the West, there was the rise of Bolshevism in Russia and the emergence of the planned economy, which was being canvassed as an alternative to *laissez-faire* capitalism. It was the particular genius of John Maynard Keynes which plotted a middle course through *laissez-faire* and authoritarian intervention, as the equilibrium theory of economists such as Walras and Marshall were overhauled and the deficiencies of perfect competition and market forces exposed. Depression equilibrium appeared to be no substitute for growth. Keynes advocated deficit financing and the multiplier effect of public spending as the way out of unemployment and unused resources, which were providing a fertile ground for radical alternatives. The consequence of such policies was an increase in government intervention in the economy.

World War II provided a much-needed boost to the industries of Western Europe, but it also set in train new precedents. The US emergend as a dominant world force, strengthened by its role in the post-war economy of the West and became increasingly anxious about the power of the Soviet Union and revolutionary socialist movements in the underdeveloped countries of Asia, Latin America and Africa. In Europe, Marshall Plan aid was a vital ingredient in the recovery of Britain and other European nations and the rapid growth achieved gave legitimacy to the concept of intervention. But US assistance was also conceived as a means of deflecting the spread of communism in Western Europe and eventually a similar concern was shown for the Third World. The US was well aware of the weakening hold of the colonial powers on their possessions, and how newly-independent countries could drift into the Soviet bloc. Also, both the US and Western Europe were concerned about the general patterns and control of world resources and the need for access to basic minerals such as iron ore, which had been severely depleted as a result of the war effort and which were under pressure again with the commencement of the Korean War. The US had basically two strategies for economic intervention, finance and trade, which made use of loans, investment, trade agreements and credits and technical assistance.

The interest in the possibilities of economic intervention were not solely confined to the US. The British and French, whose empires were still considerable, also embarked upon development schemes. The success of government intervention in the United Kingdom, especially in agriculture, combined with the return of a socialist government, provided a suitable climate for economic intervention in Africa through schemes of mechanization and irrigation, which took some of their inspiration from the success of the Gezeira cotton growing project in the Sudan which was started in the 1920s, rather than the disaster of the Groundnut scheme (see p. 146) in the 1940s. Furthermore, just as they had been expected to contribute to the war effort, so raw materials and crop exports were required to assist the post-war recovery of Britain. The British were also interested in the launching of financial initiatives to smooth deficits and eventually this led to the creation of the IMF.

The post-war posture of the US, the success of its aid policies in Europe, combined with the push towards decolonization, led to a situation where economists and politicians made common cause; the former because of the shift in theory after Keynes and the latter because the new economic orthodoxy fitted with their perceptions of the post-war world and the balance of powers. Also, there was an associated convergence of technological and political rationality, as science was to be the instrument of change. The legitimization of economic planning and intervention in the West was based on certain premises; assumptions were made about what it was that had to be changed, that it would respond to change in a predictable fashion and that intervention was to be accomplished according to a clear set of expectations. It was an essentially positivist model of growth and development.

GROWTH THEORY

As we have already noted, growth theory is rooted in Keynsian economics and arose from an intellectual and practical desire to resolve the waste of human and natural resources through their underemployment. This notion was further perfected and adapted by other economists and their models which concentrated on how growth was related to the rate of saving and investment. They did, however, realize that getting the rate of investment and saving right and accounting for such things as the rate of population growth were not easy. They based their calculations on the idea of a well-ordered society whose prosperity depended on European cultural values: on the rewarding of thriftiness and on scientific invention.

In terms of the underdeveloped countries, growth theory was popularized by the work of Lewis (1955). But these countries were radically different from those where Keynsian-type theories had first been advocated; underdeveloped countries are poor in capital resources and the problems of unemployment are difficult to handle. A primary concern was the reduction of unemployment and underemployment. Idle resources, especially labour could be diverted to public works, while domestic savings should be pitched at the level of 5 per cent per annum of national income. The problem was how to put into operation the multiplier effect where savings were so low, and where imports were so crucial for industrial progress. Deficit financing, taxation and cheap money as used in developed countries were hardly applicable. Furthermore, the concept of disguised unemployment which had been put forward by Robinson in England, as due to slack demand was not the case in many countries such as Africa. As we have noted in chapter 2, agricultural labour, even if 'underemployed' for large parts of the year, is in heavy demand for specific jobs such as harvesting and weeding and its absence can be a severe constraint on farming. There was a quick jump from theory and European practice to policy as applied to underdeveloped countries, with little questioning of the applicability of the underlying assumptions. Furthermore, the issue of most poor countries being exporters of primary products, and the problem of the terms of trade, were naively believed to be things which could eventually be sorted out.

Lewis's formal treatise (1955) on development and underdevelopment centred on increased output per head of population, through the acceleration of capital formation. However, Lewis recognized the problems of securing adequate savings and investment since the middle-class elites of underdeveloped countries tended to hoard money, as there was a lack of institutions such as banks and investment facilities. Under such circumstances, external injections of capital would be necessary in conjunction with the introduction of new technology and scientific methods. Lewis's analysis was also based on an assumption which held that the changes experienced in the developed countries would be repeated in the underdeveloped. Thus the shift from agriculture to industry formed an important part of orthodox thinking about development in the 1950s, and was encapsulated in the notion that the marginal productivity of agricultural labour was equal to zero. Such was the level of underemployment in the rural areas that any further application of labour would yield zero returns in farming enterprises, while the abstraction of agricultural labour by industry would not seriously affect agricultural productivity. This kind of thinking was based on beliefs that peasantries were homogenous and that the situation found in Asia, especially India where population densities were high, were fairly universal and characteristic of peasant farmers everywhere. But as we observed in chapter 1, Helleiner has showed the inapplicability of this kind of model to much of Africa, where population densities are low or moderate and where labour is often a constraint on production. Also, we have tried to demonstrate that 'peasantries' in Africa are far from homogenous.

TAKE-OFF AND SELF SUSTAINING GROWTH: ROSTOW

Growth theory expanded in the 1950s and continued into the 1960s aided by the increased collection of data on national economic performance for a greater range of countries. Concepts of aggregate growth-dominated policy which were finally secured by Rostow's stage theory of economic growth. Rostow's analysis was based upon long-term data available for only 15 countries, but he asserted that all societies can be located at some point along a developmental axis marked by five stages. These are: (1) traditional society, (2) pre-conditions for take-off, (3) 'take-off' into self-sustaining growth, (4) drive to maturity and (5) the age of high mass-consumption (Rostow, 1960). Only the United States has yet achieved the final stage.

The crucial period for underdeveloped countries is that of 'take-off' which can be achieved under the following conditions:

1 The rate of productive investment rises from 5 per cent to over 10 per cent of National Income.
2 One or more substantial manufacturing sectors become leading sectors in growth.
3 The political and social framework is modified to exploit the impulses of the modern sector to secure ongoing growth.

Rostow's model had its roots in earlier models and their focus on the critical rate of investment related to income and savings. But to this was added the evolutionary schema of the five stages to achieve the transition from tradition to modernity.

The popularity of Rostow's work is intriguing and it made a powerful impact on politicians in the 1960s. Part of its appeal was that it appeared to give every country an equal chance and it offered a path to progress without spelling it out in too much detail (Brookfield, 1975). As far as politicians were concerned, especially in the US during the hopeful years of the Kennedy administration, it was a comforting alternative to the programmes of communist countries and it debunked the historical progressivism of Marx based on class conflict. Rostow's work has attracted much criticism and leaving aside detailed argument about how growth and take-off is achieved, there are clearly contrary views on what is meant by development and the manner in which Rostow portrays or understands 'primitive' societies and ignores their particular histories.

MODERNIZATION THEORY

Rostow's analysis, while rooted in the concept of growth also relies heavily on economic dualism, which is also present in Lewis's work and is embraced in the logic of industrialization. By the 1960s development theory had become broader, blander and more diffuse. Not only economists but anthropoligists, sociologists, psychologists, historians and political scientists were drawn into the development debate and there emerged what had become known as the 'modernization thesis'. All of these various interdisciplinary strands were interpreted through dichotomous views of change and progress. The sectorial dualism posited by industry and agriculture had become broadened out to be presented as 'tradition' versus 'modernity'. Tradition and modernity spring from the theory of cultural change or acculturation whereby societies which had been subject to slow change, or which were relatively static, come under external influences and adopt new ways of living. Traditional societies are ones where interpersonal contacts and communal values are pervasive, whereas in modern societies, relationships are impersonal and marked by individual achievement and role specificity. Modernization is the process whereby there is a transition from the traditional to the modern, a process of slow stable change and adaptation unlike the progression of class conflict outlined by Marx. Talcott Parsons' theory of social action was another powerful influence in the shaping of modernization theory. Parsons was much concerned with sets of dichotomies which he calls 'pattern variables': any actor in any situation may choose between the variables before the meaning of the situation becomes determinate and he can act. Thus does he adopt community or self-orientation, give priority to his accepted role in society by ascription, or give priority to personal achievement and weigh up the possible success of his actions. In other words, does he behave like a 'rational economic man'? To these strands of acculturation and social action can be added another, that of the creation of nationalism as a force to transform people from a local or tribal setting, which is particularist, to one which is national and universalist. Deutsch was a particular proponent of the thesis of social mobilization of people to accept new social and political systems as a prerequisite to modernization. An important group in promoting social change of this kind are the achieving elites. Thus change for the mass of rural people is to be always through external forces: Their own urban elites will co-operate with the external economic and political forces of advanced countries who will in turn administer and supply aid. Modernization contains a consensus in that it comprises a social and cultural framework that facilitates the development of technology, because it is through the application of science that underdeveloped countries will attain similar levels of economic well-being to Western ones.

By the early 1960s development agencies, planners and economists had assembled a large body of aggregate data for the construction of models of growth and the assessment of economic performance. In addition, there was an array of dichotomies on the transition from traditional to industrial urban society. Both Myrdal (1963) and Hirschmann had recognized that spread effects may be negated by countervailing forces of 'backwater' and polarization. Myrdal in particular favoured state intervention as a means of avoiding this problem. Many industries in developing countries found it difficult to compete in international markets, while small populations with limited purchasing power meant that in order to compete with imported goods high tariff barriers would be needed. Industry could not expand without markets and without expansion there were no jobs being created. There were no 'multiplier' effects. It had also become clear that many large-scale agricultural schemes had not worked either since too little was known about the ecology and the economic behaviour and structure of rural populations. Macro-economic data was being used to solve problems at regional or local levels, where they were of little use. One of the aims of this text has been to look at the micro-and meso-levels because we feel it at the very least a prerequisite for planning changes in rural society. Myrdal (1963) and others opted for industrialization as the catalyst for a circular cumulative causation of development linked to Rostow's process model (1960). The dynamics of change were to be by means of diffusion or a 'trickle down effect' from elites, towns and economic growth-poles. These ideas paved the way for notions of 'centre and periphery' pioneered by Friedmann and Alonso (1965) who was firmly committed to the idea of cities as the core of the development process with benefits cascading down the urban hierarchy until even the smallest village benefited. It became a feature of much of the earlier development planning.

But by the late 1960s it had become obvious that industrial development was not going to push rural-based underdeveloped countries towards economic growth or 'take-off'. Also, as we noted in chapter 3, in the early 1970s lessons had to be learned about the importance of non-farm and off-farm work as crucial elements in the reproduction of rural households.

Both theorists and planners had begun to respond to new voices of disillusionment and radical reassignment. Gundar Frank (1971) was writing about a new clientship of neo-colonization. Rodney (1972), Fanon (1967) and Amin (1973) wrote with anger of the experience of underdevelopment from the other side of the racial divide. Geographers began to notice that the optimistic diffusionist maps of development were imploding into privileged core areas and wide peripheries of disadvantage. Dumont (1969) wrote of the mistakes in rural development planning which reflected a mistaken commitment, the 'centre-down' large-scale investment. Development was replaced by underdevelopment as the new prevailing recognition of the inadequacies of belief in large-scale capital investment and schemes. Marxist and neo-Marxist writers began to propose alternative frames of reference and African political leaders and scholars contributed their own perspectives (Nyerere, 1974, Kaunda, 1980).

In the early 1970s new models of economic growth and concepts of development were being propounded which embraced policies designed to help the rural sector protect the environment and to generate employment (Wilkinson, 1973). The doubts about policies based on growth through industrialization and conventional strategies which relied on large-scale production concentrated in towns led to alternative strategies which were focused on small-scale enterprises in agriculture and industry. The publication of Schumacher's book *Small is Beautiful* (1973) was an eloquent plea for labour-intensive, small-scale technology which would economize on scarce capital resources (intermediate technology), while it also contained an ethical dimension, arguing that small-scale avoids the dehumanization of labour. Another influential book was Lipton's *Why Poor People Stay Poor: Urban Bias in World Development* (1977), in which he argued that conventional analyses of class conflict needed to be replaced by a theory presenting an opposition between urban and rural interest groups. Lipton argued that rural people are discriminated against through urban-biased policies, which are expressed through the location of public services, industry, wages and the depression of agricultural prices to serve the interest of townsfolk.

As we noted earlier, these anti-urban, pro-small-scale sentiments have been placed within the history and development of populist thought by numerous writers, most recently by Kitching (1982) who has also linked populism to the rise of nationalism in Third World countries. Kitching points out that many of the arguments put forward by the small-scale development lobby of the 1970s have their roots in the nineteenth-century populism of Europe and the twentieth-century neo-populists of Russia, notably A. V. Chayanov (1966). Chayanov believed peasants constituted an important economic class, who were not transitory and destined to wither away. Rather they had a vitality of their own which should be defended from the inroads of large-scale mechanized farming. Many of the populist arguments of the 1970s had been already spelled-out in the 1969 ILO Employment Report, although its arguments are primarily economic ones and based on what was believed to be the only practicable alternatives to conventional growth strategies, which had failed or were deemed incapable of promoting change.

The ILO report was an employment-orientated strategy, at least in the short term while it admitted that long-term growth was not impossible. The objectives were to tackle the rural sector which employed most people and therefore priority was given to rural development. It envisaged that sufficient land must be made available which, together with appropriate technology and capital, could raise output and incomes of the majority of those in poorer countries. Technology which was labour-enhancing and not labour displacing should be preferred; agrarian populations should be kept *in situ* and their productivity raised by improving simple irrigation systems, rural water supplies and through the distribution of new seeds and fertilizers. The ILO report also wished to apply improved techniques to the labour-intensive informal sector in the towns and in this sense was not anti-urban. It also allowed the possibility of large-scale agriculture where population densities were low. But overall the emphasis was on small-scale labour-intensive schemes and the promotion of equity among Third World populations.

The main tenets of the ILO report were adopted by the World Bank in 1974 in its document on *Redistribution and Growth*, which set in train new initiatives in the development of the rural sector. Such initiatives were premised on distributive designs which held that economic growth must bring about a proportionate or more than proportionate increase in adequately remunerated employment (Rimmer, 1984). Development objectives were now couched in terms of 'basic needs' and the provision of adequate levels of consumption and access to public services for everyone and matched some of the objectives of the honest brokers among colonial civil servants and missionaries in the colonial years. Attention was focused on minimum calorie requirements per day and adequate floor-space per person, which allowed new quantitative criteria to be used in the place of such things as GNP. Rimmer (1984) has pointed out that this social welfare approach and a concern for the poorer sections of society is a re-run of policies advocated by the ILO in the 1930s with respect to Europe. Also he indicated that underlying these models is the assumption that the acceleration of equity is compatible with economic growth.

The basic needs approach is heavily conditioned by the ability of a nation to produce enough foodstaples to feed the population and thus the agricultural and rural sectors have to become central to planning – in theory, if not always in practice. The shift towards rural-led development was made even more attractive by the appearance of high yielding varieties of rice, wheat and maize (Cohen, 1980). When accompanied by fertilizers, irrigation techniques and improved farming practices these hybrid seeds can greatly increase yields. But new seed-fertilizer technology is equally applicable to both large and smallholdings, something which posed new policy choices for African governments. Hitherto, the large capital-intensive mechanization schemes were location specific, but the 'green revolution' strategy opened up the possibility of bringing improvements to farmers scattered over wide areas. The next step was the concept of the Integrated Rural Development Project whereby 'packages' of inputs and services can be introduced into villages, which, it is claimed, are less disruptive and less labour and land displacing than other approaches.

But even where large irrigation or mechanization schemes are preferred, there is now a tendency to leave populations *in situ* and avoid too much relocation of settlements and the consideration of landholdings. However, in both large and small schemes of rural development there has remained a commitment to the application of new technology and an emphasis on inputs such as seed, water and fertilizer. Despite the laudable intention of so many development projects, that failure, combined with rising levels of indebtedness in the 1980s, has prompted new approaches by Third World economies, especially in the rural sector. First, there has occurred a resurgence of interest in farming systems and ethno-science. In chapter 1 we referred to arguments about the innovativeness of African farming systems and the value of indigenous practice and understanding of local environments. The case for an indigenous agricultural revolution has been strongly argued by Richards (1985) wherein the agenda for rural change is set with reference to the potential of local landuse systems and practices which are frequently underperceived or misunderstood by development planners. This view has not been without its critics, notably Watts (1983) who, while accepting the soundness of African agricultural systems, nonetheless believes that they have disintegrated or become inoperable for many farmers in the face of an increasingly commoditized rural economy which is also significantly differentiated into rich and poor, powerful and weak. Furthermore, he believes that populist approaches to agrarian change would have all the benefits of competition without the disadvantages.

Second, in the 1980s, attitudes towards African agriculture have been influenced by the new economics coming out of Europe and America. There has been a resurgence of arguments for the removal of state intervention, the encouragement of market forces and the expansion of agricultural exports by peasant farmers. It is argued that what farmers need are price incentives. Policies to achieve this kind of development are held to include targeting aid to areas with the greatest potential, encouraging larger farmers and devaluing the exchange rate to facilitate exports. These policies are contained within the World Bank's 'Berg Report' to which we referred earlier. The report shifts the development issue to domestic policy within Africa and argues that past trends in the terms of trade cannot explain the slow growth of African economies. The problem lies in the bias against agriculture, import substitution industries, over-valued exchange rates, urban wages and prices and over-expansion of a subsidized state sector.

The Berg Report has been influential in shaping World Bank policies and the conditions laid down by the IMF for negotiating loans and debt repayments, while its impact has been felt in African countries in a variety of ways. Objections have been raised that it will intensify class divisions and create a class of kulak farmers while regional inequalities will also become greater. However, those in favour of freer markets believe that the development of rural and urban entrepreneurs will create sufficient forward and backward linkages with all sectors of the economy so as to promote a general rise in economic well-being. But the successful implementation of the World Bank's 'Agenda for Action' would entail far-reaching realignments of class interest and an unacceptable (if not impossible) degree of state coercion. We have already drawn attention in chapter 8 to the political instability engendered by attempts to meet IMF conditions, for example in Zambia and during 1988 in Nigeria, related to the increase in petroleum product prices. Whatever the merits of the World Bank and IMF packages may be, they have to be set against the internal political problems of implementing them, when they involved increased landlessness, job losses and the reduction of already limited health and education services. However, as we noted in chapter 8, there is now a consensus among some Marxists that the deepening of class differences was occasioned by a number of development policies which, together with IMF initiatives, will precipitate a struggle among classes which will provide the real basis for a structural change in society.

CONCLUSION

The explanations and theories of development and underdevelopment embrace a diversity of views which at times rest on diametrically opposed positions. Analyses of change, prescriptions and policies are shaped by different ideologies, and perhaps rather like beauty, 'underdevelopment' and 'development' can be deemed to lie in the eye of the beholder. We have seen movements in explanation which favour *laissez-faire* capitalism, paternalist interventionism, socialist revolution and industrialization. Programmes of development have moved from a stress on large-scale schemes aiming to secure import substitution or foreign exchange earnings, to small-scale peasant credit associations. Few have proved to be outstanding successes. Grass roots development remains a nice ideal, but integrated development projects and irrigation schemes continue as part of the political necessity which binds together national governments and foreign interests. But even when such interventions fail, as they often do, to meet their stated objectives, changes are occurring in rural Africa. The post-war interventions of the colonial regimes and especially the development projects of the post-independence period, have meant a rapid development of the forces of production, and intensification of class differences, dramatic changes in social infrastructures and redistribution of populations.

Yet state intervention has not entirely brought about socialist or capitalist transformations of society and a number of states have been marked by economic stagnation or retrogression. This is a retrogression which has been explained on the one hand by the World Bank as due to interventions by the state and on the other, by market forces dominated by the world capitalist order and degrees of dependency or articulation. The way forward for the one is the removal of state control, while for the other it is a retreat into self-sufficiency and self-reliance which at times amounts to autarky. The latter view most has led to what Sender and Smith (1986) describe as wishful thinking concerning policy options. In the view of Sender and Smith, it is not state intervention *per se* which is necessarily bad, but the failure of states to adopt coherent interventions based on an informed understanding of their economies and a belief that macro-economic policy is subject to significant degrees of domestic control. In the view of these authors there are serious lacunae in analytical and ideological frameworks outlined earlier in this chapter which inhibit relevant policies. There is a chasm between the 'Scylla' or autarky and the 'Charybdis' of market forces. There has been a failure to identify the forces of change as they already exist and are operative. In particular 'the denial of the existence of a working class and the absence of an analysis of rural structures has resulted in the ideological dominance of a "classless" nationalism, albeit expressed in the language of socialism'. This is a view with which we have a good deal of sympathy, and one of our objectives in this book has been to try to uncover some of the important dimensions of rural society and forces of change. However, as we remarked earlier about the IMF initiatives, even if you have the right policies their political implementation may be difficult and goals are not attainable overnight. In some areas at least time may well be running out, both politically and ecologically.

10

Conclusion

It is currently fashionable to view Africa as a continent in crisis: its ecology massively disrupted and possibly threatened by global climatic changes; its economies stagnant or declining; its political and social systems fractured or fragile. While there is no doubt that the combined effects of political disturbance and ecological instability have created tensions which have led to enormities of famine on a regional scale, and while we have sometimes appeared to accept the more pessimistic scenarios, we have generally taken the view in this book that it is possible to overstate the long-term impact of cataclysmic disasters. Similarly, we have argued that any view of African economies which uses the language of formal macro-economics will take little account of the unreliability of published data and of the very considerable commercial activity throughout Africa which takes place beyond the balance sheets and away from tarmac roads.

While stressing this essentially anarchic vigour of African rural life in the first part of the book, we have also been mindful of the ways in which external forces have both shaped and been conditioned by Africa. Africans have enjoyed both the benefits and problems associated with the opening up of contact with the North, first with Arab Islamic culture and then with European coastal traders, leading eventually to the traumas of the slave trade and the 'short sharp shock' of 80 years of direct colonialism. Colonialists sought to control African societies by both direct and indirect rule, buttressing their attempts in some cases by inventing an African past of tribal authority, by supporting religious superstructures, such as Islam, which were already in place, or by promoting the spread of Christianity. It has been argued by some that colonial rule was in most areas more parasitic than destructive. It has also been suggested that partial transformation of African economies was well suited to the interests of ruling elites, business-men, bureaucrats and politicians, who have had much to gain from re-maining clients of foreign powers. Whichever view one takes, the cashcrop revolution of the nineteenth and early twentieth centuries, first engineered by merchant capital and then supported by the colonial state, has had a profound and continuing effect on African communities, leading to the restructuring of domestic groups and the emergence of new kinds of conflict. The shifting control and access to resources of land and labour in rural communities coupled with colonial policies on taxation and monetization, were effective in promoting migrant labour and off-farm employment on plantations and in the towns and mines. Many traditional crafts have been replaced by new forms of small commodity production in the manufacturing and service sectors of larger villages. If they have adapted to all the forms of economic imperialism which have continued into the period of independence, Africans have also been subjected to the reactions of international guilt: a panoply of committed but frequently paternalistic services and advice offered by missionaries, by civil servants and more recently by aid agencies. As a product of all these changes, many if not most Africans are either fully or partly involved in the money economy. They are involved as wage-labourers and share-croppers, not only on plantations but as employees of other Africans. Access to off-farm work and non-farm incomes has also expanded through the proliferation of government offices and para-statal agencies, new industries, multi-national companies and mining enterprises. There is little doubt that new classes are emerging in Africa.

The gap between those with the access to scarce resources and those without is already widening in many areas, even beyond the point where one can talk sensibly about the checks and balances of kinship and reciprocity. This is not to deny the existence of domestic groups who are primarily concerned with food production but it would be surprising if they are any longer representative of the African village over wide areas of the continent. While one should never underestimate the significance of famine reserve crops like cassava, nor the importance of small domestic animals and foraging in the lives of all but the most commercial of African households, new forms of employment, changing access to resources and farming for urban markets mean that perhaps the majority of African households, rich and poor, are embedded in the small commodity sector as farmers, traders, manufacturers and service workers. At the same time, they are exposed to the vagaries of full-time or part-time wage earning. While these developments have brought new opportunities into the lives of many rural Africans, in many instances entry into the better paid segments of the labour market and salariat has been controlled by traditional rulers. Clientage of this kind has also gone hand in hand with the development of the new political parties and increasing social differentiation in communities. Those with better non-farm jobs can afford agricultural inputs associated with improved yields. Access to the development schemes is still often controlled by these older systems of patronage. But newer ones are developing. Similarly, the accumulation of land is also premised on the capital yielded by non-farm jobs. At the same time, at the other end of the spectrum, non-farm employment is sometimes the means of survival in some households and househould reproduction is entirely dependent on employment which is often unreliable given the shaky state of African economies.

All these changes have led to the restructuring of domestic groups and the emergence of new kinds of conflict. For example, the relationships have changed between elders and juniors and between men and women. Conflicts have also developed among households as their differentiation increases, premised on new forms of economic enterprise, new patterns of labour migration and non-farm jobs. While clientage is still a feature of African societies, there is evidence of new autonomies, new ways of forming beneficial alliances which go beyond the old kinship and tribal networks and evidence emerges of the development of a new indigenous bourgeoisie.

These developments are happening in ways which do not conform to the classical models of the self-regulative family household structures of peasant society provided by Chayanov and elaborated by Shanin. In many areas, in fact, the conflict between options (food production or wage labour) exacerbated by widening class differences within rural society, is disturbing the delicate balance maintained between ecological management and domestic food production. It is at this point that we confront the question of agricultural crisis in Africa.

Much has been said about the increased production of export crops and the diminution of time and land devoted to foodstuffs. This argument is often associated with demands for a retreat from the international economy which rests on simple equivalence – fewer export crops means more food for all. In reality the situation is much more complex. Even when there is little involvement in export crops, access to land and labour, as we have indicated above, is increasingly inequitable and poor households have not enough labour and land for their needs. The question of food production cannot be separated from that of resources and food distribution. Even in times of famine, food has been available, but for many of those whose crops had failed there was too little cash to buy it, even if the means to move it from one place to another existed. On the other hand, in periods of food shortage, grain has been stored against price rises and shipped to richer clients across borders by city merchants and their rural functionaries. The frequency of these food movements across borders, both legal and illegal, covert and overt, gives pause for thought about the statistics of food production adduced by governments and aid agencies. Inconsistencies both within and between official statistics produced by institutions such as the World Bank and the United Nations Food and Agriculture Organization (FAO), not to mention African governments themselves, have been noted by many writers (Berry, 1984). Such statistics are not only aggregated to scales beyond the point of potential utility but frequently miss the basic fact of African rural economies by concentrating on grain production and forgetting the crucial importance of surviving elements of the old domestic economy referred to early in this book: the significance of tubers, especially cassava and yams, and the food inputs provided by small domestic animals and by foraging which are all still underperceived and underaccounted, although some recognition is now being given to the critical importance of firewood in the domestic economy.

These comments on food supply do not mean that that there are no problems or that drought, famine and food shortages are imaginary. What it does suggest is that the food problem is complicated. It is not simply about food supply it is also about access, ecological management, entitlement and social relationships. One cannot claim that environmental problems are solely the product of political mismanagement or the erosion of indigenous structures, but there is a case to be made for the argument that shortages are exacerbated by the breakdown of indigenous production relations and techniques and that food shortage and famine do have a strong correlation with civil disturbance and warfare. Many African societies are still coping with the demands of emergent nationhood in the context of borders drawn by colonial powers with scant regard to natural polities. It is scarcely surprising that problems have arisen. The disruption of infrastructures, the loss of farmland, the feeding of armies, when they occur in zones of climatic uncertainty, more or less guarantee a food problem, as they always have done, even in environmentally more stable regions of the world. In Ethiopia, the Horn of Africa, in the Sudan, Chad, Mauritania, Uganda, Mozambique, Angola and Namibia, in Rhodesia/Zimbabwe and earlier in Nigeria, civil war and secessionist movements, often aggravated by external powers, have contributed to food shortages or famine. Many, but not all, of these disturbances have been in areas of low or uncertain rainfall.

For many observers it is the state which lies at the root of the food problem and the problem of low levels of economic development in general. As we have noted this is part of the thinking of the World Bank and IMF who see the key to development in the restructuring of economies and the removal of state control in markets and development. It is not, it would seem, dependence on world markets that causes underdevelopment but the claustrophobic influence of the state. This anti-state lobby is also joined by populists who believe that indigenous knowledge and practice are inhibited rather than assisted by state controls and interference from external agencies. But it may not be the state *per se* which is at fault, merely the kinds of policies which are pursued. In the development of Western Europe, the state has played a fundamental role in the development of both capitalism and communism. In Africa the main problem is the nature of the relationship between the state and its more energetic servants and clients.

In many states there is evidence of the virtual privatization of the public purse by those with power and influence. Large amounts of money have been channelled into existing mercantile networks, through private hands, to facilitate trade in basic commodities. Continued access to state revenues has not necessarily enhanced productivity. Food importation, lucrative building and supply contracts in the state sector and credit provisions have been the means of reproducing the bureaucrats, merchants and businessmen of the new bourgeoisie and consolidating their position.

Perhaps even more insidious is the pervasive weight of Euro-American intellectual imperialism which supplies 'detached', off-the-peg strategies for improvement with an arrogance which has lost nothing in a century of direct involvement. It may be for this reason that with some notable exceptions, African academic writers, have not been effective in this field, leaving it to the polemicists of the armed struggle and to their writers and musicians to reject both the new forms of imperialism and the corruption of elite classes and to reinterpret the potential vigour of African systems. African writers and musicians have frequently articulated radical alternatives which derive from a variety of non-African sources ranging from Marxism to American Black Power movements. Artists with a political message have had a hard time with African governments of all persuasions and politicians may be right in fearing that popular culture can forge alliances among the urban and rural poor and disaffected. But it is only in the countries of armed struggle against settler regimes that a widespread political philosophy emerged to act as a catalyst for a 'clean slate'. Despite the socialism implicit in the philosophy of the armed struggle it remains to be seen whether or not any African country can sustain a solidly socialist approach. On the evidence of those countries who have had to deal with a settler presence in evolving a new ideology, no clear view can be obtained. The very different histories of Tanzanian and Mozambiqian socialism, Zambian humanism and Kenyan capitalism leave the future direction of new states like Zimbabwe much in doubt, though there is no doubt that struggle sharpens the edge of idealism and self-discipline, which may be a critical feature of subsequent development.

So without in any way diminishing the enormity of the problems facing African societies in their struggle towards a better life, it has been one purpose of this book to explore the character of adaptation, resilience and transformation from as close as we can hope to come to an African rural perspective: to confront grand theories of modernization, development, underdevelopment and class formation with the primary evidence of rural change in the long, medium and short terms. At times we may appear to be coming close to adopting a populist position. There is no doubt this view commands much sympathy, whether expressed through political terminology or within the human ecological perspective. Where we part company with this rural-centred, 'self-help' bootstrap thinking is in the recognition of the scale of the commoditization of land, labour and exchange which has already taken place and the extent of the social and economic differentiation which exists in rural communities. We believe that populist scenarios can be idealistic; in serious danger of trying to postulate an unrealistic 'merrie Africa' populated by self-sufficient, steady-state micro-autonomies.

There also exists in all African societies, including rural ones, a gap between the idea of how life might be led and the reality. In Europe, the same sense of separation led to profound social, economic and political changes. Unlike the urban and rural peoples of nineteenth- and early twentieth-century Europe, however, the ordinary Africans have immediate access, through films, television and radio, to a wider and more opulent world in which their leaders already seem to have a share. In the struggle for improved levels of well-being, the aspirations and opinions of the poor are frequently unrecorded or ignored. The limited development of trade unions, the absence of genuine co-operatives and the indifference of local government make it difficult for views to be articulated and heard. But this does not mean that small farmers are unable to resist changes which appear unjust or inequitable. With their increasing involvement in the economy, whether in socialist Zimbabwe or Ethiopia, capitalist Ivory Coast, Kenya or Nigeria, it remains an article of faith that they alone or in alliance with others will find persuasive and effective ways of demanding a better future.

Bibliography

Allan, W. 1949: *Studies in African Land Usage in Northern Rhodesia*. Oxford: Oxford University Press.

Allan, W. 1965: *The African Husbandman*. Edinburgh: Oliver and Boyd.

Amerena, P. M. J. 1982: Farmers' participation in the cash economy: case studies of two settlements in the Kano close-settled zone of Nigeria. PhD. Thesis, University of London.

Amin, S. 1973: *Neo-colonialism in West Africa*. Harmondsworth: Penguin.

Amin, S. 1976: *Unequal Development: an essay on the social formations of peripheral capitalism*. New York: Monthly Review Press.

Anthony, K. R. *et al.* 1979: *Agricultural Change in Tropical Africa*. Ithaca: Cornell University Press.

Ardener, E. *et al.* 1960: *Plantation and Village in the Cameroons*. London: Oxford University Press.

Baran, P. A. 1957: *The Political Economy of Growth*. New York: Monthly Review Press.

Barker, J. 1979: The debate on rural socialism in Tanzania. In B. U. Mwansasu and C. Pratt (eds), *Towards Socialism in Tanzania*, Dar es Salaam: Tanzanian Publishing House.

Bassett, T. 1988: Breaking labour bottlenecks: food crops and cotton in Cote d'Ivoire. *Africa*, 58 (2), 147–74.

Bates, R. H. 1981: *Markets and States in Tropical Africa*. Berkeley: University of California Press.

Bates, R. H. 1983: *Essays on the Political Economy of Rural Africa*. Cambridge: Cambridge University Press.

Bauer, P. 1954: *West African Trade: a study of competition oligopoly and monopoly in a changing economy*. Cambridge: Cambridge University Press.

Berry, S. S. 1984: The food crisis and agrarian change in Africa. *African Studies Review*, 27 (2), 59–112.

Biebuyck, K. D. 1963: *African Agrarian Systems*. Oxford: Oxford University Press.

Boesen, J. 1986: *Tanzania: crisis and struggle for survival*. Uppsala: Scandanavian Institute of African Studies.

Bohannan, P. 1963: Land 'tenure' and land tenure. In D. Biebuyk (ed.), *African Agrarian Systems*. London: Oxford University Press.

Bohannan, P. and Bohannan, L. 1962: *The Tiv of Central Nigeria*. London: International African Institute.

Bohannan, P. and Dalton, G. (eds) 1962: *Markets in Africa*. Evanston: Northwestern University Press.

Boserup, E. 1965: *The Conditions of Agricultural Growth: the economics of agrarian change under population pressure*. London: Allen and Unwin.

Boserup, E. 1970: *Women's Role in Economic Development*. New York: St Martin's Press.

Bovill, E. D. 1968: *Golden Trade of the Moors*. London: Oxford University Press.

Brenner, R. 1977: The origins of capitalist development: a critique of neo-Smithian Marxism. *New Left Review*, 104, 29–92.

Brookfield, H. 1975: *Interdependent Development*. London: Methuen.

Buntjer, B. 1973: Rural society in the Zaria area: the changing structure of Gandu. *Samaru Research Bulletin*, 80, Samaru, Nigeria: Institute of Agricultural Research.

Burnham, P. 1980: Changing agricultural and pastoral ecologies in the West African savanna region. In D. R. Harris (ed.), *Human Ecology in Savanna Environments*, London: Academic Press.

Cardoso, F. H. 1979: *Dependency and Development in Latin America*. Berkeley: University of California Press.

Chambers, R. 1969: *Settlement Schemes in Tropical Africa: a study of organisations and development*. London: Routledge and Kegan Paul.

Chambers, R. 1983: *Rural Development: putting the last first*. London: Longman.

Chayanov, A. V. 1966: *The Theory of Peasant Economy*. (eds) D. Thorner, R. E. F. Smith and B. Kerblay. Homewood, Ill.: R. D. Irwin.

Cheater, A. P. 1982: Formal and informal rights to land in Zimbabwe's black freehold areas: a case study from Msengezi. *Africa*, vol. 52 (3), 77–91.

Chuta, E. and Liedholm, C. 1975: The role of small scale industry in employment generation and rural development: initial research results. *African Rural Employment Paper No. 11*, East Lansing: Michigan State University.

Clarke, J. 1980: Peasantization and landholding: a Nigerian case study. In M. Klein (ed.), *Peasants in Africa: historical and contemporary perspectives*, London and Beverley Hills: Sage.

Cleave, J. H. 1974: *African Farmers: Labor Use in the Development of Smallholder Agriculture*. New York: Praeger.

Cliffe, L. 1973: The policy of Ujamaa Vijijini and the class struggle in Tanzania. In L. Cliffe and J. S. Saul (eds), *Socialism in Tanzania*, Dar es Salaam: East African Publishing House.

Clothier, J. N. 1956: *Regional Planning in Northern Rhodesia*. Lusaka: Government Printer.

Clough, P. 1981: Farmers and traders in Hausaland. *Development and Change*, 12, 273–92.

Clough, P. 1985: The social relations of grain marketing in northern Nigeria. *Review of African Political Economy*, 34, 16–34.

Cohen, J. M. 1980: Land tenure and rural development in Africa. In R. H. Bates and M. F. Lofchie (eds), *Agricultural Development in Africa*, New York: Praeger.

Cohen, R. 1976: From peasants to workers. In P. C. W. Gutkind and I. Wallerstein (eds), *The Political Economy of Contemporary Africa*. London and Beverley Hills: Sage.

Cohen, R. and Hutton, C. 1978: African peasants and resistance to change: a reconsideration of sociological approaches. In I. Oxaal, T. Barnett and D. Booth (eds), *Beyond the Sociology of Development*. London: Routledge and Kegan Paul.

Colson, E. 1971: *The Social Consequences of Resettlement: the impact of the Kariba resettlement upon the Gwembe Tonga*. Manchester: Manchester University Press.

Colson, E. and Gluckman, M. (eds) (1951) *Seven Tribes of British Central Africa*. London: Oxford University Press.

Coquery-Vidrovitch, C. 1976: *Le Congo au Temps des Grandes Compagnies Concessionnaires, 1898–1919*. Paris: Mouton.

Corbridge, S. 1986: *Capitalist World Development: a critique of radical development geography*. New Jersey: Rowman and Littlefield.

Curtin, P. D. 1975: *Economic Change in Pre-colonial Africa: Senegambia in the era of the slave trade*. Madison: University of Wisconsin Press.

Davies, D. H. 1971: *Zambia in Maps*. London: University of London Press.

Davies, R. 1979: Informal sector or subordinate mode of production? A model. In R. Bromley and C. Geery (eds), *Casual Work and Poverty in Third World Cities*, Chichester: Wiley.

Dey, J. 1981: Gambian women: unequal partners in Ria development projects. *Journal of Development Studies*, 17 (3), 109–22.

Dilley, R. 1986: Tukolor weavers and the organization of their craft in village and town. *Africa*, 56 (2), 123–47.

Dinham, B. and Hines, C. 1983: *Agribusiness in Africa*. London: Earth Resources Research Ltd.

Dumont, R. 1966: *False Start in Africa*. New York: Praeger.

Dumont, R. 1969: *The Hungry Future*. London: Deutsch.

Dyson-Hudson, N. 1980: Strategies of resource exploitation among East African savanna pastoralists. In D. R. Harris (ed.) *Human Ecology in Savanna Environments*. London: Academic Press.

Emmanuel, A. 1972: *Unequal Exchange*. London: Monthly Review.

Fanon, F. 1967: *The Wretched of the Earth*. Harmondsworth: Penguin.

Faris, J. C. 1975: Social evolution, population and production. In S. Polgar (ed.), *Population, Ecology and Social Evolution*, The Hague: Mouton.

Federation of Rhodesia and Nyasaland 1961: *Agricultural Survey of Southern Rhodesia. Part I Agro-Ecological Survey*. Salisbury:

Fortes, M. 1958: Introduction. In J. Goody (ed.), *The Developmental Cycle in Domestic Groups*, Cambridge: Cambridge University Press.

Fortt, J. M. 1973: Land tenure and the emergence of large scale farming. In A. I. Richards, F. Sturrock and J. M. Fortt (eds), *Subsistence to Commercial Farming in Present Day Buganda*, Cambridge: Cambridge University Press.

Francis, P. 1984: For the use and common benefit of all Nigerians: consequences of 1978 land nationalization. *Africa*, 54 (3), 5–28.

Frank, A. G. 1971: *Sociology of Development and Underdevelopment of Sociology*. London: Pluto.

Frank, A. G. 1972: *Lumpen Bourgeoisie, Lumpen Development*. London: Monthly Review Press.

Frank, A. G. 1976: *Capitalism and Underdevelopment in Latin America*. London: Monthly Review Press.

Freund, W. M. and Shenton, R. W. 1977: 'Vent for Surplus' theory and the economic history of West Africa. *Savanna*, 6 (2) 191–6.

Friedmann, J. and Alonso, W. (1965): *Regional Development and Planning*. Cambridge, Ma.: Massachusetts Institute of Technology.

Gakou, M. H. 1987: *The Crisis in African Agriculture*. London: Zed Books.

Galletti, R., Baldwin, K. D. S. and Dina, I. O. 1956: *Nigerian Cocoa Farmers: the economic survey of Yoruba cocoa farming families*. London: Oxford University Press.

Gluckman, M. *et al.* 1948: *Land Holding and Land Usage among the Plateau Tonga of Mazabuka District*. Capetown: Oxford University Press.

Goddard, A. D. 1973: Changing family structures among the rural Hausa. *Samaru Research Bulletin, 196*. Samaru, Nigeria: Institute of Agricultural Research.

Goddard, A. D., Fine, J. C. and Norman, D. W. 1971: *A Socio-Economic Survey of Three Villages in the Sokoto Close-Settled Zone, Vol 1, Land and People*. Samaru, Nigeria: Institute of Agricultural Research.

Goodman, D. and Redcliffe, M. 1981: *From Peasant to Proletarian: capitalist development and agrarian transitions*. Oxford: Basil Blackwell.

Guyer, J. (ed.) 1987: *Feeding African Cities*. Studies in Regional Social History. Manchester: Manchester University Press for the International African Institute.

Guyer, J. I. and Peters, P. E. 1987: Introduction. Special issue on conceptualizing the household: issues of theory and policy in Africa. *Development and Change*, 18 (2), 197–215.

Hadfield, J. 1960: *Aspects of the African Agrarian Economy*. Lusaka: Northern Rhodesia Government Printer.

Hart, K. 1973: Informal income opportunities and employment in Ghana. *Journal of Modern African Studies*, 11, 61–89.

Hart, K. 1982: *The Political Economy of West African Agriculture*. Cambridge: Cambridge University Press.

Haswell, M. R. 1953: *Economics of Agriculture in a Savannah Village*. London: Her Majesty's Stationery Office.

Haswell, M. R. 1963: *The Changing Patterns of Activity in a Gambian Village*. London: Her Majesty's Stationery Office.

Helleiner, G. K. 1966: Typology in development theory: the land surplus economy (Nigeria). *Food Research Institute Studies*, 6 (2), 181–94.

Helen, J. A. 1968: *Rural Economic Development in Zambia 1890–1914*. Munich: Ifo Institut für Wirtschaftsforschung Wellform Verlag.

Hewitt, K. (ed.) 1983: *Interpretation of Calamity*. Risks and Hazard Series, 1. London: Allen and Unwin.

Hill, P. 1972: *Rural Hausa: a village and a setting*. Cambridge: Cambridge University Press.

Hill, P. 1977: *Population, Prosperity and Poverty: rural Kano 1900 and 1970*. Cambridge: Cambridge University Press.

Hobsbawm, E. J. and Ranger, T. O. (eds) 1983: *The Invention of Tradition*. Cambridge University Press.

Hodder, B. W. and Ukwu, U. I. 1969: *Markets in West Africa: studies of markets and trade among the Yoruba and Ibo*. Ibadan: Ibadan University Press.

Hogendorn, J. 1977: Vent for surplus theory and the economic history of West Africa. *Savanna*, 6 (2), 196–9.

Hogendorn, J. S. and Scott, K. M. 1983: Very large scale agricultural projects: lessons of the East Africa Groundnut Scheme. In R. I. Rotberg (ed.) *Imperialism, Colonialism and Hunger: East and Central Africa*. Lexington: Heath.

Hollier, G. P. 1981: The dynamics of rural marketing in North West Province, Cameroon. PhD thesis, Liverpool University.

Homewood, K. W., Rodgers, W. and Arhem, K. 1987: Ecology of pastoralism in Ngorongoro conservation area, Tanzania. *Journal of Agricultural Science*, 108, 47–72.

Hopen, C. E. 1958: *The Pastoral Fulbe Family in Gwandu*. London: Oxford University Press for the International African Institute.

Hopkins, A. G. 1973: *An Economic History of West Africa*. London: Longman.

Hopkins, A. G. 1975: On importing Andre Gunder Frank into Africa. *African Economic Review*, II (i), 13–21.

Hyden, G. 1980: *Beyond Ujamaa in Tanzania: underdevelopment and an uncaptured peasantry*. London: Heinemann.

Illiffe, J. 1983: *The Emergence of African Capitalism*. London: Macmillan.

Iliya, M. A. 1988: Induced agricultural change in northern Nigeria: a study of the eastern zone of the Sokoto agricultural development project. PhD thesis, University of Birmingham.

Jacobs, A. H. 1975: Maasai pastoralism in historical perspective. In T. Monod (ed.), *Pastoralism in Tropical Africa*, London: Oxford University Press.

Jones, W. O. 1959: *Manioc in Africa*. Ithaca: Cornell University Press.

Jones, W. O. 1972: *Marketing Staple Foods in Africa*. Ithaca: Cornell University Press.

Kahn, J. S. and Llobera, J. R. (eds) 1981: *The Anthropology of Pre-Capitalist Societies*. London: Macmillan.

Karimu, J. and Richards, P. 1980: The Northern Area Integrated Agricultural Development Programme. Occasional Paper No. 3. (new series) SOAS Department of Geography.

Kaunda, K. D. 1980: *Kaunda on Violence*. London: Collins.

Kaunda, K. D. and Morris, C. M. 1966: *A Humanist in Africa: letters to Colin M. Morris from Kenneth D. Kaunda, President of Zambia*. London: Longman.

Kay, G. 1967: *A Social Geography of Zambia*. London: University of London Press.

Kay, G. 1975: *Development and Underdevelopment*. London: Macmillan.

Kiernan, V. 1986: Imperialism and revolution. In R. Porter and M. Teich (eds), *Revolution in History*, Cambridge: Cambridge University Press.

Kilby, P. 1962: *The Development of Small Industry in Eastern Nigeria*. Lagos, Nigeria: U. S. A. I. D.

King, K. 1979: Petty production in Nairobi: the social context of skill acquisition and occupational differentiation. In R. Bromley and C. Geery (eds), *Casual Work and Poverty in Third World Cities*. Chichester: Wiley.

Kinsey, B. H. 1982: Forever gained: resettlement and land policy in the context of national development in Zimbabwe. *Africa*, 52 (3), 92–113.

Kitching, G. 1980: *Class and Economic Change in Kenya: the making of an African petite bourgeoisie 1905–1970*. London and New Haven: Yale University Press.

Kitching, G. 1982: *Development and Underdevelopment in Historical Perspective*. London: Methuen.

Konczacki, Z. A. 1978: *Economics of Pastoralism*. London: Cass.

Kumar, S. K. 1985: Women's agricultural work in a subsistence-orientated economy: its role in production, food consumption and nutrition. Paper prepared for the 13th International Congress of Nutrition, Brighton, UK.

Lee, R. B. 1979: *The !Kung San: men, women and work in a foraging society*. Cambridge: Cambridge University Press.

Lee, R. B. and DeVore, I. 1976: *Kalahari Hunter Gatherers: studies of the !Kung San and their neighbors*. Cambridge, Ma.: Harvard University Press.

Lericollais, A. 1972: *Sob: étude géographique d'un terroir Sérèr (Senegal) Altas des structures agraires au sud du Sahara, 7*. Paris: Mouton.

Levi, J. and Havinden, M. 1982: *Economics of African Agriculture*. London: Longman.

Lewis, W. A. 1955: *The Theory of Economic Growth*. London: Allen and Unwin.

Lipton, M. 1977: *Why Poor People Stay Poor: a study of urban bias in world development*. London: Temple Smith.

Low, A. 1986: *Agricultural Development in South Africa: a household economics perspective*. London: James Curry.

Lubeck, P. 1986: *Islam and Urban Labour: the making of a Muslim working class in northern Nigeria*. Cambridge: Cambridge University Press.

Lubeck, P. (ed.) 1987: *Capitalist Development in Nigeria, Kenya and the Ivory Coast*. Lynne Rienner: Boulder, Colorado.

Makings, S. M. 1967: *Agricultural Problems of Developing Countries in Africa*. Lusaka: Oxford University Press.

Mauss, M. 1970: *The Gift: forms and functions of exchange in archaic societies*. London: Cohen and West.

Meillassoux, C. 1964: *Anthropologie Economique des Gouro de Côte D'Ivoire: de l'économie de subsistence à l'agriculture commerciale*. Paris: Mouton.

Meillassoux, C. 1972: From reproduction to production. *Economy and Society*, 1 (1), 93–105.

Mikesell, M. W. 1962: *Readings in Cultural Geography*. Chicago: University of Chicago Press.

Mintz, S. W. 1979: The rural proletariat and the problem of rural proletarian consciousness. In R. Cohen, P. C. W. Gutkind and P. Brazier (eds), *Peasants and Proletarians*, London: Hutchinson.

Miracle, M. 1967: *Agriculture in the Congo Basin: tradition and change in African rural economies*. Madison: University of Wisconsin Press.

Monod, T. (ed.) 1975: *Pastoralism in Tropical Africa*. London: Oxford University Press for the International African Institute.

Monsted, M. 1977: *The Changing Division of Labour Within Families in Kenya*. Copenhagen: Centre for Development Research.

Moore, H. and Vaughan, M. 1987: Cutting down trees: women, nutrition and agricultural change in the Northern Province of Zambia 1920–1986. *African Affairs*, 86 (345), 523–40.

Moore, M. P. 1975: Cooperative labour in peasant agriculture. *Journal of Peasant Studies*, 2, 270–91.

Morgan, W. B. and Pugh, J. C. 1969: *West Africa*. London: Methuen.

Mortimore, M. J. 1978: Livestock Production. In J. S. Oguntoyinbo, O. O. Areola and M. Filani (eds) *A Geography of Nigerian Development.* Ibadan: Heinemann.

Mortimore, M. J. 1979: The supply of urban foodstuffs in northern Nigeria. In J. T. Coppock (eds), *Agriculture and Food Supply in Developing Countries*, Department of Geography, University of Edinburgh.

Mortimore, M. J. 1988: *Adapting to Drought: farmers, famine and desertification in West Africa.* Cambridge: Cambridge University Press.

Mwima-Mudeenya, E. 1978: A neglected component of developing economies: small scale production and employment in Uganda. PhD thesis, Cornell University.

Myint, H. 1971: *Economic Theory and the Underdeveloped Countries.* London: Oxford University Press.

Myint, H. 1988: *The Economics of Underdevelopment.* London: Hutchinson.

Myrdal, G. 1963: *Challenges to Affluence.* London: Gollancz.

Norman, D. W. 1972: *An Economic Study of Three Villages in Zaria Province, Vols 1 and 2*, Samaru, Nigeria: Institute of Agricultural Research.

Nyerere, J. K. 1974: *Man and Development.* Dar es Salam: Oxford University Press.

O'Hear, A. 1986: Pottery making in Ilorin: a study of the decorated water cooler. *Africa*, 56 (2), 175–92.

Okali, C. and Sumberg, J. E. 1986: Sheep and goats, men and women: household relations and small ruminant production in southwest Nigeria. In J. L. Moock (ed.), *Understanding Africa's Rural Households*, Boulder, Colorado and London: Westview.

Oyedype, F. P. A. 1973: Problems of socio-economic adjustment of resettlers in Nigeria. In A. L. Malsogumje (ed.), *Kainji: man made lake: socio-economic conditions*, Ibadan: Nigerian Institute of Social and Economic Research.

Palma, G. 1978: Dependency: a formal theory of underdevelopment or a methodology for the analysis of concrete situations of underdevelopment? *World Development*, 6 (7/8), 881–924.

Palmer, R. 1977: *Land and Racial Domination in Rhodesia.* London: Heinemann.

Palmer, R. 1985: White farmers in Malawi: before and after the Depression. *African Affairs*, 84 (335), 211–45.

Palmer, R. and Parsons, N. 1977: *The Roots of Rural Poverty in Central and Southern Africa.* London: Heinemann.

Pelissier, P. 1966: *Les Paysans du Senegal: les Civilizations Agraires du Cayor à la Casamance.* St Yriex: Imprimerie Fabriqué.

Perrings, C. 1979: *Black Mineworkers of Central Africa.* London: Heinemann.

Peters, D. U. 1980: *Land Usage in Serenje District: a survey of land usage and the agricultural systems of the Lala of the Serenje Plateau.* Capetown: Oxford University Press.

Phiri, G. H. 1981: Some aspects of spatial interaction and reaction to government policies in a border area: a study in the historical geography of rural development in the Zambia/Malawi/Mozambique frontier zone 1870–1979. Ph.D. thesis, University of Liverpool.

Pottier, J. 1983: Defunct labour reserve? Mambwe villages in the post-migration economy. *Africa*, 53 (2), 2–23.

Ranger, T. O. 1983: The invention of tradition in colonial Africa. In E. J.

Hobsbawm and T. O. Ranger (eds), *The Invention of Tradition*. Cambridge: Cambridge University Press.

Ranger, T. 1986: *Peasant Consciousness and Guerrilla War in Zimbabwe: a comparative study*. London: James Curry.

Raynaut, C. 1977: Lessons of a crisis. In D. Dalby (ed.), *Drought in Africa 2*, London: International African Institute.

Republic of Zambia 1971: *Second National Development Plan*. Lusaka: Ministry of Development Planning and National Guidance.

Rey, P. P. 1971: *Colonialisme, Neo-Colonialisme et Transition au Capitalisme*. Paris: Maspéro.

Rey, P. P. 1973: *Les Alliances des Classes*. Paris: Maspéro.

Richards, A. I. 1961: *Land, Labour, and Diet in Northern Rhodesia: an economic study of the Bemba tribe*. London: Oxford University Press.

Richards, P. 1983: The politics of African land use. *African Studies Review*, 26 (2), 1–72.

Richards, P. 1985: *Indigenous Agricultural Revolution*. London: Hutchinson.

Rimmer, D. 1984: *The Economies of West Africa*. London: Weidenfeld.

Robertson, A. 1987: *The Dynamics of Production Relationships*. Cambridge: Cambridge University Press.

Rodney, W. 1972: *How Europe Underdeveloped Africa*. Dar es Salaam and London: Tanzanian Publishing House and Boyle – L'Overture Publications.

Rostow, W. W. 1960: *The Stages of Economic Growth: a non-communist manifesto*. London: Cambridge University Press.

Rotberg, R. I. (ed.) 1983: *Imperialism, Colonialism and Hunger: East and Central Africa*. Lexington: Heath.

Ruthenberg, H. 1980: *Farming Systems in the Tropics*. Oxford: Clarendon Press.

Sahlins, M. 1974: *Stone Age Economics*. London: Tavistock.

Sandford, S. 1983: *Management of Pastoral Development in the Third World*. Chichester: Wiley.

Schultz, J. M. 1976: Population and agricultural change in Nigerian Hausaland the infield–outfield system of land use in Soba District, Kaduna State. Ph.D. thesis Columbia University.

Schumacher, E. F. 1962: *Small is Beautiful*. London: Sphere.

Scott, E. P. 1978: Subsistence, markets and rural development in rural Hausaland. *Journal of Developing Areas*, 12 (4), 449–69.

Scudder, T. 1962: *The Ecology of the Gwembe Tonga*. Manchester: Manchester University Press.

Sender, J. and Smith, S. 1986: *The Development of Capitalism in Africa*. London: Methuen.

Shenton, R. W. 1968: *The Development of Capitalism in Northern Nigeria*. London: James Curry.

Shenton, R. W. and Lenihan, L. 1981: Capital and class: peasant differentialism in northern Nigeria. *Journal of Peasant Studies*, 9 (1), 47–70.

Siddle, D. J. 1970: Rural development in Zambia: a spatial analysis. *Journal of Modern African Studies*, 8, 271–84.

Siddle, D. J. 1971: Young farmers clubs and radio farm forums. In D. H. Davies (ed.), *Zambia in Maps*, London: University of London Press.

Siddle, D. J. 1981: Achievement motivation and economic development: farming behaviour in the Zambian railway belt 1912–1975. *Third World Planning Review*, 33, 259–73.

Smith, C. A. 1976: *Regional Analysis*. New York: Academic Press.

Smith, M. G. 1955: *The Economy of Hausa Communities in Zaria*. London: Her Majesty's Stationery Office.

Smith, M. G. 1959: The Hausa system of social status. *Africa*, 29 (3), 239–52.

Smock, A. and Chapman, 1981: Women's economic roles. In T. Killick (ed.), *Papers on the Kenyan Economy*, Nairobi: Heinemann.

Spooner, B. 1972: *Population Growth: anthropological implications*. Cambridge, Ma.: M. I. T. Press.

Starns, W. W. 1974: *Land Tenure among the Rural Hausa*, Land Tenure Centre. Madison: University of Wisconsin.

Stichter, S. 1985: *Migrant Labourers*. Cambridge: Cambridge University Press.

Stoneman, C. 1981: *Zimbabwe's Inheritance*. London: Macmillan.

Sumra, S. 1979: Problems of agricultural production in Handeni district. In K. S. Kim, R. B. Mabele and M. J. Schultheis (eds), *Papers on the Political Economy of Tanzania*, 202–07. Nairobi: Heinemann.

Swift, J. 1980: The economics of traditional pastoralism: the Twareg of the Adrar n Iforas (Mali). PhD thesis, University of Sussex.

Swift, J. 1982: The future of African hunter gatherers and pastoral nomad peoples. *Development and Change*, 13 (2), 159–83.

Swindell, K. 1979: Serawoolies, tillibunkas and strange farmers: the development of migrant groundnut farmers along the Gambia river, 1948–59. *Journal of African History*, 2 (1), 93–104.

Swindell, K. 1981: *The Strange Farmers of the Gambia: a study in the redistribution of African population*. Monograph XV, Centre for Development Studies, University of Swansea.

Swindell, K. 1985: *Farm Labour*. Cambridge: Cambridge University Press.

Szeresewski, R. 1965: *Structural Change in the Economy of Ghana 1891–1911*. London: Weidenfeld.

Taylor, J. 1982: Changing patterns of labour supply to the South African gold mines. *Tijdschrift voor Economische en Sociale Geografie*, 73 (4), 213–20.

Terray, E. 1972: *Marxism and 'Primitive' Societies*. New York: Monthly Review Press.

Tosh, J. 1980: The cash crop revolution in tropical Africa: an agricultural reappraisal. *African Affairs*, 79, 79–94.

Tourtre, R. 1954: Perfectionnement des techniques au Senegal. *Annales du Centre de Récherches Agronomiques de Bambay au Senegal*, 13, 65.

Trapnell, C. G. and Clothier, J. N. 1953: *The Soils, Vegetation and Agriculture of North-Western Rhodesia*. Lusaka: Northern Rhodesia Government Printer.

Turnbull, C. 1961: *The Forest People*. London: Chatto and Windus.

Turnbull, C. 1976: *Man in Africa*. Newton Abbot: David and Charles.

Van Hear, N. 1982: Northern labour and development of capitalist agriculture in Ghana. PhD thesis, University of Birmingham.

Von Rotenhen, D. 1968: Cotton farming in Sukumuland. In H. Ruthenberg (ed.), *Smallholder Farming and Smallholder Development in Tanzania*, Munich: Veltforrem Verlag.

Wallace, T. 1972: Working in rural Buganda: a study of the occupational activities of young people in villages. 8th Annual conference of the East African Universities Social Science Council, Nairobi.

Wallace, T. 1979: Rural development through irrigation: studies in a town on the Kano river project. Mimeo. Zaria, Nigeria: Centre for Social and Economic Research, Ahmadu Bello University.

Wallace, T. 1980: Agricultural projects and land in northern Nigeria. *Review of African Political Economy*, 17, 59–70.

Wallerstein, I. 1974: *The Modern World System*. New York: Academic Press.

Warren, B. 1980: *Imperialism: pioneer of capitalism*. London: Verso.

Watts, M. J. 1983: 'Good try Mr Paul': populism and the politics of African land use. *African Studies Review*, 26 (2), 73–83.

Watts, M. J. 1987: Brittle trade: a political economy of food supply in Kano. In J. Guyer (ed.), *Feeding African Cities*, London: Manchester University Press for the International African Institute.

Watts, M. J. and Shenton, R. 1984: State and agrarian transformation in Nigeria. In J. Barker (ed.), *The Politics of Agriculture in Tropical Africa*. Beverley Hills: Sage.

Webb, P. 1988: The role of irrigated rice in transforming household relations in the Gambia. PhD thesis, University of Birmingham.

Wilkinson, R. G. 1973: *Poverty and Progress: an ecological model of economic development*. London: Methuen.

Williams, G. 1982: Taking the part of peasants. In J. Harriss (ed.), *Rural Developments: theories of peasant economy and agrarian change*, London: Hutchinson.

Williams, G. 1985: Marketing with and without marketing boards: the origins of state marketing boards in Nigeria. *Review of African Political Economy*, 34, 4–15.

Wolpe, H. (ed.) 1980: *The Articulation of Modes of Production*. London: Routledge and Kegan Paul.

Wood, A. P. 1983: Food production and the changing structure of Zambian agriculture. Paper presented to symposium on food production in East and Central Africa, School of Oriental and African Studies, London.

World Bank, 1981: *Accelerated Development in Sub-Saharan Africa: a joint programme of action*. Washington: World Bank.

Index

Related Titles: List of IBG Special Publications

17 Residential Segregation, the State and Constitutional Conflict in American Urban Areas
   R. J. Johnston
18 River Channels: Environment and Process
   Edited by Keith Richards
19 Technical Change and Industrial Policy
   Edited by Keith Chapman and Graham Humphrys
20 Sea-level Changes
   Edited by Michael J. Tooley and Ian Shennan
21 The Changing Face of Cities: A Study of Development Cycles and Urban Form
   J. W. R. Whitehand
22 Population and Disaster
   Edited by John I. Clarke, Peter Curson, S. L. Kayasha and Prithvish Nag
23 Rural Change in Tropical Africa: From Colonies to Nation-States
   David Siddle and Kenneth Swindell

IN PREPARATION FOR THE IBG

Salt Marshes and Coastal Wetlands
Edited by D. R. Stoddart
Demographic Patterns in the Past
Edited by Richard Smith
Wetlands: A Threatened Landscape
Edited by Michael Williams
Teaching Geography in Higher Education
Alan Jenkins, John R. Gold, Roger Lee, Janice Monk, Judith Riley, Ifan Shepherd and David Unwin
The Geography of the Retailing Industry
John A. Dawson and Leigh Sparks